PSYCHOLOGY
AND
SOCIOLOGY OF SPORT

Board of Reviewers

PSYCHOLOGY AND SOCIOLOGY OF SPORT

Current Selected Research

Volume 1

Edited by

Lee Vander Velden, Ph.D.

and

James H. Humphrey, Ed.D.

AMS PRESS, INC.
New York

About the Editors

LEE VANDER VELDEN, Ph.D., is an Assistant Professor of Physical Education at the University of Maryland, where he conducts and directs research in the sociology of sport. His personal research interest is in the area of sport heroes. One of the founders of the North American Society for the Sociology of Sport (NASSS), he currently edits the *NASSS Newsletter*.

JAMES H. HUMPHREY, Ed.D., Professor Emeritus at the University of Maryland, is the author or coauthor of 45 books and 200 articles and research reports. In the area of psychological research he has published over 30 studies involving child learning through motor activity.

PSYCHOLOGY AND SOCIOLOGY OF SPORT
Current Selected Research

Copyright © 1986 by AMS Press, Inc.
All rights reserved.

ISSN 0885−7423

Series ISBN: 0−404−63400−1
Vol. 1 ISBN: 0−404−63401−X

Library of Congress Catalog Card Number: 85−43473

MANUFACTURED IN THE UNITED STATES OF AMERICA

Published by
AMS Press, Inc.
56 East 13th Street
New York, New York 10003

CONTENTS

Part I: Psychology

Part II: Sociology

CONTRIBUTORS

Richard R. Albrecht. Institute for the Study of Sports, Michigan State University, East Lansing, Michigan

Bonnie G. Berger. Department of Physical Education, Brooklyn College, City University of New York, Brooklyn, New York

Elaine M. Blinde. Motor Behavior Laboratory, Department of Physical Education, University of Illinois at Urbana-Champaign, Champaign, Illinois

Garry E. Chick. Leisure Behavior Research Laboratory, Children's Research Center, University of Illinois at Urbana-Champaign, Champaign, Illinois

Jack S. Croxton. Department of Psychology, State University of New York—College at Fredonia, Fredonia, New York

Joan L. Duda. Department of Physical Education, Purdue University, Lafayette, Indiana

Steven W. Edwards. School of Health, Physical Education, and Leisure Services, Oklahoma State University, Stillwater, Oklahoma

Deborah L. Feltz. Institute for the Study of Sports, Michigan State University, East Lansing, Michigan

Angela B. Ginorio. Director, Women's Information Center, Seattle, Washington

Richard D. Gordin, Jr. Department of Physical Education, Utah State University, Logan, Utah

Susan L. Greendorfer. Motor Behavior Laboratory, Department of Physical Education, University of Illinois at Urbana-Champaign, Champaign, Illinois

J. Robert Grove. Department of Human Movement and Recreation Studies, University of Western Australia, Nedlands, Australia

Elizabeth Hall. Department of Physical Education, Texas Tech University, Lubbock, Texas

Douglas Halstead. Department of Kinesiological Studies, Texas Christian University, Fort Worth, Texas

Cynthia Hasbrook. Department of Human Kinetics, University of Wisconsin—Milwaukee, Milwaukee, Wisconsin

Steven Houseworth. Human Kinetic Publishers, Champaign, Illinois

Bruce G. Klonsky. Department of Psychology, State University of New York—College at Fredonia, Fredonia, New York

Eric W. Krenz. Department of Physical Education, University of Utah, Salt Lake City, Utah

John W. Loy. Department of Physical Education, University of Illinois, Champaign, Illinois

Richard V. McGehee. Department of Health and Physical Education, Southeastern Louisiana University, Hammond, Louisiana

David R. Owen. Department of Psychology, Brooklyn College, City University of New York, Brooklyn, New York

Robert Pangrazi. Department of Physical Education, Arizona State University, Tempe, Arizona

David Pargman. Department of Movement Science and Physical Education, Florida State University, Tallahassee, Florida

M. Joan Paul. Department of Health and Physical Education, Southeastern Louisiana University, Hammond, Louisiana

Gene Peterson. Mesa, Arizona Public School System

Jeffrey O. Segrave. Department of Physical Education and Dance, Skidmore College, Saratoga Springs, New York

Joe Thirer. Department of Psychology, Southern Illinois University, Carbondale, Illinois

Lee Vander Velden. Department of Physical Education, University of Maryland, College Park, Maryland

Michael Walsh. Department of Athletics, Dartmouth College, Hanover, New Hampshire

Judith C. Young. Department of Physical Education, University of Maryland, College Park, Maryland

PREFACE

This first volume of *Psychology and Sociology of Sport: Current Selected Research* presents original research on contemporary problems of interest to behavioral scientists in the areas of sport psychology and sport sociology. Papers investigating a wide variety of psychological and sociological concerns in the area of sport are included.

Psychology and sociology of sport have developed into complicated and complex subjects and involve many areas of human concern. This initial volume is well represented by researchers concerned with these considerations, some of which are relatively new areas of study. Among others, these newer areas include retirement from organized sports, reciprocity and socialization into sport, and self-efficacy as a mediating force in performance.

It is the intention of the editors and AMS Press, Inc. to provide sport psychology and sport sociology enthusiasts with an annual series reporting original research on relevant issues. The volumes should supplement and support journals and annual reviews reporting on similar topics. A volume of this nature should find use as a basic or supplementary text in courses oriented to the psychology of sport and/or the sociology of sport. In addition, it could serve as a reference for psychology and sociology of sport specialists, as well as for scholars investigating related topics.

An attempt has been made to classify the selections into the two broad categories of psychology and sociology of sport. Although these areas could be considered as more or less distinct and separate entities, there still might be some unavoidable overlapping because the classifications are, to some extent, arbitrary.

We wish to extend our gratitude to the contributors and to the members of the board of reviewers for giving their time and talent to evaluate the papers.

PART I

Psychology

1

THE INFLUENCE OF SELF-EFFICACY ON THE APPROACH/AVOIDANCE OF A HIGH-AVOIDANCE MOTOR TASK

Deborah L. Feltz

Richard R. Albrecht

Two studies, using a high-avoidance motor task, were conducted to test Bandura's (1977) theory and the reciprocal relationships he proposed. Study 1 tested Bandura's predictions using path analysis techniques in the approach/avoidance behavior of 80 female college students attempting a modified back dive. The Bandura model predicted that a reciprocal relationship existed between self-efficacy and back-diving performance and that self-efficacy was the mediator of back-diving performance. Results provided only partial support for the model. Self-efficacy was a significant predictor of performance, but not the only significant predictor. Previous performance attempts were also significant predictors of subsequent performance. A respecified model was proposed that included both previous performances and self-efficacy as predictors of back-diving performance. The respecified model was tested using a different sample in a second study along with the additional influence of perceived autonomic arousal. Results provided support for the respecified model.

Additional analyses were performed comparing divers and avoiders on self-efficacy, heart rate, cognitive anxiety, and autonomic perception. Divers had higher efficacy expectations, higher increases in heart rate, lower cognitive anxiety, and lower perceptions of autonomic arousal than avoiders. Divers were also more accurate in their efficacy judgments than were avoiders.

In physical education and sport, certain motor skills are frequently associated with anxiety and hesitancy when the learner is first confronted with attempting the skill. These skills have been termed "high-avoidance" motor skills (Feltz, Landers, & Raeder, 1979). High avoidance is defined here as a withdrawal reaction that is characteristic of a performer who may perceive a novel situation as being unpleasant or possibly dangerous. High-avoidance motor skills may include, for example, gymnastic skills, diving, rock climbing, or downhill skiing.

Numerous methods have been proposed for treating avoidance responses in motor skill acquisition, but some methods are more effective than others. For instance, participant modeling has been shown to be a more powerful technique than modeling alone for reducing avoidance in swimming and diving situations (Feltz et al., 1979; Lewis, 1974). However, the lack of an adequate theory to explain the differing effects of treatments on the avoidance responses of the individual has retarded the progress of research and treatment efforts in this area. Early research on avoidance behavior in clinical psychology was guided primarily by the anxiety-based model (Mowrer, 1947; Wolpe, 1974), according to which extinction of anxiety eliminates avoidance behavior. Subsequent research evidence cumulated, however, showing that anxiety arousal was largely unrelated to avoidance behavior (Bandura, 1969; Lang 1971; Leitenberg, Agras, Butz, & Wincze, 1971; Rachman, 1976).

More recently, Bandura (1977) proposed the theory of self-efficacy to account for the different effects accompanying the diverse methods of treating avoidance behavior. This theory proposes self-efficacy as a common cognitive mechanism for mediating behavioral responses. It states that treatment techniques, whatever their form, reduce avoidance behavior by instilling and strengthening self-perceptions of coping efficacy. According to Bandura's theory, expectations of personal efficacy are derived from four principal sources of information: performance accomplishments, vicarious experiences, verbal persuasion, and physiological arousal. Different psychological procedures rely on different sources of efficacy information and, therefore, have differing effects on the individuals' anxiety response, depending on the influence of the efficacy information it conveys. Bandura further emphasized that the relationship between efficacy expectations and performance is reciprocal. Efficacy expectations influence performance, which in turn influences further efficacy expectations. Another reciprocal relationship suggested in Bandura's theory is between self-efficacy and physiological arousal. Although Bandura does not state this explicitly, he does state that physiological arousal is a source of efficacy information and that it is a coeffect of avoidance behavior.

Two studies,[1] using a high-avoidance motor task, were conducted to test Bandura's (1977) theory and the reciprocal relationships he proposed. In order to test a network of the causal relationships in Bandura's theory without manipulating the variables, path analysis was used. This technique tested whether the hypothesized model, as a whole, fit the set of data adequately by comparing the observed relationships among the variables with the hypothesized relationships. Reciprocal causation was tested through

---

[1]These two studies are presented in greater detail elsewhere (Feltz, 1982; Feltz & Mugno, 1983). What appears in this paper is a more direct test of the respecified model proposed in Feltz (1982) and further analyses comparing divers and avoiders.

path analysis by the use of lagged variables. This was done by examining whether the change in one variable, such as self-efficacy, produced a change in another variable, such as approach/avoidance behavior, which in turn produced a further change in self-efficacy and so on.

STUDY 1

The purpose of the first study was to investigate the role of self-efficacy as a mediating variable in the performance of a high-avoidance diving task (a modified back dive) over four trials. A model based on Bandura's (1977) theory of self-efficacy was tested against an alternative or "full model" which included all possible pathways among the variables.

In Figure 1, Bandura's model is diagrammed to reflect temporal changes proceeding from past performance accomplishments on similar tasks through four performance trials on a novel diving task. In this way, the reciprocal relationship between self-efficacy and performance and between self-efficacy and physiological arousal can be examined. Each arrow or path in Figure 1 can be thought of as a hypothesis. As the diagram shows, physiological arousal and past performance accomplishments affect future performance indirectly, via self-efficacy. It should also be noted that although Bandura does not state explicitly the relationship between sources of self-efficacy, one can probably assume that past performance accomplishments and physiological arousal are correlated at the beginning of the path diagram. A double-headed arrow is drawn between these two variables to indicate that the correlation between them is not subject to causal interpretation. However, after the first performance trial, a specification of causal direction is made according to temporal order. The dotted lines represented relationships that were hypothesized to be zero.

Method

Subjects and Performance Task

The subjects were 80 female college students who were deep water swimmers and had no previous experience in performing a modified back dive, although some subjects had previous experience in performing other types of dives. The modified back dive consists of holding the arms overhead and extending the head back as far as possible, arching backward, and falling into the water. No preliminary bounce is used. The diving board could be adjusted vertically to four different heights (15, 19, 23, and 27 in. [38.1,

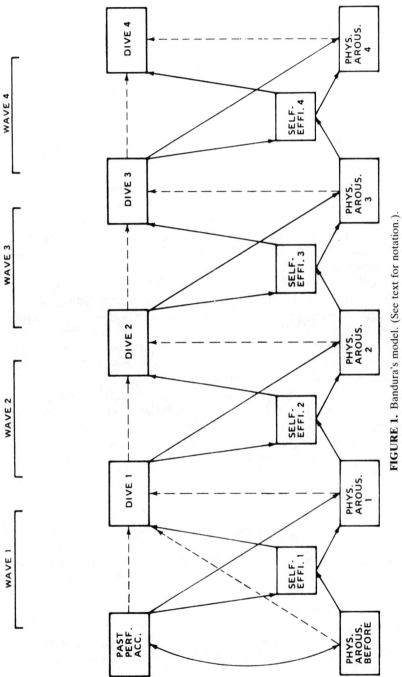

FIGURE 1. Bandura's model. (See text for notation.).

48.26, 58.42, and 68.58 cm]) above the deck of the pool so subjects could select the height form which they wished to dive. The subjects were volunteers who were given no incentive for participating other than to learn how to perform a back dive.

Dependent Measures

The dependent measures included heart rate (HR), Spielberger's state measure of the State-Trait Anxiety Inventory (Spielberger, Gorsuch, & Luchene, 1970), a diving efficacy scale, a background questionnaire, and diving performance. HR was measured via telemetry to assess physiological arousal. To equate individual differences in HR, difference scores were calculated by subtracting a basal value of HR from the measures taken prior to each trial. The self-report measures included the state anxiety scale, a diving efficacy scale, and a background questionnaire. The diving efficacy scale consisted of asking the subject to rate the strength of belief that she could accomplish the modified back dive task successfully for each of the four board heights. Each rating was made on a 100-point probability scale ranging in 10-unit intervals from great uncertainty to complete certainty. The background questionnaire contained open-ended questions concerning subjects' previous experience with swimming, diving, and other high-avoidance sports. This information was used to compile subjects' past performance accomplishments scores.

Performance was measured by the experimenter and a trained observer on a performance rating scale. The rating scale was based on a combination of the board height chosen to attempt the dive (difficulty rating) and an approach rating. No points were given if the subject refused to cross a tape placed 1 ft (0.30 m) from the end of the board. A rating of 0.5 was given if the subject stepped over the tape but refused to leave the board. Points ranged from 1.0 to 2.5 (depending on board height chosen) if the subject avoided the dive by jumping feet first into the water. Accidental loss of balance, which forced the subject to jump, did not count as an attempted dive. A rating of 3.0 to 4.5 points was given when the subject twisted her head to look at the water, or when she brought her head up out of the arched position after leaving the board. Ratings of 4.5 to 6.0 points were given for the correct dives where the head entered first, regardless of the degree of the arch. Interrater reliability was found to be 1.0.

Procedure

Subjects were tested by one of two female experimenters. After entering the test area, the subject first completed an informed consent form, along with the background questionnaire. The experimenter then took the subject's heart rate with a stethoscope three times, for 15 s each time, and the readings were then averaged to get a pretreatment measure with which to compare HR measured on the electrocardiogram (ECG). Testing protocol was explained to the subject while electrodes were being attached. After the electrodes were attached to the subject, the equipment was checked and a basal HR was taken on the ECG.

Next, the subject was given a verbal explanation of the modified back dive task by the experimenter and then shown two filmed demonstrations of the dive performed by a female model. To give the subject an idea of how much head rotation and arch were needed to perform the dive, she was asked to locate a red marker placed 9 ft (2.74 m) behind her and 6 ft (1.83 m) up a wall by tilting her head backward, arching back, and using the proper standing position (arms overhead) for the dive. HR was taken again just prior to filling out the self-report questionnaires (Heart Rate Before). The state anxiety inventory and diving self-efficacy scale were then completed.

Next, the subject was asked to select the height at which she thought she could perform the task. She was told that the higher the height the more difficult the dive. She was then asked to step up to, but not over, a red tape marker placed 1 ft (0.30 m) away from the end of the board. After she was stationary, she was connected to the transmitter and was told that she could step over the tape marker if she thought she could attempt the dive. HR was recorded continuously from the time the subject crossed the red line until the subject left the board or indicated that she could not attempt the dive. Movement was not extensive enough to create any movement artifacts in the HR recordings. If the subject refused to perform the dive, it was counted as a trial. If a back flop was performed, the experimenter said, "You did not keep your head back." The intertrial interval was kept at approximately 5 min. It took approximately 2 min to complete the questionnaires and approximately 3 min to change the height of the diving board.

Treatment of the Data

A factor analysis was employed to provide a single composite measure of each subject's past performance accomplishments that were related to the modified back dive. The measures used to calculate this composite score were subject's years of swimming, type of diving experience, and type of risk-taking experience. These were all taken from responses on the background questionnaire.

The Bandura model in Figure 1 was assumed to be recursive, meaning that the causal flow is unidirectional.[2] A recursive model permitted the use

---

[2]Although Bandura (1977) proposes reciprocal relationships between self-efficacy and performance and self-efficacy and physiological arousal, this does not mean that the causal flow is bidirectional. Bandura states these relationships in terms of a temporal order. For example, efficacy expectations influence performance, which in turn influences *future* efficacy expectations.

of ordinary least squares solutions to estimate path coefficients, which involved writing a path analytic equation for every dependent variable. The Bandura model contains fewer paths than the number of correlations between the variables, because certain path coefficients were predicted to be zero. Hypothesizing a certain path coefficient to be zero is stated as a null hypothesis and then tested against a "full model" containing all pathways for that equation by means of an *F* test (Ott, 1977). The full model contains as many path coefficients as there are possible correlations between all variables, and thus becomes the standard against which the theoretical model can be tested. Only first-order dependence was considered in structuring the full model. This means that direct paths were not drawn across waves, such as from Self-Efficacy 1 to Self-Efficacy 3.

Results and Discussion

The means and standard deviations for the variables in Study 1 are presented in Table 1. Although self-reported state anxiety was measured, it was not a variable in the Bandura model and, therefore, was not analyzed in the path analysis. Table 2 presents the path coefficients for Bandura's model.

Bandura's model predicted that past performance accomplishments and back-diving performance directly influenced self-efficacy. Results indicated that all path coefficients going from either past performance accomplishments or back-diving performance to self-efficacy were significant. The

TABLE 1
Means and Standard Deviations for All Variables in Study 1

			Variables			
Wave	Past Performance Accomplishments	Heart Rate Before	Cognitive Anxiety	Self-Efficacy	Heart Rate	Performance Dive
1						
M	.00	2.04	45.05	17.25	25.05	3.26
SD	.78	12.44	11.31	11.95	18.20	1.95
2						
M	—	—	44.61	20.08	17.83	3.89
SD	—	—	12.40	14.29	18.40	1.98
3						
M	—	—	41.09	23.70	11.89	4.28
SD	—	—	12.45	14.46	15.49	1.92
4						
M	—	—	38.24	26.19	9.18	4.56
SD	—	—	13.07	14.36	15.57	1.99

TABLE 2
Path Coefficients and Zero-Order Correlations for Bandura's Model

Pathways			Standardized Coefficients	Zero-Order Correlations	R^2 for Path Equation
Wave 1					
Past performance	→	Self-efficacy 1	.277*	.274	.082
Heart rate before	→	Self-efficacy 1	−.085	−.076	
Past performance	→	Heart rate 1	−.086	.034	.062
Self-efficacy 1	→	Heart rate 1	.269*	.236	
Self-efficacy 1	→	Dive 1	.625*	.625	.391
Wave 2					
Dive 1	→	Self-efficacy 2	.771*	.773	.597
Heart rate 1	→	Self-efficacy 2	.005	.276	
Dive 1	→	Heart rate 2	−.152	−.029	.011
Self-efficacy 2	→	Heart rate 2	.160	.043	
Self-efficacy 2	→	Dive 2	.776*	.776	.602
Wave 3					
Dive 2	→	Self-efficacy 3	.821*	.819	.672
Heart rate 2	→	Self-efficacy 3	−.033	.023	
Dive 2	→	Heart rate 3	−.048	−.061	.004
Self-efficacy 3	→	Heart rate 3	−.016	−.055	
Self-efficacy 3	→	Dive 3	.790*	.790	.624
Wave 4					
Dive 3	→	Self-efficacy 4	.834*	.829	.692
Heart rate 3	→	Self-efficacy 4	−.059	.005	
Dive 3	→	Heart rate 4	.090	−.031	.008
Self-efficacy 4	→	Heart rate 4	−.145	−.071	
Self-efficacy 4	→	Dive 4	.849*	.849	.721

*$p < .05$.

influence of past performance accomplishments for similar tasks on self-efficacy (.277) was not as large as the path coefficients between actual diving performance and self-efficacy (Wave 2 = .771; Wave 3 = .821; Wave 4 = .834). This result is in accord with Bandura's theory. Performance accomplished on the same task on which the subject is to be tested (back dive) is a more dependable source of information than performance on a different task.

Bandura's model also predicted that HR would have a direct but weaker influence on self-efficacy than past performance accomplishments or back-diving performance. However, none of the HR→Self-Efficacy path coefficients were significant. Not only were the HR→Self-Efficacy path coefficients weaker than the Diving→Self-Efficacy and the Past Performance Accomplishments→Self-Efficacy 1 path, but they were not at all useful in determining efficacy expectations for diving performance. Furthermore, no reciprocal relationship was found between self-efficacy and HR. A possible reason for this finding may be that some individuals do not have accurate perceptions of their physiological arousal.

Another prediction from Bandura's model was that self-efficacy was the primary direct influence of actual diving performance. This meant that the direct paths between past related performance (or past diving performance) and future performance were predicted to be zero, as were the direct paths between HR and performance. This prediction was tested by comparing the Bandura model to the full model. As mentioned previously, this prediction is tested by an F test between the full and reduced model for the dependent variable in question. The resulting F tests indicated a significant difference between the full and reduced equations on every wave: Wave 1, $F(2, 76) = 6.46$; Wave 2, $F(2, 76) = 31.35$; Wave 3, $F(2, 76) = 43.32$; Wave 4, $F(2, 76) = 105.75$. Significant differences between the full and reduced regression equations indicated that there were significant path coefficients other than self-efficacy that should be examined in the full model. The path coefficients and zero-order correlations for the Bandura full model are reported in Table 3. In examining the full model, it can be seen that self-efficacy was not the only significant predictor of performance, although it was the major predictor on the first trial. After Trial 1, however, performance on the previous

TABLE 3
Path Coefficients and Zero-Order Correlations for the Bandura Full Model

Pathways		Standardized Coefficients	Zero-Order Correlations	R^2 for Performance
Wave 1				.516
Past performance	→ Dive 1	.283*	.402	
Heart rate before	→ Dive 1	−.135	.032	
Self-efficacy 1	→ Dive 1	.466*	.625	
Heart rate 1	→ Dive 1	.303*	.352	
Wave 2				.782
Dive 1	→ Dive 2	.669*	.864	
Self-efficacy 2	→ Dive 2	.256*	.776	
Heart rate 2	→ Dive 2	.077	.069	
Wave 3				.824
Dive 2	→ Dive 3	.751*	.892	
Self-efficacy 3	→ Dive 3	.182*	.790	
Heart rate 3	→ Dive 3	.133*	.078	
Wave 4				.926
Dive 3	→ Dive 4	.806*	.957	
Self-efficacy 4	→ Dive 4	.183*	.849	
Heart rate 4	→ Dive 4	.029	.008	

*$p < .05$

trial was the major predictor of performance on the next trial. Regardless of what the women thought they were capable of performing on each trial after Trial 1, when they stepped up on the board, their next performance was determined more by what they actually did on the previous trial. If a subject avoided the dive on the first trial, it was likely that she would avoid the dive again. If she was successful, she was more likely to try the dive again, possibly at a greater height. Moreover, the influence of diving performance increased over trials (from .283 to .806), whereas the influence of self-efficacy on performance decreased over trials (from .466 to .183).

In accordance with Bandura's theory, there was a reciprocal relationship between self-efficacy and performance, but they were not equally reciprocal when previous diving performance was included as a predictor of performance (see Tables 2 and 3). As one gained experience on the task, back-diving performance had a greater influence on self-efficacy than self-efficacy had on performance.

When models or theories are still young in their development, it is sometimes useful to delete the nonsignificant and nonmeaningful path coefficients and reexamine the model. This approach is referred to as theory trimming (Kerlinger & Pedhazur, 1973). A respecified model was proposed which included both self-efficacy and previous performance as predictors of approach/avoidance performance as well as HR as a predictor of performance on the first trial. The path coefficients for the respecified model are contained in Table 4. When comparing the R^2s for performance in the Bandura and respecified models (see Tables 2 and 4), one can see that the respecified model accounted for more performance variance than the Bandura model. Because the respecified model was not constructed a priori, however, it needed to be evaluated with a different sample. Thus, a second study was undertaken to test this respecified model.

STUDY 2

The purpose of Study 2 was to test the respecified model proposed in Study 1 and to investigate the additional influence of perceived physiological arousal on self-efficacy and performance. Borkovec (1976) has indicated that individuals have different perceptions of the magnitude of their own physiological arousal. Some individuals perceive their physiological arousal to be high regardless of their actual arousal level. Thus, it was hypothesized that individuals' perceptions of their physiological arousal were more influential sources of efficacy information than their actual arousal.

TABLE 4
Path Coefficients for the Respecified Model

	Study 1		Study 2	
	Standardized	**R^2 for**	**Standardized**	**R^2 for Path**
Pathways	**Coefficients**	**Performance**	**Correlations**	**Equation**
Wave 1				
Past performance → Self-efficacy 1	.274*	.075	.226*	.051
Self-efficacy → Heart rate 1	.269*	.055	.245*	.061
Past performance → Dive 1	.270*		.050	
Self-efficacy → Dive 1	.495*	.502	.488*	.698
Heart rate 1 → Dive 1	.239*		.374*	
Wave 2				
Dive 1 → Self-efficacy 2	.773*	.597	.824*	.679
Dive 1 → Dive 2	.657*	.776	.827*	.920
Self-efficacy 2 → Dive 2	.268*		.156*	
Wave 3				
Dive 2 → Self-efficacy 3	.819*	.672	.880*	.775
Dive 2 → Dive 3	.745*	.807	.752*	.878
Self-efficacy 3 → Dive 3	.180*		.205*	
Wave 4				
Dive 3 → Self-efficacy 4	.829*	.688	.880*	.774
Dive 3 → Dive 4	.809*	.925	.837*	.931
Self-efficacy 4 → Dive 4	.178*		.105	

*$p < .05$

Method

The number of subjects, type of subjects, and task were the same as used in Study 1. Additionally, perceived physiological arousal was measured by the autonomic perception questionnaire (APQ) (Mandler, Mandler, & Uviller, 1958). The procedures differed slightly from those used in Study 1. The subjects in Study 2 completed the questionnaires while they were standing on the board, just prior to attempting the dive, in order to keep the state anxiety, efficacy, and APQ measure as close in time to performance as possible. Bandura (1978) has argued that if efficacy judgments and performance are not measured closely in time, self-efficacy may be altered by new experiences during the intervening period. Because efficacy expectations were measured approximately 3 min prior to HR and performance measures in the first study, changes in HR during this intervening period might have altered expectations, although results from the first study indicated that self-efficacy was still a stronger determinant of performance than HR. The time interval between completing the questionnaires and performance was held constant at about 30 s. The time interval between dives was also held constant at about 5 min.

Results and Discussion

The means and standard deviations for the variables in Study 2 are presented in Table 5. The respecified model proposed in Study 1 was tested against the full model (in Figure 1, the solid plus dotted pathways) containing all pathways. Again, only first-order dependence was considered in structuring the full model. The path coefficients for this respecified model are also contained in Table 4. The influence of autonomic perception on self-efficacy and performance was examined separately.

Results indicated that there were no significant differences between the full and respecified equations. The full equations were examined for HR in the second, third, and fourth waves because these variables were completely eliminated from the respecified model. None of these regression equations were significant. These findings, therefore, support the respecified model proposed in Study 1. The only differences between the path coefficients for the respecified models in Studies 1 and 2 were for the Past Performance Accomplishments→Dive 1 and Self-Efficacy 4→Dive 4 paths. These paths were not significant in Study 2.

The R^2s for performance reported in Table 4 were quite high. By

TABLE 5
Means and Standard Deviations for All Variables in Study 2

Wave	Past Performance Accomplishments	Heart Rate Before	Autonomic Perception	Cognitive Anxiety	Self-Efficacy	Heart Rate	Performance Dive
1							
M	.00	3.20	45.41	43.99	21.85	27.21	3.45
SD	.84	10.60	27.62	11.19	10.74	18.26	1.90
2							
M	—	—	42.23	43.99	24.13	16.09	3.83
SD	—	—	31.49	13.13	13.11	16.57	2.03
3							
M	—	—	37.43	41.46	25.93	12.40	4.00
SD	—	—	31.03	13.63	14.61	15.90	2.22
4							
M	—	—	33.56	39.30	26.93	7.75	4.38
SD	—	—	33.06	14.33	15.20	16.63	2.25

Wave 4, the model in Study 2 accounted for 93.1% of the performance variance for that trial. These large R^2s are rare in the social sciences and confirm the strength of this model. From these results, it appears that both self-efficacy and previous performance experiences are direct influences of subsequent performance, and that HR is influential only in the first performance attempt. Although the results from these studies suggest that Bandura's (1977) model may have been too simplistic to account for all behavioral change in motor performance attempts, self-efficacy was still found to be an important and necessary cognitive mechanism in explaining motor behavior, especially in initial performance attempts.

Another purpose of Study 2 was to investigate the influence of perceived physiological arousal on self-efficacy and performance. When autonomic perception was included in the revised model as a predictor of self-efficacy, it was a significant predictor on every trial along with previous performance. The path coefficients were APQ1 = $-.225$; APQ2 = $-.212$, Dive 1 = .720; APQ3 = $-.203$, Dive 2 = .777; APQ4 = $-.233$, Dive 3 = .760. None of the HR→Self-Efficacy path coefficients from the full model were significant; thus the hypothesis that perceived arousal is a more influential source of self-efficacy than actual arousal was supported. These results indicate that the higher the perceived autonomic arousal, the lower the expectation of self-efficacy. Although perceived autonomic arousal was a significant predictor of self-efficacy, it was not a significant predictor of back-diving performance. This supports Bandura's (1977) hypothesis that perceived arousal influences performance through its effect on self-efficacy. In the initial performance attempt, perceived arousal appears to be the strongest source of efficacy information. After the first attempt, however, previous performance becomes the strongest source of efficacy information. This supports Bandura's contention that mastery experiences provide the most dependable source of efficacy information.

The path analyses in Studies 1 and 2 indicate support for certain causal networks in the self-efficacy/motor behavior relationships. However, the path coefficients do not show how individuals who made mastery attempts differed from individuals who avoided the task completely. In order to examine in greater detail the responses of divers compared to avoiders, further analyses were performed.

DIVERS VERSUS AVOIDERS

Subjects were classified as divers if they left the board on every diving attempt, even if the attempt resulted in a back flop or jump in. Subjects were classified as avoiders if they did not leave the board on any of the four attempts. Six subjects who avoided some attempts but made others were eliminated from analysis. Separate analyses were conducted for each sample population in a Group (Divers/Avoiders) × Trials (2 × 4) factorial design with repeated measures on the trials factor. Cognitive anxiety, self-efficacy, and HR were the dependent measures examined. Autonomic perception was added as a dependent measure in Study 2. Univariate rather than multivariate analyses of variance (ANOVAs) were performed on each of the dependent measures because of the small sample sizes in the avoiders group which may have violated the assumptions of the MANOVA model. In order to reduce the possibility of Type 1 errors with the number of ANOVAs performed, the alpha level was set at .01 for all analyses. Upon evidence of significant interactions, post hoc individual mean comparisons were made on trial means using Tukey WSD and on between-subject means using Behren's Fisher t tests for unequal ns. Means and standard deviations of the groups are presented in Tables 6 and 7.

The results of all of the ANOVAs revealed significant group main effects, trials effects, and Group × Trials interactions for all dependent measures in both studies. The F values for all of these analyses are contained in Table 8.

TABLE 6
Means and Standard Deviations for Divers and Avoiders on Three Dependent Measures in Study 1

Group	Trial	Cognitive Anxiety		Self-Efficacy		Heart Rate	
		M	*SD*	*M*	*SD*	*M*	*SD*
Divers ($n = 63$)							
	1	43.41	10.62	19.73	11.87	28.49	17.99
	2	41 38	10.65	24.21	13.14	18.00	18.74
	3	37.30	9.71	27.94	12.70	11.33	15.24
	4	33.87	9.28	30.56	11.72	8.08	15.40
Avoiders ($n = 11$)							
	1	54.18	10.53	4.91	4.95	9.36	10.88
	2	57.55	8.55	2.55	3.11	10.82	8.23
	3	58.55	11.08	4.55	6.92	8.18	7.56
	4	58.73	12.35	4.45	7.45	9.00	8.23

TABLE 7
Means and Standard Deviations for Divers and Avoiders on Four Dependent Measures in Study 2

Group	Trial	Cognitive Anxiety		Self-Efficacy		Heart Rate		Autonomic Perception	
		M	*SD*	*M*	*SD*	*M*	*SD*	*M*	*SD*
Divers (*n* = 59)									
	1	42.31	11.40	24.58	9.67	30.25	17.15	44.03	29.79
	2	40.20	11.68	28.93	9.95	16.92	16.03	35.24	29.57
	3	37.67	11.69	32.00	10.01	13.73	15.99	30.64	28.42
	4	35.39	12.05	33.29	10.07	6.95	16.47	26.24	28.25
Avoiders (*n* = 15)									
	1	49.33	9.70	12.07	8.51	12.13	14.55	50.60	21.64
	2	57.60	11.03	6.20	6.27	11.27	16.91	65.60	27.99
	3	55.67	12.92	3.87	4.81	4.13	12.12	61.07	31.65
	4	54.73	13.65	3.67	6.48	7.47	17.06	60.78	39.52

TABLE 8
ANOVA Summary Table for Each Dependent Measure for Study 1 and Study 2

Variable	Study 1			Study 2		
	df	*F*	*p*	*df*	*F*	*p*
Group main effect						
Cognitive anxiety	1/72	38.75	.001	1/72	25.50	.001
Self-efficacy	1/72	34.99	.001	1/72	90.69	.001
Heart rate	1/72	9.21	.003	1/72	7.79	.007
Autonomic perception				1/72	14.06	.001
Trials main effect[a]						
Cognitive anxiety	2/162	27.34	.001	2/156	13.44	.001
Self-efficacy	2/125	69.12	.001	2/121	23.16	.001
Heart rate	2/175	38.60	.001	3/189	68.56	.001
Autonomic perception				2/149	10.93	.001
Group × Trials effect[a]						
Cognitive anxiety	2/162	11.51	.001	2/156	13.81	.001
Self-efficacy	2/125	12.57	.001	2/121	40.27	.001
Heart rate	2/175	4.75	.001	3/189	10.44	.001
Autonomic perception				2/149	10.57	.001

[a]The lambda hat adjustment for degrees of freedom was used in this analysis to correct for non-symmetry in the variance-covariance matrix.

Cognitive Anxiety

Divers reported less anxiety (Study 1 M = 38.99, Study 2 M = 38.01) than avoiders (Study 1 M = 57.25, Study 2 M = 54.09). Post hoc t tests indicated that this difference occurred on the last two trials, t's (58) = 3.45 and 4.03 respectively for Study 1 and on the last three trials for Study 2, t's (24) = 2.96, 3.02, and 3.22, respectively. Moreover, post hoc tests using Tukey WSD for trials comparisons indicated in Study 1 that cognitive anxiety significantly decreased for divers from Trial 1 to Trial 4. In Study 2, divers again significantly decreased in their reported cognitive anxiety; however, avoiders significantly increased. These results are diagrammed in Figure 2.

Self-Efficacy

As expected, divers reported having higher efficacy expectations (Study 1 M = 25.61, Study 2 M = 30.27) than avoiders (Study 1 M = 4.11, Study 2 M = 6.06). Post hoc t' tests indicated that this difference occurred on every trial, t's (21) = 3.33, 4.85, 5.24, and 5.84 in Study 1 and t's (39) = 3.61, 6.31, 7.68, and 8.09 in Study 2. Analyses on the trial means indicated in Study 1 that divers significantly increased their expectations from Trial 1 to Trial 4, whereas avoiders did not change over trials. In study 2, divers again significantly increased their self-efficacy, but avoiders significantly decreased their self-efficacy over trials. These results are diagrammed in Figure 3.

Heart Rate

Divers had significantly higher increases in HR (Study 1 M = 20.08, Study 2 M = 18.77) than avoiders (Study 1 M = 9.93, Study 2 M = 8.09), even though their reported cognitive anxiety was lower than avoiders. However, post hoc t' tests did not reveal any significant differences by trial at the .01 level. Analyses on the trial means indicated that in both studies, divers significantly decreased in HR change over trials, whereas avoiders did not change. These results are diagrammed in Figure 4.

Autonomic Perception

Study 2 was the only study that measured autonomic perception. The main effect showed that divers had lower APQ scores (M = 33.15) than avoiders (M = 59.19). However, post hoc t tests did not reveal any significant differences by trial at the .01 level. Post hoc tests across trials revealed that divers significantly decreased their perception of physiological arousal

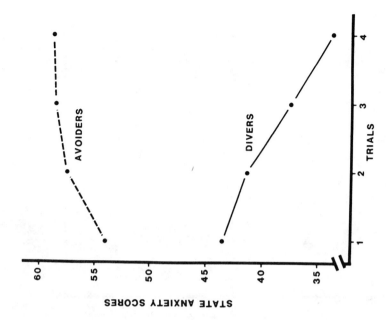

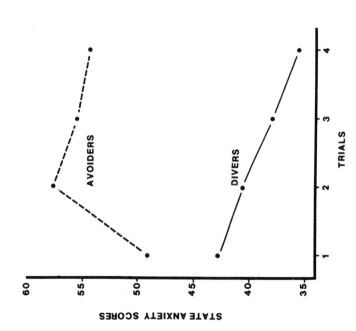

FIGURE 2. Mean comparisons of cognitive anxiety scores between divers and avoiders in Study 1 (left) and Study 2 (right).

19

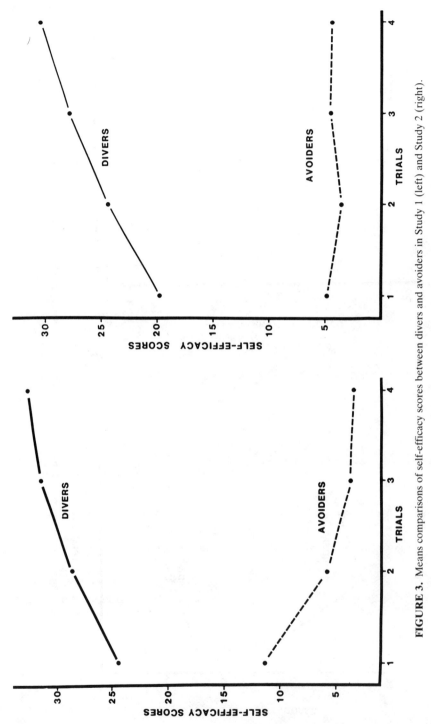

FIGURE 3. Means comparisons of self-efficacy scores between divers and avoiders in Study 1 (left) and Study 2 (right).

20

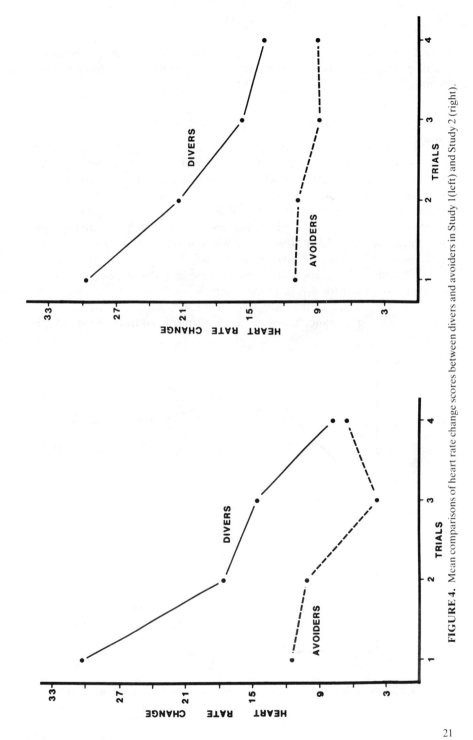

FIGURE 4. Mean comparisons of heart rate change scores between divers and avoiders in Study 1(left) and Study 2 (right).

from Trial 1 to Trial 4, whereas avoiders significantly increased their autonomic perception from Trial 1 to Trial 2. These results are diagrammed in
Figure 5.

Accuracy of Efficacy Judgments

Although the results from the present studies showed that self-efficacy
was a significant predictor of performance and that mastery attempts increased efficacy expectations whereas avoidance decreased expectation,
they do not show that self-efficacy is necessarily an accurate predictor of
performance. Bandura (1977) has noted that discrepancies between efficacy
judgment and behavior will occur when tasks or circumstances are ambiguous, when one has little information on which to base efficacy expectations,
or when there are no incentives to perform.

To examine the relationship between efficacy judgment and approach/
avoidance behavior for divers and avoiders, self-efficacy scores and performance scores for the entire sample in each study were standardized. The
standardized performance scores were then subtracted from the standard-

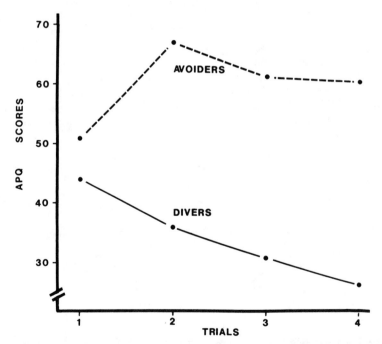

FIGURE 5. Mean comparisons of autonomic perception between divers and avoiders in
Study 2.

ized efficacy scores to get an estimate of efficacy judgment accuracy. Positive scores indicated that efficacy judgments were higher than actual performance and negative scores indicated that efficacy judgments were lower than actual performance.

Divers and avoiders were compared on their average judgment accuracy scores. One would expect that the avoiders would be less accurate than the divers because they did not have the mastery experiences and, therefore, had less information on which to base their judgments. Results of the t test were in the expected direction. In both Study 1 and Study 2, divers were more accurate in their efficacy judgment (Study 1 $M = -.124$, Study 2 M = .149) than were avoiders (Study 1 $M = .596$, Study 2 $M = .712$), Study 1 t (16) = 4.92, $p < .001$; Study 2 t (30) = 4.82, $p < .001$.

GENERAL DISCUSSION

The overall results of both studies support Bandura's (1977) hypothesis that self-efficacy is a cognitive mediator of approach/avoidance behavior. Although self-efficacy appears to play an important and necessary role in the initial learning of a high-avoidance motor task such as a modified back dive, these results indicate that performance accomplishments are also important in predicting future performance behavior. Our findings are consistent with those found in other studies (McAuley, 1983; Schunk, 1981). These results suggest that instructors of high-avoidance tasks should not only provide plenty of practice opportunities but also ensure that these experiences result in successes that will raise efficacy expectations. Participant modeling (Feltz et al., 1979; Lewis, 1974) and proximal goal setting (Schunk, 1983) are two techniques that have been shown to enhance self-efficacy and performance.

The source of efficacy information that appeared to be most predictive of self-efficacy prior to the initial performance attempt was autonomic perception. According to Bandura (1977), past performance accomplishments should be a stronger source of efficacy information than perceived autonomic arousal. However, the past performance accomplishments in the present studies were measured on related performance tasks and may not have been related closely enough to the modified back dive to influence subjects' self-efficacy. After the initial performance attempt, however, performance accomplishments on the diving task was the strongest influence on subjects' self-efficacy. This finding is consistent with Bandura's (1977) theory and with previous research which has found clinical techniques based on performance accomplishments to have the strongest influence on subjects' self-efficacy (Bandura & Adams, 1977; Feltz et al., 1979; McAuley, 1983).

The comparison of divers and avoiders supported Bandura's (1977) contention that successes will raise efficacy expectations and failure (or avoidance) will lower them. Subjects who attempted the task also perceived that they were less anxious and had less autonomic arousal than subjects who avoided the task, even though subjects who attempted the task actually had higher increases in HR than avoiders. Borkovec (1978) has suggested that when individuals avoid the behavior their physiological arousal is not high because they now have nothing to fear. This does not explain why avoiders' perceptions of arousal and anxiety were high and in some cases increased over trials. Perhaps avoiders and divers cognitively processed their arousal differently. Divers may have interpreted their arousal as facilitative, whereas avoiders may have interpreted theirs as debilitative. In a study of test anxiety, investigators found that low-anxious subjects labeled their arousal as facilitative, whereas high-anxious subjects labeled their arousal as debilitative, even though low-anxious subjects had higher HRs than their counterparts (Hollandsworth, Glazeski, Kirkland, Jones, & Van Norman, 1979). Future research may wish to assess how subjects interpret their arousal along with measures of actual arousal.

The present findings also indicated that subjects who avoided the back dive made less accurate efficacy judgments than subjects who attempted the task. The efficacy expectations of avoiders exceeded their actual performance. These inflated efficacy expectations may have been due to a lack of actual performance accomplishments on which to base judgments or a lack of motiviation. The reason for these inaccurate judgments cannot be determined from the results of the present studies. Future investigators may wish to ensure a high level of motivation in their subjects when testing self-efficacy in approach/avoidance behavior.

REFERENCES

Bandura, A. (1969). *Principles of behavior modification*. New York: Holt, Rinehart & Winston.
Bandura, A. (1977). Self-efficacy: Toward a unifying theory of behavioral change. *Psychological Review, 84*, 191–215.
Bandura, A. (1978). Reflections on self-efficacy. In S. Rachman (Ed.), *Advances in behaviour research and therapy* (Vol. 1, pp. 237–269). Oxford: Pergamon Press.
Bandura, A., & Adams, N.E. (1977). Analysis of self-efficacy theory of behavioral change. *Cognitive Therapy and Research, 1*, 287–310.
Borkovec, T.D. (1976). Physiological and cognitive processes in the regulation of anxiety. In G.E. Schwartz & D. Shapiro (Eds.), *Conciousness and self-regulation: Advances in research* (Vol. 1 pp. 261–312. New York: Plenum.
Borkovec, T.D. (1078). Self-efficacy: Cause or reflection of behavioral change. In S. Rachman (Ed.), *Advances in behaviour research and therapy* (Vol. 1, pp. 163–170). Oxford: Pergamon Press.

Feltz, D.L. (1982). Path analysis of the causal elements in Bandura's theory of self-efficacy and an anxiety-based model of avoidance behavior. *Journal of Personality and Social Psychology, 42,* 764–781.

Feltz, D.L., Landers, D.M., & Raeder, U. (1979). Enhancing self-efficacy in a high-avoidance motor task: A comparison of modeling techniques. *Journal of Sport Psychology, 1,* 112–122.

Feltz, D.L., & Mugno, D.A. (1983). A replication of the path analysis of the causal elements in Bandura's theory of self-efficacy and the influence of autonomic perception. *Journal of Sport Psychology, 5,* 263–277.

Hollandsworth, J.G., Jr., Glazeski, R.C., Kirkland, K., Jones, G.E., & Van Norman, I.R. (1979). An analysis of the nature and effects of test anxiety: Cognitive, behavioral, and physiological components. *Cognitive Therapy and Research, 3,* 165–180.

Kerlinger, F.N., & Pedhazuer, E. (1973). *Multiple regressions in behavioral research.* New York: Holt, Rinehart & Winston.

Lang, P. (1971). The application of psychophysiological methods to the study of psychotherapy and behavior modification. In A.E. Bergin & S.L. Garfield (Eds.), *Handbook of psychotherapy and behavior change* (pp. 75–125). New York: Wiley.

Leitenberg, H., Agras, W.S., Butz, R., & Wincze, J. (1971). Relationship between heart rate and behavioral change during the treatment of phobias. *Journal of Abnormal Psychology, 78,* 59–68.

Lewis, S. (1974). A comparison of behavior therapy techniques in the reduction of fearful avoidance behavior. *Behavior Therapy, 5,* 648–655.

Mandler, G., Mandler, J.M., & Uviller, E.T. (1958). Autonomic feedback: The perception of autonomic activity. *Journal of Abnormal and Social Psychology, 56,* 367–373.

McAuley, E. (1983, May). *Modeling and self-efficacy: An examination of Bandura's model of behavioral change.* Paper presented at the annual meeting of the North American Society for the Psychology of Sport and Physical Activity, East Lansing, MI.

Mowrer, O.H. (1947). On the dual nature of learning: A re-interpretation of "conditioning" and "problem-solving." *Harvard Education Review, 17,* 102–148.

Ott, L. (1977). *An introduction to statistical methods and data analysis.* North Scituate, MA: Duxburg Press.

Rachman, S. (1976). The passing of the two-stage theory of fear and avoidance: Fresh possibilities. *Behaviour Research and Therapy, 14,* 125–131.

Schunk, D.H. (1981). Modeling and attributional effects on children's achievement: A self-efficacy analysis. *Journal of Educational Psychology, 73,* 93–105.

Schunk, D.H. (1983). Developing children's self-efficacy and skills: The roles of social comparative information and goal setting. *Contemporary Educational Psychology, 8,* 76–86.

Spielberger, C.D., Gorsuch, R.L., & Lushene, R.E. (1970). *The state-trait anxiety inventory.* Palo Alto, CA: Consulting Psychologists Press.

Wolpe, J. (1974). *The practice of behavior therapy.* New York: Pergamon Press.

2

NEED FOR STIMULATION AND SPORT INVOLVEMENT AMONG ADOLESCENT MALES

Garry E. Chick
John W. Loy
Michael Walsh

This study examined "need for stimulation" (nStim) as a factor in sport involvement for a sample of 145 male, private secondary school students. Individual differences in nStim were assessed by means of Vando's Reducing-Augmenting Scale (RAS) and Zuckerman's Sensation Seeking Scale (SSS). Forms of sport involvement were analyzed in terms of five dimensions: (1) degree of risk, (2) degree of spatial/temporal uncertainty, (3) self-paced or reactive emphasis, (4) direct or parallel competition, and (5) degree of body contact. Correlational and discriminant function analyses demonstrated that subjects' scores on the RAS and SSS were positively related, and that subjects high in nStim participated more often in sports characterized by stimulating sensory conditions than subjects low in nStim. Overall findings of the study indicated that the concepts of stimulus intensity modulation and sensation seeking have certain similarities and, thus, suggest that selected facets from both of these lines of research should be incorporated in future studies of nStim in sport situations.

INTRODUCTION

Research regarding individual differences in degree and kind of sport involvement represents a long-standing interest of sport psychologists. In recent years several investigators of this topic have specifically sought to explain individual differences in patterns of sport involvement in terms of what can be broadly labeled as "need for stimulation" (nStim). Studies of individual differences in nStim in sport situations have largely emphasized one of two personality dimensions; namely, stimulus intensity modulation and sensation seeking.

Stimulus Intensity Modulation Perspective

The major tenet of the stimulus intensity modulation perspective is that individuals differ in their subjective experience and response to the intensity of identical stimuli (Barnes, 1976; Petrie, 1960, 1967; Sales, 1971, 1972;

Sales, Guydosh, & Iacono, 1974; Sales & Throop 1972; Vando, 1969, 1974).
Although several specific theories are associated with the stimulus intensity
modulation perspective, the majority of studies in sport situations have
drawn upon Petrie's perceptual augmenting-reducing theory (see reviews by
Donnelly, 1976; Loy & Donnelly, 1976),

Petrie proposed that individuals can be classified as sensory augmenters, moderates, or reducers. "The key assumption in Petrie's view of perceptual modulation is that reducers have an abnormally high need for stimulation because their nervous systems dampen down incoming stimuli, whereas
augmenters, whose nervous systems amplify stimuli, attempt to avoid excessive stimulation" (Davis, Cowles, & Kohn, 1983, p. 491). Petrie measured
individual differences in augmenting-reducing by means of a modified version of the kinesthetic aftereffect task (KAE) developed by Kohler and
Dinnerstein (1947). In this task blindfolded subjects "match the width of a
standard bar which is felt with one hand, with an area on a tapered bar which
is felt with the other hand. A large (or smaller) block is then rubbed.
Thereafter, the original test bar is again equated with the tapered bar, and
the difference between the two subjective estimations is measured." (Ryan
& Foster, 1967, p. 472) Reducers tend to underestimate (reduce) and
augmenters tend to overestimate (augment) kinesthetically perceived size
after stimulation, while moderates tend to accurately estimate the correct
size.

A substantial body of research has been addressed to Petrie's theory,
and many behavioral correlates of the KAE have been identified (see review
by Barnes, 1976). Predictions from Petrie's theory have been especially
successful in sport situations. For example, drawing upon samples of male
high school and university students and using the KAE to assess nStim,
Ryan and colleagues (Ryan, 1969; Ryan & Foster, 1967; Ryan & Kovacic,
1966) have shown that athletes in contact sports tend to be reducers, nonathletes tend to be augmenters, and athletes in noncontact sports tend to be
moderates with respect to their degree of stimulus intensity modulation.
More specifically, Ryan and his colleagues have demonstrated that contact
athletes, relative to noncontact athletes and nonathletes, (1) underestimate
kinesthetically perceived size after stimulation, (2) tolerate more pain, and
(3) underestimate various measures of elapsed time.

Although predictions from Petrie's theory have been fairly successful,
concerns have been raised about her measuring procedure (see, e.g., Gardner, 1961; Hoff, 1979; Morgan & Hilgard, 1972; Spilker & Callaway, 1969).
These concerns include questions about the reliability and validity of the
KAE, and the fact that the KAE is a very time-consuming procedure; for
example, it requires a subject to rest his or her hands for 45 minutes before

testing begins. Thus, several researchers have used Vando's (1969, 1974) Reducing-Augmenting Scale (RAS) to assess individual differences in nStim. His paper-and-pencil instrument is composed of 54 forced-choice items, each pair presenting a high-stimulation and a low-stimulation choice. High scorers on the RAS are identified as reducers and low scorers are classified as augmenters. Vando's theoretical framework is compatible with that of Petrie but specifically emphasizes the dimension of pain tolerance. Based on data collected from a sample of 80 female university students, Vando (1969) obtained a correlation of .839 between subjects' scores on the RAS and a measure of pain tolerance (i.e., the amount of gross pressure subjects would tolerate on their shins).

Berger (1970) administered the RAS to selected samples of "Ivy League" university athletes and found that the most marked reducers participated in sports characterized by a combination of a high probability of physical harm and a high degree of spatial/temporal uncertainty. More specifically, she discovered that divers, skiers, and wrestlers had the highest scores on the RAS, followed in relative rank order by tumblers, swimmers, discus throwers, shot-putters, golfers, tennis players, and hurdlers. Similarly, Donnelly (1976) found a substantial relationship between nStim and sport environmental dimensions. For a sample of 315 general university students (139 males, 176 females), Donnelly found that high scorers on the RAS preferred sport situations characterized by risk, speed, vertigo, combativeness, probability of physical harm, and a high level of competition.

Sensation Seeking Perspective

Proponents of the sensation seeking perspective of nStim in sport situations have generally drawn upon various versions of Zuckerman's (1979) theory of sensation seeking and have typically assessed nStim by means of various forms of the Sensation Seeking Scale (SSS) initially developed by Zuckerman, Kolin, Price, and Zoob (1964). The SSS was specifically designed as a psychometric measure of "the need for varied, novel and complex sensations and experiences and the willingness to take physical and social risks for the sake of such experiences" (Zuckerman, 1979, p. 10). This scale has undergone several revisions (Forms II through V) and has been shown to be a reliable and valid measure of sensation seeking (Zuckerman, 1978, 1979). Unlike the RAS, the SSS has several subscales intended to measure more specific aspects of nStim, including a general sensation seeking subscale (Gen, Form IV) or a total score (Form V) and subscales directed at thrill and adventure seeking (TAS), experience seeking (ES), disinhibition (Dis), and boredom susceptibility (BS) (Zuckerman, 1971).

Zuckerman (1983) reviewed 12 studies[1] of the relationship of sensation seeking, as measured by the SSS, to involvement in sports that differ on the dimension of risk of either physical injury or of a social nature. He concluded that "the broad trait of SS is related to participation in specific kinds of sports, namely those that provide unusual sensations and novel experiences such as those involved in sky-diving, hand-gliding, skiing and scuba diving" (Zuckerman, 1983, pp. 290−291). A recent example of this line of investigation in sport psychology is Straub's (1982a) study of sensation seeking among participants in high- and low-risk sports. He found that hang gliders and auto racers (groups exemplifying high-risk sports) have significantly higher levels of sensation seeking, especially in terms of scores on the Total and TAS subscales of the SSS, than bowlers (a group exemplifying a low-risk sport).

Problem and Purpose

On the one hand, the two theoretical perspectives of stimulus intensity modulation and sensation seeking show certain similarities. For example, both perspectives were initially associated with research focused on sensory deprivation; both perspectives deal with the notion of optimal levels of arousal; both perspectives posit neural and physiological bases of nStim; and both perspectives seem to share four implicit assumptions when utilized in a sport context, namely:

> (1) individuals differ in the need for stimulation, (2) sport situations have varying stimulus value, (3) the interaction between individuals (sport-persons) and environments (sport situations) influences the emotional state of individuals with respect to the degree of arousal effected, and (4) individual levels of arousal influence behavioral responses toward and in sport situations. (Loy & Donnelly, 1976, p. 80)

On the other hand, the two theoretical perspectives have been held to represent conflicting viewpoints regarding nStim. Zuckerman, for example, baldly states that "the correlates of sensation seeking are not in accord with the predictions that would logically be made from Petrie's augmenting-reducing theory" (1979, p. 228). However, contrary to Zuckerman's contention, several recent studies have indicated a positive relationship between perceptual reduction as measured by the RAS, and sensation seeking as

---

[1]The 12 studies are Bacon (1974), Cellini (1982), Connolly (1981), Fowler, Knorring, and Oreland (1980), Heyman and Ross (1980), Hymbaugh and Garrett (1974), Kusyszyn, Steinberg, and Elliot (1974), McCutcheon (1980), Stirling (1977), Straub (1982a, 1982b), and Wickoff (1982).

measured by the Gen subscale of the SSS (Coulas, 1981; Goldman, Kohn, & Hunt, 1983; Kohn, Hunt, & Hoffman, 1982).

Granted the problematic nature of the relationship between stimulus intensity modulation and sensation seeking, and given the fact that no study to date in a sport context has compared the relationship of nStim and sport involvement from the two viewpoints, the general purpose of the present study was to examine the relationships between the RAS and the SSS and to compare the degree of variance in patterns of sport involvement accounted for by psychometric scores on the RAS and the SSS, respectively, for a sample of male adolescents.

This study emphasized individual differences as they relate to decisions about sport involvement rather than differences among participants in specific sports selected as polar exemplars of some dimension, such as risk. It was assumed that if individual differences in nStim, as measured by the RAS and the SSS, influence the choice of sports, then the choices should show some consistency across seasons. Because different sports are often played during different seasons, it was necessary to utilize some means of categorizing sports in order to determine whether or not choices demonstrated consistency. To this end, five sport models, each representing a dimension hypothesized to be related to nStim, were selected. These models of sport involvement emphasized, respectively, (1) the degree of risk of physical injury, (2) the degree of spatial/temporal uncertainty, (3) self-paced versus reactive emphasis, (4) parallel versus direct competition, and (5) the degree of body contact involved in play.

Hypotheses

The basic assumption of the present study was that augmenting-reducing and sensation seeking represent underlying dimensions of nStim, thus it was hypothesized that the scale scores on the RAS and the SSS would be positively correlated. The principal hypotheses of the study, however, concerned the relationship of nStim, as measured by the RAS and the SSS, for each of the five sport models. Specifically, two separate hypotheses were set forth for each of the sport classification models as follows:

Model 1. *Degree of Risk of Physical Injury*
    H1a: Individuals with high nStim will participate in more high-risk sports than will those who are low in nStim.
    H1b: Measures of nStim will significantly differentiate group membership in high- and low-risk sports.

Model 2. *Degree of Spatial/Temporal Uncertainty*

    H2a: Individuals with high nStim will participate in more sports that are high in spatial/temporal uncertainty than will those who are low in nStim.

    H2b: Measures of nStim will significantly differentiate group membership in sports that are high and low in spatial/temporal uncertainty.

Model 3. *Self-Paced versus Reactive Emphasis*

    H3a: Individuals with high nStim will participate in more reactive, versus self-paced, sports than will those who are low in nStim.

    H3b: Measures of nStim will significantly differentiate group membership in self-paced and reactive sports.

Model 4. *Parallel versus Direct Competition*

    H4a: Individuals with high nStim will participate in more sports involving direct, versus parallel, competition than will those who are low in nStim.

    H4b: Measures of nStim will significantly differentiate group membership in parallel and direct competition sports.

Model 5. *Degree of Body Contact*

    H5a: Individuals with high nStim will participate in more sports involving a high degree of body contact than will those who are low in nStim.

    H5b: Measures of nStim will significantly differentiate group membership in sports that are high or low in body contact.

METHOD

Subjects

The subjects in this study were 145 male students enrolled in grades 8 through 12 at a private New England secondary school. Subjects ranged in age from 13 to 19 years with a mean age of 16.56.

Subjects were required to participate in a physical activity (typically a sport)[2] of their choice during each term of the school year (i.e., Fall, Winter, and Spring). The variety of sport activities selected and the number of participants in each per season are shown in Table 1.[3]

---

[2]A number of activities in which some individuals participated were eliminated from consideration because they did not conform to a general definition of sport and could not be readily classified in each of the sport models used in this study. These activities included physical conditioning, dance, lifesaving, mountaineering, outdoor skill, riding, sailing, and yoga.

Data Collection

Subjects were given questionnaires by school counselors and selected teachers and were permitted to complete them at their convenience in their dormitory rooms. The questionnaires were designed to elicit basic demographic data and information about patterns of sport participation from each subject. In addition, each questionnaire included Vando's RAS and Zucker-

TABLE 1
Sports and Number of Participants per Season for 145 Male Secondary School Students

Sport	Number of Participants—Fall	Number of Participants—Winter	Number of Participants—Spring
1. Archery	0	0	1
2. Badminton	2	1	0
3. Baseball	0	0	10
4. Basketball	1	28	1
5. Crew	5	0	10
6. Cycling	1	0	2
7. Diving	0	4	0
8. Football	24	0	0
9. Golf	0	0	4
10. Hockey	0	29	0
11. Kayaking	0	0	3
12. Lacrosse	0	0	17
13. Skiing	0	24	0
14. Soccer	52	0	7
15. Softball	0	0	2
16. Swimming	2	10	0
17. Tennis	5	0	23
18. Track	13	9	15
19. Volleyball	2	1	0
20. Water polo	10	0	0
21. Weight lifting	2	2	3
22. Wrestling	0	9	0
Totals	122	124	100

*Note. N*s for this table and subsequent analyses vary owing to missing responses and the fact that several activities that some individuals participated in were excluded from the analyses because they were not readily classifiable in terms of the sport models used in this study.

[3]In addition to having a variety of sport activities to choose from in meeting their school requirement, subjects had the option of selecting one of six levels of competition per season: (1) Varsity, (2) Junior Varsity, (3) Junior League, (4) Ivy League, (5) C Squad, or (6) physical education sport instruction classes.

man's SSS (Form IV). Completed questionnaires were returned by 86% of the male students enrolled at the school.

Variables and Measures

Independent Variables (Psychometric Measures).

Scores on the two psychometric inventories (i.e., the RAS and the Gen, TAS, ED, Dis, and BS subscales of the SSS) constituted the independent variables in this study.

Dependent Variables (Behavioral Measures).

Forms of sport involvement were considered to be the dependent variables in this study. The list of sports in which the subjects participated were dichotomized in terms of five dimensions: (1) degree of risk (or injury) (2) degree of spatial/temporal uncertainty, (3) self-paced or reactive emphasis, (4) parallel or direct competition;[4] and (5) degree of body contact. Although the sports were dichotomized in terms of these dimensions, it is recognized that, with the possible exception of parallel and direct competition, the dimensions are more or less continuous. These dimensions were used to classify sports in terms of five models of sport involvement as shown in Table 2.

This classification procedure was employed for both pragmatic and theoretical reasons. Practically considered, it was not reasonable to examine the degree of nStim of participants in specific sports because the majority of sports had relatively few participants per season. Theoretically considered, sports were classified according to selected dimensions because some authorities have hypothezied that sports having similar underlying dimensions make similar psychological demands upon participants (cf., e.g., Kroll, Loy, Hosek, & Vanek, 1973, Vanek & Cratty, 1970). The dimensions of sport involvement used for classification purposes in the present study intuitively appear to be related to the degree and kind of sensory stimulation experienced by participants. Thus, for each sport model, subjects were grouped into those who (1) participated each season in sports of the same type, for example, three high-risk sports; or (2) participated in one type for two seasons and the other type for the third season, for example, one high-risk

---

[4]Although the self-paced/reactive and direct/parallel models constitute conceptually distinct classifications, it was found that the same sports activities were grouped under the self-paced and parallel categories and the reactive and direct competition categories (see Table 2). Accordingly, results of data analyses are the same for each model and, for the sake of parsimony, results are reported only for the self-paced/reactive emphasis model.

TABLE 2
Dichotomous Categorization of Sports for Five Sport Models

	Sport Model				
Sport	**Degree of Risk**	**Degree of Spatial/Temporal Uncertainty**	**Self-Paced or Reactive**	**Parallel or Direct Competition**	**Degree of Body Contact**
1. Archery	Low	Low	Self-paced	Parallel	Low
2. Badminton	Low	Low	Reactive	Direct	Low
3. Baseball	Low	Low	Reactive	Direct	Low
4. Basketball	Low	High	Reactive	Direct	High
5. Crew	Low	Low	Self-paced	Parallel	Low
6. Cycling	Low	Low	Self-paced	Parallel	Low
7. Diving	High	High	Self-paced	Parallel	Low
8. Football	High	High	Reactive	Direct	High
9. Golf	Low	Low	Self-paced	Parrallel	Low
10. Hockey	High	High	Reactive	Direct	High
11. Kayaking	Low	High	Self-paced	Parallel	Low
12. Lacrosse	High	High	Reactive	Direct	High
13. Skiing	High	High	Self-paced	Parallel	Low
14. Soccer	High	High	Reactive	Direct	High
15. Softball	Low	Low	Reactive	Direct	Low
16. Swimming	Low	Low	Self-paced	Parallel	Low
17. Tennis	Low	High	Reactive	Direct	Low
18. Track	Low	Low	Self-paced	Parallel	Low
19. Volleyball	Low	High	Reactive	Direct	Low
20. Water polo	High	High	Reactive	Direct	High
21. Weight lifting	Low	Low	Self-paced	Parallel	Low
22. Wrestling	High	High	Reactive	Direct	High

and two low-risk sports. This placed the subjects, in terms of each of the models, into one of four possible groups: 3 and 0; 2 and 1; 1 and 2; or 0 and 3.

Tests of Hypotheses

The degree of relationship between the two psychometric inventories was ascertained by correlating the RAS with each of the SSS subscales using Pearson product-moment correlation coefficients. The relationship of the psychometric variables to each of the sport models was ascertained by correlating subjects' scores on the RAS and the SSS with the number of sports in which they participated across the three seasons that (1) were high risk, (2) were high in spatial/temporal uncertainty, (3) were reactive, (4) involved direct competition, and (5) were high in body contact.

The primary research hypotheses were examined through the use of discriminant function analysis (Nie, Hull, Jenkins, Steinbrenner, & Bent, 1975). In the case of the RAS, only one discriminating variable (the RAS score) was used; whereas a stepwise procedure was used for the SSS because it was of interest to determine which of the five subscales contributed to discrimination between the groups as well as the relative contribution of each. The stepwise procedure was controlled by the minimization of Wilk's lambda. Since discriminant analysis provides a classification matrix of known cases, the percentage of cases that are correctly classified can be used, along with the Wilk's lambda and the canonical correlations, to evaluate the discrimination power of the independent variable(s). In addition, Klecka (1980, pp. 50−51) has suggested a proportional reduction in error statistic, tau, that gives a standardized measure of the improvement in the classification of cases over random assignment. Tau was calculated for each of the discriminant analyses. Because there was a substantially different number of subjects in each of the four groups of the various sport models, it was decided, for analytic purposes, to collapse the four groups in each of the models into two groups, each representing participation in a majority two or three of sports of one type (e.g., high risk) or the other (e.g., low risk).

RESULTS

Relationships between Inventories

As shown in Table 3, all scale and subscale scores for the RAS and SSS were significantly related ($p < .005$) with positive correlations ranging from a low of .214 to a high of .712. The highest correlations obtained were between the Gen and the TAS and ES subscales of the SSS (i.e., .712 and .621, respectively).

The data reported in Table 3 provide empirical support for the general hypothesis predicting that the scale scores of the RAS and the SSS would be positively correlated. Specifically, significant ($p < .005$) positive correlations were obtained between subjects' scores on the RAS and all five subscales of the SSS. The most substantial correlations between the two inventories were found for the relationships between the RAS and the TAS subscale of the SSS ($r = .557$); and between the RAS and the Gen subscale of the SSS ($r = .548$).

Relationships between Psychometric Measures and Degree of Sport Involvement

Hypotheses 1a, 2a, 3a, 4a, and 5a predicted that subjects high in nStim would participate more often in sports characterized by stimulating sensory conditions than subjects low in nStim. The data reported in Table 4 offer

TABLE 3
Intercorrelations of Vando's Reducer-Augmenter Scale
(RAS) and Zuckerman's Sensation Seeking Scale (SSS)
for 145 Male Students

	RAS	Gen	TAS	ES	Dis
Gen	.548				
TAS	.557	.712			
ES	.357	.621	.342		
Dis	.424	.356	.374	.400	
BS	.248	.497	.214*	.466	.315

*Significant at the .005 level. All others significant at the .001 level.

TABLE 4
Correlations Between the Number of Sports (0−3) Participated in for Each of the
Sport Models and Scores on the Psychometric Inventories

Sport Model	Psychometric Scales					
	RAS	Gen	TAS	ES	Dis	BS
Degree of risk	$r =$ .414	.242	.261	.124	.181	.096
	$n =$ 99	102	102	102	102	102
	$p =$ .001	.007	.004	.108	.034	.169
Degree of spatial/ temporal uncertainty	$r =$ .338	.120	.063	.173	.257	.115
	$n =$ 106	109	109	109	109	109
	$p =$ .001	.108	.257	.036	.004	.118
Self-paced/ Reactive	$r =$ .295	.079	−.054	.126	.148	.108
	$n =$ 107	110	110	110	110	110
	$p =$ .001	.207	.287	.095	.062	.131
Degree of body contact	$r =$ .258	.051	−.040	−.003	.028	.062
	$n =$ 105	108	108	108	108	108
	$p =$ .004	.301	.340	.489	.387	.264

generally empirical support for these hypotheses. However, as is evident from the table, RAS scores were more strongly correlated with each of the classifications of sport involvement than were any of the SSS subscales. Specifically, RAS scores were significantly correlated ($p < .05$) with all models of sport involvement; whereas only 5 of the 20 correlations between the SSS subscales and the sport models were statistically significant ($p < .05$), namely, degree of risk and Gen, TAS, and Dis; and degree of spatial/ temporal uncertainty and ES and Dis. As indicated in Table 4, the highest obtained correlation was between the RAS and Degree of Risk ($r = .414$, $p < .001$).

TABLE 5
Summary Statistics for the Discriminant Function Analysis of the RAS and Sport Models.

Sport Model	Percentage of Correct Predictions	Canonical Correlation	Wilk's Lambda	χ^2	df	p	tau
Degree of risk	65.66	.40	.837	17.23	1	.000	.31
Degree of spatial/ temporal uncertainty	65.09	.29	.915	9.18	1	.003	.29
Self-paced/ Reactive	59.81	.23	.947	5.71	1	.019	.23
Degree of body contact	51.43	.17	.971	2.99	1	.084	.03

TABLE 6
Summary Statistics for the Discriminant Function Analysis of the SSS and Sport Models

Sport Model	Discriminating Variables	Percentage of Correct Predictions	Canonical Correlation	Wilk's Lambda	χ^2	df	p	tau
Degree of risk	Gen, TAS	60.78	.30	.912	8.85	2	.012	.22
Degree of spatial/ temporal uncertainty	Dis	57.80	.19	.962	3.99	1	.046	.16
Self-paced/ reactive	TAS, BS	58.18	.19	.966	3.64	2	.162	.16
Degree of body contact	Dis	54.63	.11	.987	1.30	1	.254	.09

Relationships between Psychometric Measures and Sport Group Memberships

Tables 5 and 6 summarize the results of the discriminant analyses of the sport models and psychometric variables. As could be expected from the correlational results reported in Table 4, the RAS proved, with one exception, to provide better classification accuracy than the SSS. For each sport model, the canonical correlations were higher and the values of Wilk's lambda were lower for the RAS scores than for the SSS scores.

The stepwise procedure selected more than one discriminating variable from the SSS subscales in only two models (i.e., degree of risk and self-paced/reactive emphasis). For degree of risk, the standardized discriminant function coefficients were .757 for the TAS and .317 for the Gen subscale, indicating the greater contribution of TAS to differentiating between the two groups. The standardized discriminant function coefficients for the TAS and BS subscales, in the self-paced/reactive sport model, were $-.598$ and .936, respectively. However, as indicated in Table 6, this function was not statistically significant.

The results reported in Tables 5 and 6 offer empirical support for Hypotheses 1b through 4b with respect to the RAS as a measure of nStim. However, neither individual differences in reducing-augmenting nor individual differences in sensation seeking permitted significant discrimination between subjects who chose to participate in two or more sports that are high in degree of body contact and those who participated in two or more sports that are low in degree of body contact. Hypotheses 1a and 2a were supported for the SSS as a measure of nStim, while hypotheses 3a, 4a, and 5a were not.

As the square of the canonical correlation indicates the proportion of the variance in a discriminant function that is related to group differences, it is evident from Tables 5 and 6 that relatively low amounts of the variance in group membership were accounted for by scores on the RAS or the SSS. For the degree of risk and the degree of spatial/temporal uncertainty models, the values of tau do indicate that a reasonable improvement (31% and 29%, respectively) in the classification of cases, over random assignment, was accomplished by individual differences in RAS scores.

DISCUSSION

Relationships with Past Studies

The results reported above indicate that individuals who vary in terms of nStim will tend, given the opportunity for making sport participation choices, to select sports that are most in accord with their style of stimulus intensity modulation and sensation seeking. The results are also in general accord with those of earlier studies using the RAS in sport contexts. Specifically, the results agree with the conclusions of Berger (1970) that individuals who participate in sports that are high in spatial/temporal uncertainty are reducers, as are those who participate in sports having high probability of harm (e.g., risky sports). In addition, reducers tend to select sports that involve direct rather than parallel competition and that emphasize reactive rather than self-paced activities. However, in the present study reducing-augmenting was found to be only weakly related to the degree of body contact in the various sports. This result runs counter to findings reported by Berger (1970), Donnelly (1976), and Ryan and Foster (1967).

Sensation seeking appeared to be influential only in the choice of sports that differed in terms of degree of risk and degree of spatial/temporal uncertainty. This result is unsurprising inasmuch as Zuckerman (1983) hypothesized that "SS will only be related to participation in the more risky sports" (p. 287). For sports differing in degree of risk, the SSS subscales that contributed to discrimination between the groups were the Gen and TAS, a result that accords with several earlier studies (for a review, see Zuckerman, 1983). On the other hand, the Dis subscale was the most discriminating variable for sports categorized according to degree of spatial/temporal uncertainty.

The results of this study are somewhat at variance with those of Stirling (1977). Using the KAE rather than the RAS, Stirling compared male athletes participating in body contact sports with athletes participating in non-body-contact sports, and with nonathletes. He found that, while the three groups did not differ overall on the Gen subscale of the SSS (Form IV), the analyses of variance were significant for the TAS and Dis subscales with body contact athletes scoring highest and nonathletes scoring lowest. Body contact athletes were greater reducers that either of the other groups.

Although RAS was consistently superior to the SSS in the classification of subjects, neither accounted for a large amount of the variance in any of the sport models. Additionally, as can be seen from Table 2, the sport models are all rather similar; indeed, two are identical (self-paced versus reactive and parallel versus direct) in terms of how the various sports were classified.

Implications

Several authors have called attention to possible parallels between research regarding stimulus intensity modulation and research regarding sensation seeking in sport situations (see, e.g., Browne & Mahoney, 1984; Donnelly, 1976; Loy & Donnelly, 1976; Morgan, 1980). However, the present study is the first attempt to compare these two lines of investigation in a sport context. The results reported above show that, contrary to the contention of Zuckerman (1979), measures of augmenting-reducing and sensation seeking are positively related and have similar correlates with respect to patterns of sport involvement. But, given the exploratory nature of the present study, further research is required regarding the relationship between individual differences in nStim and patterns of sport involvement. Findings of the present study suggest that the following lines of investigation would be worthy of pursuit.

First, there is a clear need to assess the relative merits of the various forms of psychometric and psychophysical measurement of nStim as well as to examine their interrelationships. Recent research has demonstrated substantial intercorrelations among a variety of measures of nStim and arousal, including absolute auditory threshold, average evoked cortical response, extraversion, kinesthetic aftereffect, neuroticism, sensation seeking, stimulus screening, and type "A" behavior patterns (see, e.g., Davis, Cowles, & Kohn, 1983; Eysenck & Zuckerman, 1978; Furnham, 1984,; Goldman, Kohn, & Hunt, 1983; Paisey & Mangan, 1980; Ridgeway & Hare, 1981). This body of research needs to be integrated and replicated in sport situations.

Second, there is an evident need to assess the relative merits of the various theories of nStim and arousal, including those of Brebner, 1983; Ellis, 1973; Eysenck, 1955; Gray, 1967; Mehrabian and Russell, 1974; Petrie, 1967; Sales, 1971; Schultz, 1965; Strelau, 1970; Vando, 1969; and Zuckerman, 1979. Initial efforts to synthesize the tenets and research findings of theories of nStim and arousal suggest that works to date might be accommodated within a "strength of the nervous system" perspective (see, e.g., Davis, Cowles, & Kohn, 1983). However, as Gale and Edwards (1983) have warned: "Because both psychophysiology and individual differences sample physiological, behavioral and experimental domains, a variety of logical and technical problems make research in this field extremely difficult." (p. 361).[5] Notwithstanding this cautionary note, sport situations seem to offer ideal proving grounds for examining the interrelationships among the behavioral, experimental, and physiological domains of nStim.

Third, given the fact that most theories of nStim and arousal posit neurological, physiological, and sometimes hormonal bases (see, e.g., Daitzman & Zuckerman, 1980; Daitzman, Zuckerman, Sammelwitz, & Ganjam, 1978), a further area of investigation should be the degree to which nStim reflects innate biological predispositions versus learned attributes. For example, Roberts and Luxbacher (1982) found that, among college soccer players, attackers are greater reducers while defenders are greater augmenters, as measured by the RAS. It may then be asked whether this result is due to biologically predisposed reducers and augmenters gravitating toward attacker and defender positions, respectively; or whether such styles of stimulus intensity modulation are learned as part of playing different positions and, hence, are useful in the performance of attacking or defending roles.

Fourth, the failure of the RAS and the SSS to account for a substantial amount of the variance in the various sport models used in the present study suggests that there is a need to develop better models of sport involvement.

---

[5]See *Australian Journal of Psychology*, 1983, *35*(3), for a special issue devoted to "personality and temperament."

It is, additionally, important that more precise methods of measurement of the dimensions of these sport models be developed so that there is no need to make assumptions concerning attributes such as "degree of body contact" which may not only differ among sports but may also differ within the same sport at varied levels of competition. In part, the weakness of the sport models used in this study may result from the fact that the models do not reflect the way that the subjects themselves perceive the sports. The sport models used in the present study are, in the terminology of Kempton (1981, pp. 3–4), "devised classifications" rather than "folk classifications" in that they were deliberately created for a particular purpose. It is highly unlikely that individuals would verbalize that they chose to participate in particular sports because those sports were "high risk" or "high in spatial/temporal uncertainty." Future research, using empirically derived folk classifications, may demonstrate a stronger relationship between measures of nStim and involvement in different types of sports.

Conclusion

In summary, the study showed that subjects' scores on the RAS and the SSS were positively related, and that subjects high in nStim participated more often in sports characterized by stimulating sensory conditions than subjects low in nStim. These two sets of findings in combination indicate that the concepts of stimulus intensity modulation and sensation seeking have certain similarities; and they suggest that both theoretical viewpoints should be incorporated in future studies of nStim in sport situations.

ACKNOWLEDGMENTS

This paper is a revised version of a paper presented at the annual meeting of the Association for the Anthropological Study of Play, Clemson University, Clemson, South Carolina, 1984. The authors wish to thank Lynn Barnett-Morris for her suggestions for data analysis and Peter Donnelly for his comments on the theoretical content of the paper.

REFERENCES

Bacon, J. (1974). *Sensation seeking levels for members of high-risk organizations.* Unpublished manuscript.

Barnes, G.E. (1976). Individual differences in perceptual reactance: A review of the stimulus intensity modulation individual difference dimension. *Canadian Psychological Review, 17,* 29–52.

Berger, B.G. (1970). *Relationships between the environmental factors of temporal-spatial uncertainty, probability of physical harm, and nature of competition, and selected personality characteristics of athletes.* Unpublished doctoral dissertation, Teachers College, Columbia University.

Brebner, J. (1983). A model of extraversion. *Australian Journal of Psychology, 35*, 349−359.

Browne, M.A., & Mahoney, M.J. (1984). Sport psychology. In M. R. Rosenzweig & L.W. Porter (Eds), *Annual Review of Psychology* (Vol. 35, pp. 605−625). Palo Alto, CA: Annual Reviews.

Cellini, H.R. (1982). *Cognitive and personality trait differences of youthful offenders of property, violent impulsive, and violent premeditated offensive groups.* Unpublished doctoral dissertation, Southern Illinois University.

Connolly, P.M. (1981). *An exploratory study of adults engaging in the high-risk sport of skiing.* Unpublished master's thesis, Rutgers University.

Coulas, J.T. (1981). *Sensation seeking and the perceived and preferred effects of drugs.* Unpublished Honors B.A. Thesis, York University, Downsview, Ontario.

Daitzman, R.J., & Zuckerman, M. (1980). Disinhibitory sensation seeking, personality and gonadal hormones. *Personality and Individual Differences, 1*, 103−110.

Daitzman, R.J.,Zuckerman, M., Sammelwitz, P., & Ganjam, V. (1978). Sensation seeking and gonadal hormones. *Journal of Biosocial Science, 10*, 401−408.

Davis, C., Cowles, M., & Kohn, P. (1983). Strength of the nervous system and augmenting-reducing: Paradox lost. *Personality and Individual Differences, 4*, 491−498.

Donnelly, P. (1976). *A study of need for stimulation and its relationship to sport involvement and childhood environmental variables.* Unpublished master's thesis, University of Massachusetts.

Ellis, M.J. (1973). *Why people play.* Englewood Cliffs, NJ: Prentice-Hall.

Eysenck, J.H. (1955). Cortical inhibition, figural after-effect and theory of personality. *Journal of Abnormal and Social Psychology, 51*, 94−106.

Eysenck, S.B.G., & Zuckerman, M. (1978). The relationship between sensation-seeking and Eysenck's dimensions of personality. *British Journal of Psychology, 69*, 483−487.

Fowler, C.J.,Knorring, L. von, & Oreland, L. (1980). Platelet monoamine oxidase activity in sensation seekers. *Psychiatric research, 3*, 273−279.

Furnham, A. (1984). Extraversion, sensation seeking, stimulus screening and type "A" behaviour pattern: the relationship between various measures of arousal. *Personality and Individual Differences, 5*, 133−140.

Gale, A., & Edwards, J. (1983). Psychophysiology, and individual differences: Theory, research procedures, and the interpretation of data. *Australian Journal of Psychology, 35*, 361−379.

Gardner, R.W. (1961). Individual differences in figural after-effects and response to reversible figures. *British Journal of Psychology, 52*, 269−272.

Goldman, D., Kohn, P.M., & Hunt, R.W. (1983). Sensation seeking, augmenting-reducing, and absolute auditory threshold: A strength-of-the-nervous-system perspective. *Journal of Personality and Social Psychology, 45*, 405−411.

Gray, J.A. (1967). Strength of the nervous system, introversion-extraversion, conditionability and arousal. *Behavioral Research and Therapy, 5*, 151−169.

Heyman, S.R. & Ross, K.G. (1980). Psychological variables affecting SCUBA performance. In C.H. Nadeau, W.R. Halliwell, K.M. Newell, & G.C. Roberts (Eds.), *Psychology of motor behavior and sport—1979* (pp. 180−188). Champaign, IL: Human Kinetics.

Hoff, P.A. (1979). Kinesthetic augmentation and reduction in adult females. *Perceptual and Motor Skills, 48*, 711−720.

Hymbaugh, K.I., & Garrett, J. (1974). Sensation seeking among skydivers. *Perceptual and Motor Skills, 38*, 118.

Kempton, W. (1981). *The folk classification of ceramics.* New York: Academic Press.

Klecka, W.R. (1980). *Discriminant analysis* (Sage University Paper on Quantitative Applications in the Social Sciences, 07-019). Beverly Hills, CA: Sage.

Kohler, W., & Dinnerstein, D. (1947). Figural after-effects in kinesthesis. In A. Michotte (Ed.), *Miscellanea Psychological* (pp. 196–220). Paris: Joseph Vrin.

Kohn, P.M., Hunt, R.W., & Hoffman, E.M. (1982). Aspects of experience seeking. *Canadian Journal of Behavioral Science, 14*, 13–23.

Kroll, W., Loy, J.W., Hosek, V., & Vanek, M. (1973). Multivariate analysis of the personality profiles of championship Czechoslovakian athletes. *International Journal of Sport Psychology, 4*(3), 131–147.

Kusyszyn, I., Steinberg, P., & Elliott, B. (1974, July). *Arousal seeking, physical risk taking, and personality*. Paper presented at the 18th International Congress of Applied Psychology, Montreal.

Loy, J.W., & Donnelly, P. (1976). Need for stimulation as a factor in sport involvement. In T.T. Craig (Ed.), *The humanistic and mental health aspects of sports, exercise and recreation* (pp. 80–89). Chicago: American Medical Association.

McCutcheon, L. (1980, Fall). Running and sensation seeking. *North Virginia Community College Journal*, p. 11.

Mehrabian, A., & Russell, J.A. (1974). *An approach to environmental psychology*. Cambridge, MA: MIT Press.

Morgan, A.H., & Hilgard, E.R. (1972). The lack of retest reliability in individual differences in the kinesthetic after effect. *Education and Psychological Measurement, 32*, 871–878.

Morgan, W.P. (1980). The trait psychology controversy. *Research Quarterly for Exercise and Sport, 51*, 50–76.

Nie, W.H., Hull, C.H., Jenkins, J.G., Steinbrenner, K., & Bent, D.H. (1975). *Statistical package for the social sciences* (2nd ed.). New York: McGraw-Hill.

Paisey, T.J.H., & Mangan, G.L. (1980). The relationship of extraversion, neuroticism and sensation-seeking to questionnaire-derived measures of nervous system properties. *Pavlovian Journal of Biological Science, 15*, 123–130.

Petrie, A. (1960). Some psychological aspects of pain and the relief of suffering. *Annals of the New York Academy of Sciences, 86*, 13–27.

Petrie, A. (1967). *Individuality in pain and suffering*. Chicago: University of Chicago Press.

Ridgeway, D., & Hare, R.D. (1981). Sensation seeking and psychological responses to auditory stimulation. *Psychophysiology, 18*, 613–618.

Roberts, J.M., & Luxbacher, J.A. (1982). Offensive and defensive perspectives in soccer. In J.W. Loy (Ed.), *The paradoxes of play* (pp. 225–238). West Point, NY: Leisure Press.

Ryan, E.D. (1969). Perceptual characteristics of vigorous people. In R.C. Brown, Jr., & B.J. Cratty (Eds.), *New perspectives of man in action* (pp. 88–101). Englewood Cliffs, NJ: Prentice-Hall.

Ryan, E.D., & Foster, R. (1967). Athletic participation and perceptual augmentation and reduction. *Journal of Personality and Social Psychology, 6*, 472–476.

Ryan, E.D., & Kovacic, C.R. (1966). Pain tolerance and athletic participation. *Perceptual and Motor Skills, 22*, 383–390.

Sales, S.M. (1971). Need for stimulation as a factor in social behavior. *Journal of Personality and Social Psychology, 19*, 124–134.

Sales, S.M. (1972). Need for stimulation as a factor in preference for different stimuli. *Journal of Personality Assessment, 36*, 55–61.

Sales, S.M., Guydosh, R.M., & Iacono, W. (1974). Relationship between "strength of the nervous system" and the need for stimulation. *Journal of Personality and Social Psychology, 29*, 16–22.

Sales, S.M., & Throop, W.F. (1972). Relationship between kinesthetic after effects and "strength of the nervous system." *Psychophysiology, 9*, 492–497.

Schultz, D.D. (1965). *Sensory restriction: Effects on behavior*. New York: Academic Press.

Spilker, B., & Callaway, E. (1969). "Augmenting" and "reducing" in averaged visual evoked responses to sine wave light. *Psychophysiology, 6*, 49−57.

Stirling, J. (1977). *Strength of the nervous system extraversion-introversion, and kinesthetic and cortical augmenting and reducing.* Unpublished doctoral dissertation, University of York, England.

Straub, W.F. (1982a). Sensation seeking among high and low-risk male athletes. *Journal of Sport Psychology, 4*, 246−253.

Straub, W.F. (1982b). *Sensation seeking and locus of control of high and low-risk female athletes.* Unpublished manuscript.

Strelau, J. (1970). Nervous system type and extraversion-intraversion: A comparison of Eysenck's theory with Pavlov's typology. *Polish Psychological Bulletin, 1*, 17−24.

Vando, A. (1969). *A personality dimension related to pain tolerance.* Unpublished doctoral dissertation, Columbia University.

Vando, A. (1974). The development of the R-A Scale: A paper-and-pencil measure of pain tolerance. *Personality and Social Psychology Bulletin, 1*, 28−29.

Vanek, M., & Cratty, B.J. (1970). *Psychology and the superior athlete.* New York: Macmillan.

Wickoff, W.L. (1982). *Are physical education majors sensation seekers?* Unpublished Manuscript.

Zuckerman, M. (1971). Dimensions of sensation seeking. *Journal of Consulting and Clinical Psychology, 36*, 45−52.

Zuckerman, M. (1978). Sensation seeking. In H. London & J. Exner (Eds.), *Dimensions of personality* (pp. 487−559). New York: Wiley.

Zuckerman, M. (1979). *Sensation seeking: Beyond the optimal level of arousal.* Hillsdale, NJ: Erlbaum.

Zuckerman, M. (1983). Sensation seeking and sports. *Personality and Individual Differences, 4*, 285−293.

Zuckerman, M., Kolin, E.A., Price, L., & Zoob, I. (1964). Development of a sensation-seeking scale. *Journal of Consulting and Clinical Psychology, 28*, 477−482.

3

EFFECTS OF HYPNOSIS ON STATE ANXIETY AND STRESS IN MALE AND FEMALE INTERCOLLEGIATE ATHLETES

Eric W. Krenz

Richard D. Gordin, Jr.

Steven W. Edwards

Male (N = 20) and female (N = 23) athletes at the University of Utah were studied to determine the effects of hypnosis on state anxiety and stress during the performance of a pursuit rotor task. Experimental (N = 22) and control (N = 21) group subjects were administered the state-anxiety portion of the State—Trait Anxiety Inventory (STAI) following a pretest which consisted of 15 trials of 30 s each on the pursuit rotor task while under verbal stress. Heart rate was recorded for each minute for the 25-min—pretest period.

The treatment consisted of 18 hypnosis sessions of 30 min each, administered during the 6 weeks following the pretest period. The hypnosis treatment was designed to allow each athlete to attain his or her optimum level of performance while under stress. Control group subjects read unrelated literature in 18 sessions during the 6 weeks of treatment. Posttest measurements, identical to the pretest were taken following the 6 weeks of treatment.

Using a two-way repeated measures analysis of variance with two grouping factors (experimental/control group and male/female group) and one trial factor (pre- and posttest), significant (p < .10) pursuit rotor differences were indicated between the male (X = 20.07) and female (X = 17.80) groups. A significant decrease in heart rate (p < .05) during the pursuit rotor task was noted between the pretest (X = 85.51) and posttest (X = 81.47) periods. A significant (p < .10) Group × Sex interaction indicated that both the experimental and the control groups significantly decreased their state anxiety from the pre- to posttest periods. However, state anxiety for the experimental group (X = 38.04) was significantly lower than for the control group (X = 59.10) at the posttest. It was concluded that the hypnosis treatment was effective in lowering anxiety while performing a fine motor task under stress.

Traditionally, the training of athletes has emphasized the development and refinement of fine and gross motor skills. Although many hours of practice are utilized for the perfection of movements necessary for optimal performance in a competitive situation, little attention has been given to the mental preparation of athletes for competition. When placed in a stressful competitive situation, athletes experience varying amounts of stress and anxiety. These heightened states of stress and state anxiety may sometimes enhance performance. However, increased amounts of stress and state anxiety are most often detrimental to performance. Therefore, it is important to control this psychological aspect of preparation for and participation during competitive performance. Sarason (1961) has reported a direct relationship between stress and anxiety and poor performance in complex motor skills. Martens (1977) reported that as stress and state anxiety (or arousal) increased to an optimal point, performance was enhanced. However, increases in state anxiety beyond this point had a detrimental effect on performance. Similarly, research by Castaneda, McCandless, and Palermo (1956) and Sarason and Palola (1960) have supported this theory that high levels of stress and anxiety have negative effects upon the performance of complex motor skills.

Posthypnotic suggestion has been utilized in a variety of settings to reduce or control excessive levels of stress and anxiety. Researchers have investigated the enhancement of motor performance through the use of posthypnotic suggestion (Johnson & Kramer, 1961; Pulos, 1969). Other studies have been conducted to investigate the positive effects of posthypnotic suggestion on stress and anxiety in fine motor performance (DeMers, 1980; London, Ogle, & Unikel, 1968).

Research has indicated that male and female subjects respond to stress and anxiety differently. Researchers in the area of sex differences have reported that female subjects exhibit a higher fear of success while male subjects exhibit a greater fear of failure (Patty & Safford, 1977). Studies by Hill and Sarason (1966) and Lehanczyk and Hill (1969) indicated that male subjects are more defensive, that is to say, less willing to admit to weakness.

Since research has indicated that higher levels of stress and anxiety are detrimental to the performance of fine motor skills and that sex differences may exist in this area, the use of posthypnotic suggestion as a technique to control excess stress and anxiety was investigated in this study. The purpose of this study was to determine the effects of posthypnotic suggestion on stress and state anxiety in male and female athletes while performing a fine motor skill under verbal stress.

METHOD

Subjects

The subjects were 24 male and 23 female intercollegiate athletes representing a variety of sports who volunteered for participation in this study.

Following a pretest assessment, all subjects were administered the *State—Trait Anxiety Inventory* (STAI) (Spielberger, Gorsuch, & Lushene, 1970) to assess state anxiety and were then assigned equally to either the experimental ($N = 24$) or control groups ($N = 23$). If the subject completed all requirements of voluntary participation, he or she received one credit hour of university credit. During the treatment stage of the study, two male experimental subjects and two male control group subjects withdrew from the study and were not replaced. Thus, for purposes of analysis, there were 22 experimental subjects and 21 control group subjects.

Apparatus

Electrocardiograph

A Parke-Davis 2100A electrocardiograph was utilized to record the heart rate of each subject during the last 10 s of each minute of both the pretest and posttest assessments. Although five leads were provided, the subjects were only monitored on the four leads which were attached to the left and right forearms and left and right calves. The paper speed was set at 25 mm/s and the sensitivity was set at 1 mV.

Pursuit Rotor

The pursuit rotor task was performed on the Lafayette Pursuit Rotor Model 30012. This fine perceptual motor skill was scored to the hundredths of a second by recording the total time the stylus was in contact with the moving disk. This on-time was recorded automatically by the Lafayette Timer Model 30012. The speed was calibrated at 60 rpm for each subject.

Procedure

After consent was obtained from the Review Committee for Research with Human Subjects, all subjects were given a pretest assessment during the initial meeting with the researcher. During this introductory period, course credit and any previous experience with the pursuit rotor was discussed (none of the subjects had such experience). While the subject listened to an audio cassette tape which briefly explained the study and the role of each subject in the experiment, he or she was asked to read and sign a consent form and to fill out a data card. During this time, the researcher attached all the necessary equipment in order to measure heart rate. The subject was then instructed concerning his or her upcoming performance with the pursuit rotor.

The stressor used in this study consisted of a previously prepared statement that implied a false relationship about the subject's performance on the pursuit rotor and overall athletic ability, as well as suggesting competition between subjects. Each subject was then given 15 trials of 30-s duration interspersed by rest intervals of 30 s on the pursuit rotor. Total time on target was recorded for each trial. At the conclusion of the pursuit rotor task, each subject was administered the STAI. The subject was given the standard instructions regarding this inventory but completed only form X-1, the state anxiety portion of the inventory.

Each subject's percentile rank on the STAI was determined and then each subject was assigned to either the experimental or control group so that approximately the same number of low (1st–35th percentile), medium (36th–65th percentile), and high (66th and above) subjects were in each group.

The treatment used in this study was applied during three sessions per week for 6 weeks. The posthypnotic suggestion treatment consisted of an initial session of 30 min in which the subject was assured by the researcher about the use of hypnosis and the researcher answered questions concerning its myths. At that time, the subject signed a second consent form, and a personalized tape for each experimental subject was made. The posthypnotic suggestion treatment was designed to allow each subject to attain the proper level of nontightness during a stressful situation. Sessions 2–18 were 20 min each, when the subject listened to his or her personal tape in the laboratory. The control group returned to the laboratory three times a week, 20 min per visit, for 6 weeks to read unrelated material.

A posttest assessment, which was identical to the pretest assessment, was administered to all subjects during the 8th week. At this time all subjects were debriefed and the stressor was disavowed.

RESULTS

A three-way repeated measures analysis of variance (ANOVA) was used to statistically analyze the data. Two grouping factors were used: group (hypnosis or control) and sex (male or female). One trial factor was used: time (pre or post). This analysis permitted testing the main effects of group, sex, and time as well as the two-way and single three-way interaction effects (Keppel, 1973).

Pretest means and standard deviations for the variables of interest in each of the four comparison groups are presented in Table 1. Posttest data are presented in Table 2.

The pursuit rotor variable represents the average of Trials 13, 14, and 15. The STAI variable is the percentile rank obtained from the norms presented for the test. The heart rate variables are the average of the minute-by-

TABLE 1
Means and Standard Deviations for Pretest Data

Variable	Hypnosis/Male (n=10)	Hypnosis/Female (n=12)	Control/Male (n=10)	Control/Female (n=11)
Pursuit rotor	18.04 ± 4.53	16.21 ± 4.26	18.42 ± 3.59	16.37 ± 4.84
STAI	66.40 ±21.81	73.67 ±24.54	75.50 ±20.49	80.91 ±25.53
Heart Rate− Baseline	68.41 ±11.69	71.49 ±12.42	73.67 ±16.33	70.47 ±10.58
Heart Rate− Verbal Stressor	78.07 ±13.65	79.08 ±12.62	82.53 ±15.60	80.06 ±16.03
Heart Rate− Pursuit Rotor	82.40 ±13.38	83.48 ±11.99	88.14 ±13.99	88.16 ±18.80

TABLE 2
Means and Standard Deviations for Posttest Data

Variable	Hypnosis/Male (n=10)	Hypnosis/Female (n=12)	Control/Male (n=10)	Control/Female (n=11)
Pursuit rotor	22.20 ± 2.99	18.87 ± 4.39	21.63 ± 3.48	19.81 ± 3.25
STAI	37.40 ±12.19	38.58 ± 6.91	59.40 ±10.96	58.82 ±23.45
Heart Rate− Baseline	74.89 ±12.19	73.63 ± 6.91	69.28 ±10.96	71.38 ±13.77
Heart Rate− Verbal Stressor	79.16 ±12.42	79.11 ± 8.24	75.93 ± 8.28	80.03 ±19.68
Heart Rate− Pursuit Rotor	82.52 ±14.56	81.03 ± 7.43	78.77 ± 8.22	83.43 ±15.78

minute heart rates obtained during each of the three phases of the data collection: 7 min of baseline, 3 min during introduction of the verbal stressor, and 15 min during the performance on the pursuit rotor.

Pursuit Rotor

Table 3 represents the repeated measures ANOVA results for the pursuit rotor data. There are two significant main effects: one for sex and one for time. The males ($X = 20.07$) performed significantly higher than the females ($X = 17.80$) in the overall experiment. Regarding the main effect of

TABLE 3
Results of ANOVA Including Repeated Measures for Pursuit Rotor

Source	SS	df	MS	F
Group	1.10	1	1.10	.04
Sex	108.90	1	108.90	4.07*
Group × Sex	2.24	1	2.24	.08
Error	1044.66	39	26.77	
Time	242.54	1	242.54	48.04**
Time × Group	.04	1	.04	.01
Time × Sex	2.12	1	2.12	.42
Time X Group × Sex	4.06	1	4.06	.80
Error	196.91	39	5.05	
Total	1602.57	85		

$^*p < .05. ^{**}p < .01$

time, posttime performance $(X = 20.53)$ was significantly greater than pretest performance $(X = 17.19)$ for the total group in the study.

There were no significant differences between the experimental and control groups on this variable, and there were no significant interaction effects considering either the two-way interactions or the three-way interaction.

STAI

Table 4 presents the repeated measures ANOVA results for the performance on the STAI. There are two significant main effects: one for group and one for time. The hypnosis group $(X = 54.20)$ had significantly lower STAI scores than the control group $(X = 68.71)$ for the overall experiment. Regarding the main effect of time, posttest scores $(X = 48.33)$ were significantly lower than the pretest scores $(X = 74.26)$ for the total group in the study.

A significant two-way interaction, Time × Group, was also noted in Table 4. A Newman-Keuls Sequential Range Test was used to compare the means for the four cells in this interaction: hypnosis group pretest, hypnosis group posttest, control group pretest, and control group posttest. In the hypnosis group, the posttest mean $(X = 38.04)$ was significantly lower than the pretest mean $(X = 70.36)$. Similarly, in the control group the posttest mean $(X = 59.10)$ was significantly lower than the pretest mean $(X = 78.33)$. Although the hypnosis and control group means were not significantly different at the pretest, the posttest means were significantly different from one another.

Heart Rate

The three-way repeated measures ANOVA results for Heart Rate—Baseline and Heart Rate—Verbal Stressor yielded no significant main effects or interaction effects for either the two-way interactions or the three-way interaction.

A significant main effect for time was noted for Heart Rate—Pursuit Rotor Phase as indicated in Table 5. Posttest heart rates ($X = 81.47$) were significantly lower than pretest heart rates ($X = 85.51$) for all subjects during the pursuit rotor performance phase of testing.

TABLE 4
Results of ANOVA Including Repeated Measures for STAI

Source	SS	df	MS	F
Group	4584.32	1	4584.32	5.27
Sex	235.52	1	235.52	.27
Group × Sex	17.53	1	17.53	.02
Error	33936.47	39	870.17	
Time	13974.93	1	13974.93	44.65**
Time × Group	895.70	1	895.70	2.86*
Time × Sex	194.78	1	194.78	.62
Time × Group × Sex	.01	1	.01	.00
Error	12207.36	39	313.01	
Total	66046.62	85		

*$p < .10.$ **$p < .05$

TABLE 5
Results of ANOVA Including Repeated Measures for Heart Rate—Pursuit Rotor

Source	SS	df	MS	F
Group	110.22	1	110.22	.40
Sex	24.19	1	24.19	.09
Group × Sex	34.55	1	34.55	.13
Error	10666.03	39	273.49	
Time	360.50	1	360.50	4.09*
Time × Group	185.09	1	185.09	2.10
Time × Sex	5.76	1	5.76	.07
Time × Group × Sex	69.56	1	69.56	.79
Error	3437.01	39	88.13	
Total	14892.91	85		

*$p < .05.$

DISCUSSION

Pursuit Rotor

The mean differences between the male and female subjects indicated that the male subjects out-performed the female subjects in this study by 2.27 s on the 30-s pursuit rotor task. This difference is statistically significant but, more importantly, represents substantially better performance by the male subjects on the fine motor task of ocular pursuit. Since there was no significant difference between the hypnosis and control group on this task, it can only be concluded that the male subjects brought superior fine motor performance capabilities with them to the experiment. The reason for this disparity is unclear at this time, particularly in light of the fact that differences between male and female athletes are not typically reported in research studies using the pursuit rotor task.

STAI

Both the hypnosis group and the control group decreased significantly in STAI scores, and ordinarily this finding would make interpretation of the treatment effects of posthypnotic suggestion difficult at best. However, since the groups were equated at the pretest and the posttest means were significantly different, it can be concluded that the hypnotic suggestions was effective in reducing state anxiety in the male and female athletes in the treatment group. The significant decrease in STAI scores in the control group was attributable to familiarity with the testing situation and the reactive nature of the pretest situation. By dividing the 0−99 percentile range into thirds and labeling the 0−33 range as low state anxiety, the 34−67 range as medium state anxiety, and the 68−99 range as high state anxiety, another interesting finding emerges. Familiarity with the testing situation caused the control group to change from high to medium state anxiety, while the hypnosis group changed from high to nearly low state anxiety. It seems evidently, then, that posthypnotic suggestion can be effectively used to lower state anxiety in male and female athletes.

The decrease in state anxiety due to treatment effects was not, however, associated with a commensurate increase in motor performance as was expected. This finding does not preclude association between increased levels of state anxiety and decreased motor performances. It merely means that this particular measure of fine motor performance, the pursuit rotor, was not affected by a decrease in state anxiety. Other fine or gross motor performances, be they laboratory tasks or field-oriented sports skills, may indeed be related to state anxiety as inverted-U hypothesis thinking might suggest. Further investigations in this area should include a variety of motor performance tasks to elucidate relationships that may exist.

Heart Rate Measures

Heart rate remained consistent from pretest to posttest with the exception of the pursuit rotor phase of heart rate measurement. A decrease of 4.04 beats/min was noted from the pretest to the posttest for the total group of subjects. Table 6 helps clarify the importance of this finding.

Because of this decrease in heart rate, the stress due to motor performance was deemed to be less effective in manifesting a physiological response, an increase in heart rate. Familiarity with the testing situation was the probable cause for this decrease across all subjects. It should be noted that significant differences did exist among all three phases at the pretest and among all but the last two phases at the posttest.

Implications for Study Design

This study has shown conclusively that a verbal stressor can be used in a laboratory setting to create stress as measured by increased heart rate. Also, since state anxiety was remediated by posthypnotic suggestion and, for the most part, increased levels of stress were maintained, it can be concluded that stress and state anxiety as they were measured in this context were independent phenomena. Authorities disagree on the independence of stress and anxiety, but these findings suggest that they are indeed two independent characteristics when viewed in a motor performance context (Eliot, 1979; Selye, 1974).

Summary

Using male and female intercollegiate athletes, state anxiety due to performing a fine motor skill under verbal stress can be reduced through the utilization of posthypnotic suggestion.

TABLE 6
Mean Heart Rate Data According to Time and Phase

Time	Baseline	Verbal Stressor	Pursuit Rotor
Pretest	71.02	79.90	85.50
Posttest	72.33	78.62	81.47

Although increased levels of state anxiety are associated with increased stress and decreased motor performance, the findings from this investigation suggest that state anxiety and stress may be independent phenomena. Also, only selected fine or gross motor performance may suffer decrements due to introduction of verbal stress or the stress of actually performing a motor task.

REFERENCES

Castaneda, A., McCandless, B., & Palermo, D. (1956). Complex learning and performance as a function of anxiety in children and task difficulty. *Child Development, 27*, 327–332.

DeMers, G.E. (1980). Effects of post-hypnotic suggestion on the performance of a fine motor skill under stress. *Dissertation Abstracts International, 1980, 40*, 4955A–4956A. (University Microfilms No. 8005315)

Eliot, R.S. (1979). *Stress and the major cardiovascular disorders.* Mount Kisco, NY: Futura.

Hill, K.T., & Sarason, S.B. (1966). The relation of test anxiety and defensiveness to test and school performance over the elementary-school years. *Monographs of the Society for Research in Child Development, 31*(104).

Johnson, W., & Kramer, G. (1961). Effects of stereotyped nonhypnotic, hypnotic and posthypnotic suggestions upon strength, power and endurance. *Research Quarterly, 32*, 522–529.

Keppel. G. (1973). *Design and analysis: A researcher's handbook.* Englewood Cliffs, NJ. Prentice-Hall.

Lehanczyk, D.T., & Hill, K.T. (1969). Self-esteem, test anxiety, stress and verbal learning. *Developmental Psychology, 1*, 147–154.

London, R., Ogle, M., & Unikel, I. (1968). The effects of hypnosis and motivation on resistance to heat stress. *Journal of Abnormal Psychology, 73*, 532–541.

Martens, R. (1977). *Sport competition anxiety test.* Champaign, IL: Human Kinetics.

Patty, R.A., & Safford, S.F. (1977). Motive to avoid success, motive to avoid failure, state-trait anxiety, and performance. In C.D. Spielberger & I.G. Sarason (Eds.), *Stress and anxiety* (Vol. 4, pp. 221–238). Washington, DC: Hemisphere.

Pulos, L. (1969). *Hypnosis and think training with athletes.* Paper presented at the 12th Annual Scientific Meeting, American Society of Clinical Hypnosis, San Francisco.

Sarason, I.G. (1961). The effects of anxiety and threat on the solution of a difficult task. *Journal of Abnormal and Social Psychology, 62*, 165–168.

Sarason, I.G., & Palola, E. (1960). The relationship of test and general anxiety, difficulty of task, and experimental instructions to task performance. *Journal of Experimental Psychology, 59*, 186–191.

Selye, J. (1974). *Stress without distress.* New York: J.B. Lippincott.

Spielberger, C.D., Gorsuch, R.L., & Lushene, R.E. (1970). *STAI manual.* Palo Alto, CA: Consulting Psychologists Press.

4

PERCEPTIONS OF MALE AND FEMALE ATHLETES AS A FUNCTION OF PERFORMANCE OUTCOME AND TYPE OF SPORT

Bruce G. Klonsky

Jack S. Croxton

Angela B. Ginorio

The present study investigates college students' perceptions of male and female athletic performance. The 337 undergraduate volunteers (167 males, 170 females) were randomly assigned to consider either a successful or unsuccessful performance by an athlete. Independent 2 (Sex of Perceiver) × 2 (Sex of Target) × 2 (Sex-Orientation of Activity: Male-Oriented vs. Non Male-Oriented) × 2 (Type of Competition: Individual vs. Team) analyses of variance were carried out for the successful and unsuccessful performance conditions, respectively. Assessments took the form of causal attributions about performance and personality impressions of the target person. Results indicated that the personality impressions (particularly on the masculine-feminine dimension) which college students form about males and females performing in sports are more strongly influenced by the sex-typing of the activity than are their causal attributions about such performance. Gender-role stereotypes were most in evidence when the female was successful in a male-oriented sport and the perceiver was male. However, when the female was unsuccessful in a male-oriented sport, little negative bias appeared to exist.

The impetus for the present study comes from the literature exploring how gender-role stereotypes and attribution processes affect performance evaluation. Many researchers have investigated the effect of gender-role stereotypes upon the evaluation of others. One of the most consistent findings is the lower evaluation of females' than males' achievements by both males and females (e.g., Deaux & Emswiller, 1974; Goldberg, 1968; Nicholls, 1975; Pheterson, Kiesler, & Goldberg, 1971).

Another form of evaluation bias associated with gender labeling is illustrated in studies of causal attributions. The four causal factors which have received the most attention in achievement situations have been ability, effort, task difficulty, and luck (e.g., Bar-Tal & Frieze, 1977; Frieze & Weiner, 1971; Weiner et al., 1971). Under identical circumstances, and when they are engaged in identical tasks, the performances of males and females are attributed to different sources. The successful performance of males is typically seen as resulting from hard work or ability, whereas the successful performance of females is often seen as influenced by luck. This attributional pattern appears to be particularly strong when masculine tasks (e.g., using mechanical objects) and occupations (e.g., medicine) are involved (Deaux & Emswiller, 1974; Feather & Simon, 1975; Feldman-Summers & Kiesler, 1974). A similar attributional pattern has emerged when sport activities are utilized (Bird & Williams, 1980).

The causal attributions made about a person have important implications not only for the affect and expectancies of that person, but also for the rewards given that individual by others. The kinds of attributions made by decision makers such as coaches have important consequences for those being judged. For example, if a coach felt that poor performance was the result of the individual being incompetent or lazy, the person might be dropped from the unit. If, however, the coach perceived the poor performance to have been caused by circumstances beyond the individual's control (e.g., an overly difficult assignment or temporary illness), the individual would be more likely to get a second chance (Frieze, Parsons, Johnson, Ruble, & Zellman, 1978).

A few studies have been designed to look specifically at the types of attributions made by sports participants. Frieze, McHugh, and Duquin (1976) created a hypothetical win-lose situation for male and female college athletes and nonathletes. A number of gender differences in attributions were obtained. Males tended to attribute a success to stable characteristics more than did females, whereas females tended to emphasize team attributes more than did males. Another study (Croxton & Klonsky, 1982) found that losing male athletes rated internal characteristics as less important in determining the outcome than did losing females. Winning females rated the opponent's characteristics as less important in determining the outcome than did winning males. Successful female athletes were generally just as inclined to take responsibility for the victory as successful males. Also, there is suggestive evidence, based on data obtained from a sample of undergraduates, that as females are given the opportunity to develop their athletic abilities and gain athletic experience, their attributions for performance outcomes more closely approximate those of males (Klonsky & Croxton, 1981).

Society still remains ambivalent, however, about certain types of sports participation on the part of females (King & Chi, 1979). Evidence for this comes from Snyder and Spreitzer (1983), whose literature review indicated that gymnastics and volleyball are perceived as more appropriate sports for females than basketball and track and field. Also, the majority of college female basketball players felt that there was a stigma attached to their participation.

The present study explores the effects of gender-role stereotypes on college students' perception of successful and unsuccessful males and females in several types of sport activities. The activities included both individual (floor exercise in gymnastics and the shot put in track and field) and team (volleyball and basketball) events. Causal attributions for the target person's performance and impressions of the target person were assessed.

One purpose of this study was to determine to what degree gender-role stereotypes operate in the world of sports in the 1980s. A second purpose was to determine whether perceptions of an athlete and attributions regarding the athlete's performance might depend to some extent on the nature of the sport. For example, some sports are obviously more male-oriented than others. Reactions to a female who participates in a male-oriented sport might differ from reactions to a female who participates in a sport that is regarded as more appropriate for females. Another variable that might potentially influence reactions to an athlete's performance is whether the sport involves a team or whether the athlete performs as an individual.

The incidence of gender-role stereotypes in sports has been well documented. We feel that the issue may be more complex, however, given the variety of sports available to athletes. Our goal was to determine how the identity of the sport might influence perceivers' reactions to the performance outcomes of male and female athletes. Our hypotheses were based on earlier research on the operation of gender-role stereotypes and on our assumptions about how the nature of the sport might influence perceivers' reactions. We created a model which incorporates a number of variables having the potential to influence causal attributions and personality impressions in sports-related settings, and the major components of the model were utilized in the development of our hypotheses.

Valle and Frieze (1976) proposed a model indicating that when an actor's performance is consistent with an observer's expectations, the observer should make an internal attribution, whereas when the actor's performance is inconsistent with an observer's expectations, the observer should make an external attribution. Coakley (1982) pointed out that there is still a pervasive myth that males will be more successful than females when competing in athletics. Therefore, the following hypotheses were formulated:

Hypothesis 1A. A successful performance by a male athlete should more likely be attributed to an internal characteristic such as high ability, relative to a successful performance by a female athlete.

Hypothesis 1B. An unsuccessful performance by a female athlete should more likely be attributed to an internal characteristic such as a lack of ability, relative to an unsuccessful performance by a male athlete.

Hypothesis 2A. A successful performance by a female athlete should more likely be attributed to an external characteristic such as good luck, relative to a successful performance by a male athlete.

Hypothesis 2B. An unsuccessful performance by a male athlete should more likely be attributed to an external characteristic such as bad luck, relative to an unsuccessful performance by a female athlete.

Maloney and Petrie (1972), Petrie (1971), and Reis and Jelsma (1978) obtained data indicating that males place more value on achievement in sport than females. Since sports are likely to be perceived as more ego-involving for males, we presumed that the performance outcome would be perceived to have a greater emotional impact on males than on females.

Hypothesis 3A. A male athlete who is successful should be perceived as happier than a female athlete who is successful.

Hypothesis 3B. A male athlete who is unsuccessful should be perceived as sadder than a female athlete who is unsuccesful.

Broverman, Vogal, Broverman, Clarkson, and Rosenkrantz (1972) found that males and females are typically perceived to possess different types of characteristics. More specifically, they discovered that males tend to be seen as more aggressive and more active, and as having a greater number of masculine qualities relating to instrumental competencies (e.g., competitiveness, independence, strength, and dominance) than their female counterparts. Also, much psychological literature (e.g., Cratty, 1967; Kagan & Moss, 1962) supports the view that sport and athletics are generally perceived as a male sex-typed activity. By second-grade, both girls and boys view athletics as a masculine activity (Stein & Smithells, 1969).

One effect of sex-typing sport as masculine is that physical activities and coordinations become associated with males. As a result of this association, teachers often expect much less of their female pupils in the early grades, and offer less to them in the upper grades. Some evidence (Wyrick, 1974) indicates that teachers and tests will often set much lower standards for the physical skill performance of prepubescent females or expect less of them. Females apparently learn that correct and coordinated movement patterns are typically associated with males, and uncoordinated and incorrect ones typically with females (Smith & Clifton, 1962).

Given the pattern of perceptions of males and females both inside and outside sport situations found in previous studies, the following hypotheses about male versus female athletes were generated:

Hypothesis 4A. A male athlete should be perceived as more masculine than a female athlete, regardless of performance outcome.

Hypothesis 4B. A male athlete should be perceived as more active than a female athlete, regardless of performance outcome.

Hypothesis 4C. A male athlete should be perceived as stronger than a female athlete, regardless of performance outcome.

The participation rate among females in sports continues to increase. Yet it is still true today that many more males than females participate in organized sports. Coakley (1982) pointed out that there are various physiological, performance, and social psychological myths still in existence today which discourage sports participation by females. King and Chi (1979) argued that American society tends to encourage sports participation by males but does not provide equal opportunities for females. Snyder and Spreitzer (1983) emphasized that certain sports are viewed as more appropriate for females than others and that females are often discouraged from participating in the more stereotypically masculine sports. We assumed that the subjects in our study should be aware, perhaps through their own experiences, that females generally receive less encouragement when it comes to sports participation, relative to their male counterparts.

Hypothesis 5. A female athlete's unsuccessful performance should more likely be attributed to a lack of prior support relative to a male athlete's unsuccessful performance. This attributional tendency should be more likely when the sport is male-oriented.

Both Reis and Jelsma (1978) and Snyder and Spreitzer (1983) reported that male athletes are more likely to stress the importance of winning than female athletes. Petrie (1971) observed that males tend to emphasize personal achievement as the primary reason for sports participation. We assumed that more male-oriented sports might be perceived as encouraging this type of motivating tendency. Therefore, the following hypotheses were formulated:

Hypothesis 6A. Effort should be perceived as a more important determinant of an outcome in a male-oriented sport than in a sport that is not male-oriented, regardless of the outcome.

Hypothesis 6B. Training should be perceived as a more important determinant of an outcome in a male-oriented sport than in a sport that is not male-oriented, regardless of the outcome.

Metheny (1965) found that male-oriented sports were believed to involve more physical exertion than sports that were not male-oriented. Coakley (1982) stated that the stereotypically masculine sports often involve power, strength, or speed. Because of these differences in the nature of male-oriented versus non-male-oriented sports, perceptions of those who participate in such sports could be affected accordingly.

Hypothesis 7A. The sports participant should be perceived as more masculine when participating in a male-oriented sport than when participating in a sport that is not male-oriented.

Hypothesis 7B. The sports participant should be perceived as stronger when participating in a male-oriented sport than when participating in a sport that is not male-oriented.

Hypothesis 7C. The sports participant should be perceived as more active when participating in a male-oriented sport than when participating in a sport that is not male-oriented. Hypotheses 7A−7C should be supported regardless of the performance outcome.

Over the years, society has been at best ambivalent about female participation in sport, particularly in male-oriented sports (Snyder & Spreitzer, 1983). A study by Fisher, Genovese, Morris, and Morris (1977) provided some data relevant to this issue. These authors investigated college student perceptions of females in sport. Subjects in this study viewed slides of female athletes participating in various sports (e.g., track and field events, and basketball). They discovered that nonathletes perceived women in sports as less ideal than did athletes. They also found that female participation in traditional male-oriented sports (e.g., track and field events such as the shot put) was viewed as less appropriate than participation in female-oriented sports, and as making the female athlete less feminine and less valued. Therefore, the following hypotheses were formulated:

Hypothesis 8A. Successful female athletes in male-oriented sports should be rated as more masculine than successful female athletes in sports that are not male-oriented. Perceptions of males should be less affected by the orientation of the sport.

Hypothesis 8B. The evaluation of female athletes should be lower than the evaluation of male athletes in male-oriented sports regardless of the performance outcome.

METHOD

Subjects

The subjects were 337 undergraduate volunteers (167 males and 170 females) from various courses in psychology at a 4-year liberal arts college.

Procedure

Subjects were randomly assigned to consider one of the following four types of target persons: successful male, successful female, unsuccessful male, or unsuccessful female. Each subject learned that the target person experienced either a positive or negative outcome in one of the following types of sports: a male-oriented team sport activity (basketball), a male-oriented individual sport activity (the shot put in track and field), a non-male-oriented team sport activity (volleyball), and a non-male-oriented individual sport activity (the floor exercise in gymnastics). Each of the activities and the resulting outcome was described in a short paragraph. The choice of gender-typed sport activities was based on the data presented by Snyder and Spreitzer (1983) and on the work of Metheny (1965).

Each subject received one of 16 different scenarios. Varied were the sex of the target, the performance outcome, the sex orientation of the sport activity, and team versus individual performance. For example, one group of subjects received the following scenario: "Mary Smith is a member of the gymnastics team at her college. During her team's competition against its arch rival, Mary turns in an outstanding overall performance in the floor exercise and as a result her team wins the match."

After reading the scenario, subjects rated the importance of eight potential causal factors relating to the target person's performance on a 1 (not at all important) to 10 (extremely important) scale. The attribution measures are listed in Table 1.

The wording of the items differed slightly, depending on the performance outcome. For example, a potential causal explanation for an unsuccessful outcome was, "The person was unlucky," and a potential causal explanation was for a successful outcome was, "The person was lucky."

TABLE 1
Attribution Factors Included in Questionnaire

Successful Outcome	Unsuccessful Outcome
The person tried very hard.	The person did not try very hard.
The person had a lot of natural ability.	The person had little natural ability.
The person was lucky.	The person was unlucky.
The task was not very difficult.	The task was extremely difficult.
The person was loose and relaxed.	The person was nervous.
The person trained very hard.	The person did not train very hard.
The person had previously received a lot of support from others.	The person had previously received very little support from others.
The person received a lot of support from others during the event.	The person received very little support from others during the event.

Subjects also indicated their impressions of the target person on a series of 11-point scales anchored at each end by bipolar trait adjectives. The dimensions were *active−passive, happy−sad, energetic−relaxed, masculine−feminine, weak−strong*, and *good−bad.*

Because the attribution measures were worded differently in the successful and unsuccessful performance outcome conditions, separate 2 (Sex of Perceiver) × 2 (Sex of Target) × 2 (Sex Orientation of Activity: Male-Oriented or Non-Male-Oriented Activity) × 2 (Type of Competition: Individual or Team Performance) analyses of variance (ANOVAs) were carried out for each of these two conditions, respectively. Twenty subjects (10 males, 10 females) were randomly assigned to consider one of the 16 target persons within each condition.

RESULTS

Major Findings

No evidence was obtained in support of either Hypothesis 1A or Hypothesis 1B. Attributions to ability were unaffected by the sex of the target person.

No evidence was obtained in support of Hypothesis 2A or Hypothesis 2B. Attributions to luck were unaffected by the sex of the target person.

Attributions differed on only one characteristic as a function of the sex of the target person. An unsuccessful performance was more likely to be attributed to a lack of effort when the performer was male than when the performer was female (Male Target: $M = 7.36$; Female Target: $M = 6.33$, $F(1,44) = 4.79, p < .05$).

No evidence was obtained in support of Hypothesis 3A. A successful male athlete was not perceived to be any happier than a successful female athlete. However, as predicted in Hypothesis 3B, the losing male athlete was perceived as sadder than the losing female athlete (Male Target: $M = 6.05$; Female Target: $M = 5.25., F(1, 145) = 5.37, p < .05$).

Ratings on the masculine-feminine dimension provided support for Hypothesis 4A. Males were rated more toward the masculine end of the dimension in both the successful performance (Male Target: $M = 2.25$; Female Target: $M = 4.73, F(1, 158) = 61.55, p < .01$) and unsuccessful performance (Male Target: $M = 3.76$; Female Target: $M = 5.46, F(1, 144) = 22.87, p < .01$) conditions. However, ratings on the active-passive and weak-strong dimensions did not differ as a function of the sex of the target person in either the successful performance or unsuccessful performance conditions. Therefore, Hypotheses 4B and 4C were not supported.

The only other significant effect relating to the sex of the target person was obtained on the energetic-relaxed dimension in the unsuccessful performance condition. The female athlete was perceived to be more energetic than the male target person (Female Target: $M = 2.82$; Male Target: $M = 4.27$, $F(1, 144) = 12.03$, $p < .01$).

Hypothesis 5 was not supported. Lack of prior support was not perceived as more instrumental in contributing to an unsuccessful performance by a female athlete than to an unsuccessful performance by a male athlete. Furthermore, there was no interaction involving the orientation of the sport.

Hypotheses 6A and 6B were not supported. Attributions to effort and training did not differ as a function of the orientation of the sport in either the successful performance or unsuccessful performance conditions.

Some evidence was obtained in support of Hypotheses 7A and 7B when the performance was successful. Participants in male-oriented sports were rated as more toward the masculine end of the masculine-feminine dimension than participants in non-male-oriented sports (Male-Oriented Sport: $M = 3.00$; Non-Male Oriented Sport: $M = 3.94$, $F(1, 158) = 7.52$, $p < .01$), and rated more toward the strong end of the weak-strong dimension than participants in non-male-oriented sports (Male-Oriented Sport: $M = 8.19$; Non-Male-Oriented Sport: $M = 7.73$, $F(1, 158) = 3.30$, $p < .10$). No differences were obtained on the active-passive dimension. In the unsuccessful performance condition, no significant differences were obtained on any of the three dimensions. However, those in male-oriented sports were rated more toward the good end of the good-bad dimension than those in non-male-oriented sports (Male-Oriented Sport: $M = 3.47$; Non-Male-Oriented Sport: $M = 4.19$; $F(1, 144) = 5.08$, $p < .05$).

Hypothesis 8A was supported. Successful female athletes in male-oriented sports were rated as more toward the masculine end of the masculine-feminine dimension than successful female athletes in non-male-oriented sports (Male-Oriented Sport: $M = 3.88$; Non-Male-Oriented Sport: $M = 5.56$, $F(1, 83) = 11.00$, $p < .01$). Ratings of winning male athletes on this dimension did not differ as a function of the orientation of the sport (Male-Oriented Sport: $M = 2.21$; Non-Male-Oriented Sport: $M = 2.29$, $F(1, 87) = 1$, $p = $ ns).

The sex of the perceiver interacted with the other two variables on this measure, resulting in a three-way interaction between sex of perceiver, sex of target, and orientation of sport within the successful performance outcome condition, $F(1, 158) = 6.66$, $p < .05$. These results are displayed in Table 2. When the sport was male-oriented, male perceivers rated the male

TABLE 2
Assessment of Winning Athletes on the Masculine-Feminine
Dimension as a Function of Sex of the Perceiver,
Sex of Target, and Sex Orientation of Sport

		Sex of Perceiver			
		Male		Female	
		Target		Target	
		Male	Female	Male	Female
	Male-oriented	3.20	2.84	1.17	4.74
Orientation of Sport					
	Non-male-oriented	2.36	5.27	2.20	5.86

Note. Ratings were based on an 11-point bipolar scale with masculine at the low end and feminine at the high end.

and female athletes as approximately equally masculine, $F(1, 41) < 1, p =$ ns, whereas female perceivers rated the male athlete as more toward the masculine end of the masculine–feminine dimension than the female athlete, $F(1,44) = 37.02, p < .01$. When the sport was not male-oriented, both male and female perceivers rated the male athlete as more toward the masculine end of the masculine-feminine dimension than the female athlete (Male Perceivers: $F(1, 42) = 22.54, p < .01$; Female Perceivers: $F(1, 39) = 35.68, p < .01$).

Hypothesis 8B was not supported. No bias appeared to exist against female athletes who participated in male-oriented sports. In fact, when the performance was unsuccessful, female athletes were perceived as more toward the active end of the active-passive dimension (Female Athlete: $M = 3.39$; Male Athlete: $M = 4.82, F(1, 78) = 5.54, p < .05$), more toward the energetic end of the energetic-relaxed dimension (Female Athlete: $M = 2.46$; Male Athlete: $M = 4.98, F(1, 78) = 24.37, p < .01$), more toward the strong end of the weak-strong dimension (Female Athlete: $M = 6.42$; Male Athlete: $M = 5.25, F(1, 78) = 4.43, p < .05$), and more toward the good end of the good-bad dimension (Female Athlete: $M = 2.63$; Male Athlete: $M = 4.33, F(1, 79) = 15.13, p < .01$), relative to their male counterparts.

Subsidiary Findings

A number of marginally significant effects were obtained when comparing team versus individual sports. Lack of support during the event was perceived as more important for a team's unsuccessful outcome than for an individual's unsuccessful outcome (Team Sport: $M = 7.21$; Individual Sport: $M = 6.56$, $F(1, 145) = 3.57$, $p < .10$). In the successful performance condition, attributions to support during the event were unaffected by the team versus individual nature of the sport.

A marginally significant effect was obtained on attributions to training in both the successful performance and unsuccessful performance conditions. When the performance was successful, attributions to training were greater for an individual than a team sport (Individual Sport: $M = 8.96$; Team Sport: $M = 8.57$, $F(1, 159) -= 3.15$, $p < .10$). When the performance was unsuccessful, attributions to a lack of training were greater for an individual than a team sport (Individual Sport: $M = 7.23$; Team Sport: $M =6.59$, $F(1, 145) = 2.85$, $p < .10$).

DISCUSSION

The results of the present study indicate that in order to understand the gender-role stereotypes that affect college students' perceptions of athletes, one must take into consideration the performance outcome, sex orientation of the sport, and the type of sport (i.e., team vs. individual).

The evaluation of the data generated from testing this study's hypotheses indicates two major patterns with regard to the existence and operation of gender-role stereotypes. The *first pattern* is that there were few significant differences in the *causal attributions* made about males and females participating in sports. Attributions differed only in the area of effort as a function of the sex of the target person. More specifically, an unsuccessful performance was more likely to be attributed to a lack of effort when the performer was male rather than female. This finding is probably due to the greater expectations held for males performing in sporting events (Duquin, 1978) and to the fact that effort is often seen as the factor which will "tip the scales" in such events (Frieze et al., 1976). The findings of Duquin and Frieze et al. are also consistent with the present study's finding that male athletes are perceived as more unhappy when failing than female athletes are.

Attributions to ability and luck were unaffected by the sex of the target person. This may have been due to the level of performance already achieved by the athletes whose performance was being considered. Perceivers were made aware that the athletes were members of the varsity team and competing at the intercollegiate level. Both male and female athletes had presumably already achieved a certain status in their particular sport. Therefore, perceivers may have been reluctant to assume that a successful female athlete was merely lucky or that an unsuccessful female athlete lacked ability.

Perceivers did not assume that a female athlete's unsuccessful performance was due to a lack of prior support. Because the female athlete had reached the level of intercollegiate competition, perceivers may have inferred that either she had overcome this lack of support or perhaps was by this time unaffected by it. For this reason the perceivers may have elected not to focus on this variable as a potential cause of her unsuccessful performance.

Effort and training were not perceived as any more important in determining the outcome in a male-oriented sport than in a non-male-oriented sport. Perceivers may have assumed that these factors are prerequisites in order to be able to compete at the varsity level, regardless of the nature of the sport.

Overall, our data indicate that attributional biases appear not to exist against female athletes, at least in the eyes of college students when competing at the intercollegiate level. It would be instructive to determine whether attributional biases operate when females are first entering the world of sports and whether such biases perhaps discourage them from attempting to excel in this area.

The *second pattern* is that there were a number of significant differences in the *personality impressions* made about males and females, particularly when participating in sex-typed sports. More specifically, gender-role stereotypes were operating most strongly when a female was *successsful* in a male-oriented sport and the perceiver was male. Such stereotypes centered around the masculine-feminine dimension. Female athletes in male-oriented sports appear to have been "masculinized" in the ratings by male perceivers (seen as about as masculine as male athletes in such sports). Female perceivers did not show the same tendency to "masculinize" the female athlete in male-oriented sports. Additionally, there was no tendency on the part of either male or female perceivers to "feminize" the male participant in non-male-oriented sports. The pattern of these findings fits in well with the existing literature, which indicates that athletic achievement has been equated with a loss of femininity, particularly when females are participating in socially stigmatized masculine sports emphasizing strength, bodily contact, and endurance (Malumphy, 1968; Metheny, 1965; Snyder, Kivlin, & Spreitzer, 1975).

When the female was *unsuccessful* in her athletic endeavors, however, perceptions of her took a different form. Little negative bias appeared to exist against female athletes participating in male-oriented sports, at least when the performance was unsuccessful. Interestingly, unsuccessful female athletes were viewed as more active, more energetic, and stronger than their male counterparts in a male-oriented sport. No such significant differences were discovered when a non-male-oriented sport was involved.

How might these findings be explained? Perhaps equity theory is operating in this situation. Earlier research indicates that people who perform well in spite of a "handicap" (e.g., being a "short" high jumper) may have their performance viewed more favorably (Leventhal & Michaels, 1971; Taynor & Deaux, 1975). In the present research, the female's handicap may have been perceived as less physical strength than is necessary in a male-oriented sport.

There are several studies (e.g., Spence & Helmreich, 1972; Spence, Helmreich, & Stapp, 1975) indicating that a female who deviates from typically feminine interests can be rated favorably if she is generally competent. However, the data from the present study indicate that evaluations in sports-related contexts may only be favorable if the female is successful (in the sense of being able to compete on a varsity level) but not too successful (i.e., not necessarily performing well in competition).

The findings of the present study raise several questions. First it would be interesting to know whether the perceptions of male and female athletic performance by college students in the present study are typical of adult evaluators of such performance (e.g., coaches, fans, etc.). Second, it would be useful to investigate in more depth the impact of participating in a team versus individual sport on attributions and personality impressions using a greater variety of activities. It is also possible that stronger differences on this dimension may emerge during the evaluation of performance in actual as opposed to hypothetical sport situation.

A current controversy on college campuses is the implementation of Title IX and the budgeting of men's and women's athletic programs (Coakley, 1982; Snyder & Spreitzer, 1983). The positions of administrators on this issue may be partially based on their current gender-role stereotypes about college athletes. One also wonders what the long-term impact of Title IX will be on the way others view females and evaluate their performance as well as on the way females view their own performance. It is hoped that the present research, by providing insight into the nature of gender-role stereotypes and attribution biases operating in sport settings, can increase the likelihood that such biases can be reduced or perhaps even eliminated.

REFERENCES

Bar-Tal, D., & Frieze, I. (1977). Achievement motivation for males and females as a determinant of attributions for success and failure. *Sex Roles, 3,* 301–313.

Bird, A.M., & Williams, J.M. (1980). A developmental-attributional analysis of sex-role stereotypes for sport performance. *Developmental Psychology, 16,* 319–322.

Broverman, I.K., Vogel, S.R., Broverman, D.M., Clarkson, F.E., Rosenkrantz, P.S. (1972). Sex-role stereotypes: A current appraisal. *Journal of Social Issues, 28,* 59–78.

Coakley, J.J. (1982). *Sport in society: Issues and controversies.* St. Louis: Mosby.

Cratty, B. (1967). *Social dimensions of physical activity.* Englewood Cliffs, NJ: Prentice-Hall.

Croxton, J.S., & Klonsky, B.G. (1982). Sex differences in causal attributions for success and failure in real and hypothetical sport settings. *Sex Roles, 8*, 399–409.

Deaux, K., & Emswiller, T. (1974). Explanations of successful performance on sex-linked tasks: What is skill for the male is luck for the female. *Journal of Personality and Social Psychology, 29*, 80–85.

Duquin, M.E. (1978). The androgynous advantage. In C.A. Oglesby (Ed.), *Women in sport: From myth to reality* (pp. 471–483). Philadelphia: Lea & Febiger.

Feather, N.T., & Simon, J.G. (1975). Reactions to male and female success and failure in sex-linked occupations: Impressions of personality, causal attributions and perceived likelihood of different consequences. *Journal of Personality and Social Psychology, 31*, 20–31.

Feldman-Summers, S., & Kiesler, S.B. (1974). Those who are number two try harder: The effect of sex on attributions of causality. *Journal of Personality and Social Psychology, 30*, 846–855.

Fisher, A.C, Genovese, P.P., Morris, K.J., Morris, H.H. (1977). Perceptions of women in sport. In D.M. Landers & R.W. Christina (Eds.). *Psychology of motor behavior and sport—1977* (pp. 447–461). Champaign, IL: Human Kinetics.

Frieze, I.H., McHugh, M.C., & Duquin, M. (1976). *Causal attributions for women and men and sports participation.* Paper presented at the annual meeting of the American Psychological Association, Washington, DC.

Frieze, I.H., Parsons, J.E., Johnson, P.B., Ruble, D.N., & Zellman, G.L. (1978). *Women and sex roles: A social psychological perspective.* New York: W.W. Norton.

Frieze, I.H., & Weiner, B. (1971). Cue utilization and attribution judgements for success and failure. *Journal of Personality, 39*, 591–605.

Goldberg, P.A. (1968). Are women prejudiced against women? *Trans-action, 5*, 28–30.

Kagan, J., & Moss, H. (1962). *Birth to maturity.* New York: Wiley.

King, J.P., & Chi, P.S. (1979). Social structure, sex roles, and personality: Comparisons of male/female athletes/nonathletes. In J. H. Goldstein (Ed.), *Sports, games and play: Social and psychological viewpoints* (pp. 115–148). Hillsdale, NJ: Erlbaum.

Klonsky, B.G., & Croxton, J.S. (1981). *Causal attributions in sport situations a a function of sex, performance outcome, and athletic ability and experience.* Paper presented at the meeting of the Eastern Psychological Association, New York.

Leventhal, G.S., & Michaels, J.W. (1971). Locus of cause and equity motivation as determinants of reward allocation. *Journal of Personality and Social Psychology, 17*, 229–235.

Maloney, T.L., & Petrie, B. (1972). Professionalization of attitude toward play among Canadian school pupils as a function of sex, grade, and athletic participation. *Journal of Leisure Research, 4*, 184–195.

Malumphy, T.M. (1968). Personality of women athletes in intercollegiate competition. *Research Quarterly, 39*, 610–620.

Metheny, E. (1965). *Connotations of movement in sport and dance.* Dubuque, IA: Brown.

Nicholls, J. (1975). Causal attributions and other achievement-related cognitions: Effect of task outcome, attainment value, and sex. *Journal of Personality and Social Psychology, 31*, 379–389.

Petrie, B.M. (1971). Achievement orientations in adolescent attitudes toward play. *International Review of Sport Sociology, 6*, 89–99.

Pheterson, G.I., Kiesler, S.B., & Goldberg, P.A. (1971). Evaluation of the performance of women as a function of their sex, achievement, and personal history. *Journal of Personality and Social Psychology, 19*, 114–118.

Reis, H.T., & Jelsma, B. (1978). A social psychology of sex differences in sport. In W.G. Straub (Ed.), *Sport psychology: An analysis of athlete behavior* (pp. 178–188).

Smith, H., & Clifton, M. (1962). Sex differences in expressed self-concepts concerning the performance of selected motor skills. *Perceptual and Motor Skills, 14*, 71–73.

Snyder, E.E., Kivlin, J., & Spreitzer, E. (1975). The female athlete: An analysis of objective and subjective role conflict. In D. Landers (Ed.), *Psychology of sport and motor behavior II* (pp. 165–180). University Park: Pennsylvania State University Press.

Snyder, E.E., & Spreitzer, E. (1983). *Social aspects of sport.* Englewood Cliffs, NJ: Prentice-Hall.

Spence, J.T., & Helmreich, R. (1972). Who likes competent women: Competence, sex-role congruence of interests, and subjects' attitudes toward women as determinants of interpersonal attraction. *Journal of Applied Social Psychology, 2*, 197–213.

Spence, J.T., Helmreich, R., & Stapp, J. (1975). Likability, sex-role congruence of interest, and competence: It all depends on how you ask. *Journal of Applied Social Psychology, 5*, 93–109.

Stein, A., & Smithells, J. (1969). Age and sex differences in children's sex role standards about achievement. *Developmental Psychology, 1*, 252–259.

Taynor, J., & Deaux, K. (1975). When women are more deserving than men: Equity, attribution, and perceived sex differences. *Journal of Personality and Social Psychology, 32*, 381–390.

Valle, V.A., & Frieze, I.H. (1976). Stability of causal attributions as a mediator in changing expectations for success. *Journal of Personality and Social Psychology, 33*, 579–587.

Weiner, B., Frieze, I., Kukla, A., Reed, L., Rest, S., & Rosenbaum, R. (1971). Perceiving the causes of success and failure. In E.E. Jones et al. (Eds.), *Attribution: Perceiving the causes of behaviour.* Morristown, NJ: General Learning Press.

Wyrick, W. (1974). Biophysical perspectives. In E. Gerber, J. Felshin, P. Berlin, and W. Wyrick (Eds.), *The American woman in sport* (pp. 403–515). Reading, MA: Addison-Wesley.

5

COMPARISON OF MOTIVE TO SUCCEED, MOTIVE TO AVOID FAILURE, AND FEAR OF SUCCESS LEVELS BETWEEN MALE AND FEMALE INTERCOLLEGIATE SWIMMERS

Steven Houseworth

Joel Thirer

Application of achievement motivation to competitive athletic situations has been limited by the inadequacy of fabricating realistic competitive situations. This results in questioning the degree to which achievement motive factors actually influence competitive performance. This study investigated sex-based differences among intercollegiate athletes for the following variables: motive to succeed (Ms), motive to avoid failure (Maf), and fear of success (FOS). Athletic competitions for 121 NCAA I and II swimmers (males=55; females=66) during the 1982–1983 season were used as target situations in order to elicit feelings of these achievement motives. The Mehrabian Scale of Achieving Tendency (Mehrabian & Bank, 1978), Marten's (1977) Sport Competition Anxiety Test (SCAT), and Pappo's (1972) Fear of Success Inventory (FOSI) were used to assess Ms, Maf, and FOS, respectively, one week prior to each targeted competition. Additionally, a state anxiety inventory (Illinois Self Evaluation Questionnaire, ISEQ) (Martens, 1977)) was used to assess Maf immediately prior to actual competition. It was hypothesized that (1) males would evidence higher levels of Ms than females, and females would evidence higher levels of Maf and FOS than males; and (2) Ms levels would be higher for athletes than for a nonathletic population. Post hoc correlations indicated low FOSI scores to be more positively correlated with Ms, and more negatively correlated with the two measures of Maf. This study indicates that females who compete against females, rather than against males, do not evidence increased FOS levels.

As a psychological construct motivation is conceived as that which stimulates an organism to action (Atkinson & Birch, 1978; Ferguson, 1876). The achievement motivation theory developed by McClelland, Atkinson, Clark, and Lowell (1953) has attempted to account for those factors that stimulate individuals to action in evaluative situations. The importance of such as theory not only has revolutionized motivational research in educational settings, but also has provided new directions for evaluating competitive athletic behavior.

One of the specifications of achievement motivation theory is that it accounts for human behavior in any evaluative setting. Since athletic competitions are evaluated by spectators, coaches, and the athletes themselves, it is reasonable to assume that achievement motivation theory is applicable to competitive-evaluative settings. Unfortunately, studies utilizing achievement motivation theory in competitive-evaluative situations have been few in number, especially when compared to the large number of studies conducted in educational or academic settings. One of the difficulties in conducting achievement motivation research within competitive-evaluative settings is the control limitations of artificially induced competition (Ostrow, 1976). This is evidenced by the number of studies noting that the findings are "not consistent with previous research," or that the attempt to induce competition "may not have been successful" (Grove & Pargman, 1982; Healey & Landers, 1978; Scanlan & Ragan, 1978; Stadulis, 1976). Recognition of this limitation directs researchers to be more rigorous in their laboratory settings, and to more thoroughly investigate actual competitive-evaluative contests.

According to achievement motivation theory, the major factors that influence one's tendency to engage in an evaluative task are motive to succeed (Ms), motive to avoid failure (Maf), probability of successful task completion (Ps), and incentive value of successful task completion (Is). The factors of Ms and Maf are conceived as enduring, internal factors or traits. That is, one's motive to succeed and motive to avoid failure are motives within each individual which are relatively stable in their influence of achievement-motivated behavior (Atkinson & Birch, 1978). The factors of Ms and Maf are also opposing or competing motives. If one's Maf is greater than one's Ms, the behavioral tendency will be to avoid engaging in that activity. Therefore, Ms is conceived of as a facilitating achievement motive and Maf is conceived of as an inhibitory achievement motive. Ultimately the resultant tendency (Trn) of participation or nonparticipation is also a function of one's perceived Ps and Is. These factors are conceived of as external, nonstable factors which are dependent upon the immediate evaluative situation (Atkinson & Birch, 1978). Predictions of achievement-oriented behavior are therefore seen as a resultant interaction of these internal and external factors. For example, when Ms is stronger than Maf, and Ps and Is are high, the tendency to engage in or pursue a task to completion (Trn) will be high. Conversely, when Maf is stronger than Ms, and Ps and Is are moderate, the tendency to become involved in or complete a task (Trn) will be low. Obviously, there are numerous interactions among achievement motives that would influence the resultant tendency. These possible interactions should caution researchers when designing experimental settings.

Research by Horner (1968) was instrumental in the development of another stable, internal factor which affected one's Trn; this factor is the fear of success (FOS). Fear of success is defined as an inhibitory motive against achievement-oriented behavior which develops as a result of the negative consequences anticipated for success. Therefore, in terms of producing achievement-oriented behavior, FOS is similar in effect to Maf.

Since the time of Horner's original study and formulation of FOS, a great amount of study has focused on this motive. In separate reviews of the available literature, Zuckerman and Wheeler (1975) and Levine and Crumrine (1975) concluded that FOS is much less an actual phenomena than it is an artifact of other factors. One of these factors, suggested by Jackaway and Teevan (1976) and Saad, Lenauer, Shaver, and Dunivant (1978), is social affiliation. These researchers have proposed FOS as a form of Maf which is elicited by one's social acceptance and affiliative needs. This proposition is also supported by Kimball and Leahy (1976), who found that increasing peer affiliation influenced an increase in FOS for high school—aged females. Similarly, Makosky (1976) found that women with high FOS levels rated having a home and family as more important than a professional career; the opposite was found for women with low FOS levels. The most supportive evidence for this proposition was provided by Argote, Fisher, McDonald, and O'Neal (1976). In a study where actual acceptance and rejection in evaluative task outcomes were manipulated, it was found that one's level of FOS was mediated by one's need for social affiliation. Tresemer (1976a) has concluded that (1) women do not show more FOS imagery than do men, (2) the proportions of FOS imagery by both men and women have decreased since Horner's (1968) study, (3) the correlates of FOS appear to be few in number, and (4) the actual relationship between FOS and behavioral performance is unclear. However, Tresemer (1976b) also notes that an exact replication of Horner's study has not been conducted.

Thus, the question persists: Do males and females differ with regard to FOS levels? An examination of the available literature studying achievement motivation and FOS differences among male and female athletes has not provided conclusive evidence to answer this question. Lefebvre (1979) found higher Maf levels among female athletes, but not significant differences in FOS among male and female athletes. Weinberg and Jackson (1979) found that female and male athletes responded similarly to intrinsic and extrinsic motivation. Gillis (1979) found that female athletes more often attributed successful performance to luck rather than ability, while male athletes did not evidence this trend. In a study investigating the sex-role orientation of female athletes versus nonathletes, Henschen, Edwards, and Mathinos (1982) found a significant relationship between sex-role orientation and achievement motivation. High levels of Ms were associated with masculine and androgynous sex roles, while low levels of Ms were associated with feminine and undifferentiated sex-role orientations.

An additional factor which has not been investigated is the comparison of males competing against males, and females competing against females, rather than males competing against females. Significant differences in FOS between sexes may be dependent upon perceived social evaluation by females when compared with males. That is, a situation in which females are compared to other females poses different social evaluations than a situation in which females are compared to males. Most athletic teams are composed of a single sex (male or female) who compete against the same sex. Such situations provide an opportunity to investigate the question of achievement motivation and FOS differences among males and females without the confusion of sex role evaluation.

This question is compounded by the veracity of trait measures themselves. The controversy concerning use of sport-specific inventories (Martens, 1977; Singer, Harris, Kroll, Martens, & Sechrest, 1977) as opposed to general inventories (Nideffer, 1976; Zuckerman, 1979) is ongoing and deftly presented by Morgan (1980).

PROBLEM AND PURPOSE

The research problem addressed in this study was as follows: Do differences in achievement motives (Ms, Maf, and FOS) exist between male and female athletes? The purpose of this study was to determine if male athletes and female athletes differ in their levels of Ms, Maf, and FOS when oriented toward competitive-evaluative situations against the same sex. This study was conducted because of inconclusive findings of prior investigators. Based on the hypothesized direction of Horner's (1968) earlier results with the FOS motive, the following research hypotheses were formulated: (1) male athletes would have significantly higher Ms levels than would female athletes, (2) female athletes would have significantly higher Maf levels than would male athletes, (3) female athletes would have significantly higher FOS levels than would male athletes.

METHODS

The subjects were 121 (male, $N=55$; female, $N=66$) intercollegiate swimmers and divers ranging in age from 18 to 24 years. All athletes belonged to NCAA Division I and II swimming teams. The actual test administration occurred at four separate meets.

The Mehrabian Scale of Achieving Tendency (Mehrabian & Bank, 1978) was used to measure levels of Ms. Pappo's Fear of Success Inventory (FOSI) was used to measure levels of FOS (Pappo, 1972). Marten's (1977) Sport Competition Anxiety Test (SCAT) was used to measure levels of Maf. This follows the accepted procedure using anxiety as an indicant of Maf (Atkinson, 1964; Martire, 1956; Raphaelson, 1957; Scanlan & Ragan, 1978). The SCAT was used as an indicant of one's stable Maf and the Illinois Self Evaluation Questionaire (ISEQ) was used to measure situational levels of Maf, following the design of Scanlan and Ragan (1978). The ISEQ was chosen over other state anxiety instruments because it is a sport-specific instrument and therefore is appropriate for such a study. Also, the ISEQ was developed in a manner similar to the SCAT (Martens, 1977), and therefore, increases the concurrent validity of the construct assessed.

One team of male athletes was tested during a highly competitive shave meet. This meet was designed to allow swimmers the opportunity to qualify for the NCAA national championship meet. All other male teams were tested during a highly competitive collegiate invitational during the 1982–1983 swimming season. One nationally ranked team of female athletes (Southern Illinois University, Carbondale) was tested at a dual meet against another nationally ranked swim team (University of California, Berkeley). All other female teams were tested at the Gateway Collegiate Athletic Conference Championships and the National Independent Conference Championships, which were held concurrently. It was believed that these competitions would sufficiently elicit behavioral responses corresponding to each athlete's motive to succeed, motive to avoid failure, and motive to fear success.

Reliability of each inventory was analyzed using the Cronbach alpha procedure. Internal consistency was then calculated using the Spearman-Brown formula. Comparison of athletes on the variables of Ms, Maf, and FOS was conducted by a *t* test of group mean differences. Additionally, the magnitude of effect and estimated percent misclassification of subjects was calculated. Such statistics provided an indication as to the strength or magnitude of statistical differences found, and an indication of their practical significance in addition to statistical significance levels.

RESULTS

The Cronbach alpha coefficients and internal consistency coefficients for the scales used are reported in Table 1. The Mehrabian Scale of Achieving Tendency was found to have a reliability of $r = .40$ and internal consistency of $r = .92$. These values differed from the $r = .69$ and $r = .72$ respectively

TABLE 1
Cronbach Alpha and Internal Consistency Coefficients of
Intercollegiate Swimmers, and Normative Statistics

Intercollegiate Athletes (N=121)	Mehrabian Scale	SCAT	FOSI	ISEQ
Cronbach alpha	.40	.49	.93	.72
Internal consistency	.92	.83	.99	.97
Normative Statistics	Mehrabian Scale	SCAT	FOSI	ISEQ
Reliability	.69[a]	.77[b]	—	—
Internal consistency	.72[a]	.96[b]	—	—

[a]Reliability from test−retest method; internal consistency from Spearman Brown formula.
[b]Reliability from test−retest method; internal consistency from Kuder−Richardson 20 formula.

found by Mehrabian and Bank (1978). However, it would be noted that Mehrabian and Bank's values were acquired using a test-retest method to determine reliability. The Cronbach alpha coefficient ($r=.49$) and internal consistency coefficient ($r=.83$) for the SCAT are lower than the reliability values reported by Martens (1977). However, Rupnow and Ludwig (1980) have criticized the use of the Kuder-Richardson formula by Martens. The coefficients reported here more closely conform to the values reported by Rupnow and Ludwing using a split-half method to determine reliability. Normative statistics are not available for the ISEQ and FOSI, therefore, comparisons of ISEQ and FOSI values found in this study to normative data were not possible.

Comparison of athletes on the variables of Ms, Maf, and FOS was conducted by a t test comparison of group mean differences, and results can be found in Table 2. For the variable of Ms no significant difference was found between the mean value for males ($M=57.21$) and females ($M=57.22$). Comparison of the mean value of Ms for female athletes to the normative female mean score reported by Mehrabian & Bank (1978) is shown in Table 3. These data indicate that female athletes demonstrated a significantly higher mean score ($M=46.00$) with $t=2.30$, $df=699$, $p < .05$. It should be noted that the estimated magnitude of effect for $t=2.30$, $df=699$ is $r=.60$, with a misclassification of 23% based upon Ms scores alone (Freidman, 1968).

For the variable of Maf assessed by the SCAT, there were no significant differences found between male and female athletes, or between athletes in this study and normative data for the SCAT. No significant differences were

TABLE 2
Comparison of *t* test of Mean Differences, and Magnitude of Effect by Sex for Intercollegiate Swimmers

| Variable | X | SD | df | t | p | Magnitude of Effect | |
						r	Misclassified
Female	57.20	30.12					
Ms			118	.005	.99	—	—
Female	57.22	28.20					
Male	22.85	3.94					
Maf			118	2.59	.01	.20	42%
Female	20.96	4.03					
Male	11.65	1.69					
FOS			118	2.05	.04	.20	42%
Female	16.96	1.89					
Male	57.09	1.87					
Situational							
Maf			118	.86	.38	—	—
Female	54.90	1.69					

TABLE 3
Comparison of *t* test of Mean Difference between Intercollegiate Swimmers and Normative Statistics

	Intercollegiate Athletes	X	SD	Normative Statistics	X	SD
Ms	Overall (N=121)	57.21	28.97	Overall	51.00	35.00
	Male (n=55)	57.20	30.12	Male	55.00	34.00
	Female (n=66)	57.22	28.20	Female	46.00	36.00
Maf	Overall	21.82	4.08	Overall	21.17	4.36
	Male	22.85	3.94	Male	19.44	4.68
	Female	20.96	4.03	Female	22.60	4.87
FOS	Overall	14.55	14.43	Overall	—	—
	Male	11.65	12.65	Male	—	—
	Female	16.96	15.37	Female	—	—
Situational Maf	Overall	55.90	13.70	Overall	—	—
	Male	57.09	13.87	Male	—	—
	Female	54.10	13.90	Female	—	—

found between male and female athletes for the variables of FOS or Maf as assessed by the ISEQ immediately prior to competition. Again, normative data for the FOSI and ISEQ are not available, therefore, comparisons of athletes' scores to normative data were not possible.

CONCLUSIONS

Results of data analysis did not support the hypothesis that male athletes would have higher Ms levels than would female athletes. The mean scores for male and female athletes were almost identical (male $M=57.21$; female $M=57.22$). There was a significant difference found between female athletes and females used to establish the normative data for the Mehrabian Scale of Achieving Tendency. This finding indicates that female athletes have more of an achievement orientation than do females who are not specifically known to be athletes. This finding is not considered unusual. Athletes are involved in competitive-evaluative situations, and train specifically for competitions. Consequently an achievement orientation for athletes regardless of sex would be expected. The magnitude of effect estimation ($r=.60$) and percent misclassification (23%) indicate a moderate level of statistical power in differentiating female athletes in this study from female nonathletes based upon Ms levels alone.

ˋ The hypothesis that female athletes would have significantly higher levels of Maf than would male athletes was not supported. Scores for Maf as measured by the SCAT indicated a difference between males ($M=22.85$) and females ($M=20.96$) with a $t=2.59$, $df=116$, $p<.01$. However, estimation of the correlation equivalent from the t value was found to be $r=.20$, with an estimated misclassification of 42%. The practical interpretation of these findings is that, even though a statistical difference was evidenced, they are not practically significant in terms of statistical power and ability to separate male and female athletes based upon SCAT scores alone. No significant differences were found between male and female athletes on Maf as assessed situationally by the ISEQ. This finding is not considered unusual because athletes train for competition. The competition of females against other females does not seem to elicit motives different from males training for competition against other males.

The hypothesis that female athletes would have significantly higher levels of FOS than would male athletes was not supported by the research findings. Mean score differences were found to be statistically significant with $t=2.05$, $df=118$, $p<.01$ (male $M=11.65$; female $M=16.95$). However, the estimated correlation equivalent was computed to be $r=20$, with an estimated 42% misclassification of males and females based upon FOSI scores alone. Another factor to consider is the range of scores for Pappo's (1972) FOSI (-83 to $+83$). Scores found for the male and female athletes used in this study tend to indicate low to moderate scores within the scoring range. Additionally, a difference of 5.31 between males and females out of such a great range of possible scores does not seem to indicate practical significance. It is concluded that females who train for and are oriented toward competitive situations against other females do not differ from males in their FOS motive. Based upon the scoring range of the FOSI, the reported levels of FOS for male and female athletes are considered to indicate a low motive to fear success. Lack of normative data for Pappo's FOSI limits further interpretation of this data.

Considering the theoretical relationship of these motives a post hoc Pearson product-moment analysis was conducted. The intended direction of such an analysis should have revealed negative relationships between the facilitating dimension of Ms and the inhibitory dimensions of Maf/FOS. Additionally, if FOS is a form of Maf as suggested by Jackaway and Teevan (1976) and Saad, Lenauer, Shaver, and Dunivant (1978), then these motives should be positively correlated. The results of this correlational analysis are reported in Table 4.

Although the ISEQ and SCAT were highly correlated with each other ($r=.42$), the SCAT and ISEQ were found to have low negative correlations with the FOSI ($r=-.29$ and $r=-.19$, respectively). Similarly, the Mehrabian scale demonstrated a low positive correlation with the FOSI ($r=.26$) and low negative correlations with the SCAT and ISEQ ($r=.-.26$ and $r-.28$, respectively). Although the strongest correlation was found for assessments of Maf which were measured by tests similar in design (Martens, 1977), a trend seems to be evident. Fear of success, assessed in this study by the FOSI, is more closely related to Ms than MAF. Theoretically, the opposite relationship should have been found. A possible explanation is that the

TABLE 4
Pearson Product-Moment Correlations among Independent Variables for Intercollegiate Swimmers and Divers

	Motive	**Maf**	**FOS**	**Situational Maf**
r value	Ms	$-.26$	.26	$-.28$
alpha level		.004	.004	.001
r valve	Maf	—	$-.29$	.42
alpha level			.001	.001
r valve	FOS	—	—	$-.19$
alpha level				.03

extreme range of the FOSI (-83 to $+83$) would actually indicate a strong Ms with low to moderate scores, and a strong FOS motive with high scores. These findings suggest that the FOSI may assess Ms and FOS along a continuum rather than FOS singularly. This conclusion is tentative and based upon theoretical relationships. However, it is suggested that further examination of the actual motives assessed by Pappo's FOSI be conducted.

In conclusion, this study did not find support for a sex-based FOS motive among male and female athletes who compete against the same sex. It is believed that competitive athletes who train for competition against the same sex are highly motivated to succeed in their competitions. One problem which should be investigated further is the ability of Pappo's (1972) FOSI to assess FOS independent of Ms. Although the FOSI has been used in prior studies (Jackaway & Teevan, 1976; Saad, Lenauer, Shaver, & Dunivant, 1978) this investigation found low to moderate scores on the FOSI to correlate more positively with the Mehrabian scale. Thus the FOSI may assess Ms and FOS along a continuum, rather than FOS independent of other achievement motives.

REFERENCES

Argote, L., Fisher, J., McDonald, P., and O'Neal, E. (1976). Competitiveness in males and females: Situational determinants of fear of success behavior. *Sex Roles, 2,* 295–305.

Atkinson, J.W. (1964). *Introduction to motivation,* New York: Van Nostrand.

Atkinson, J. & Birch, D. (1978). *Introduction to motivation* (2nd ed.). New York: Van Nostrand.

Ferguson, E. (1976). *Motivation: An experimental approach.* New York: Holt, Rinehart & Winston.

Gillis, J. (1979). Effects of achieving tendency, gender, and outcome on causal attributions following motor performance. *Research Quarterly, 50,* 610–619.

Grove, J. , & Pargman, D. (1982). *Effects of achievement tendencies and competitive outcomes on performance.* Paper presented at the annual meeting of the American Alliance for Health, Physical Education, Recreation and Dance, Houston.

Freidman, H. (1968). Magnitude of experimental effect and a table for its rapid estimation. *Psychological Bulletin, 70,* 245–251.

Healey, T., & Landers, D. (1978). Effect of need achievement and task difficulty on competitive and noncompetitive motor performance. *Journal of Motor Behavior, 5,* 121–128.

Henschen, K., Edwards, S. & Mathinos, L. (1982). Achievement motivation and sex role orientation of high school female track and field athletes and non-athletes. *Perceptual and Motor Skills, 55,* 183–187.

Horner, M. (1968). Sex differences in achievement motivation and performance in competitive and non-competitive situations. *Dissertation-Abstracts International, 30,* 407B. (University Microfilms No. 69-12, 135)

Jackaway, R., & Teevan, R. (1976). Fear of failure and fear of success: Two dimensions of the same motive. *Sex Roles, 3,* 283–293.

Kimball, B., & Leahy, R. (1976). Fear of success in males and females: Effects of developmental level and sex linked course of study. *Sex Roles, 2,* 269–272.

Lefebvre, L. (1979). Achievement motivation and causal attribution in male and female athletes. *International Journal of Sport Psychology, 10,* 31–41.

Levine, A., & Crumrine, J. (1975). Women and the fear of success: A problem in replication. *American Journal of Sociology, 80,* 964–974.

Makosky, V. (1976). Sex role compatibility of task and of competitor, and fear of success as variables affecting women's performance. *Sex Roles, 2,* 217–236.

Martens, R. (1977). *Sport competition anxiety test.* Champaign, IL: Human Kinetics.

Martire, J. (1956). Relationships between the self-concept and differences in strength and generality of achievement motivation. *Journal of Personality, 24,* 364–375.

McClelland, D., Atkinson, J., Clark, R., & Lowell, E. (1953). *The achievement motive.* New York: Appleton-Century-Crofts.

Mehrabian, A., & Bank, I. (1978). A questionnaire measure of individual differences in achieving tendency. *Educational and Psychological Measurement, 38,* 475–478.

Morgan, W. (1980). Trait psychology controversy. *Research Quarterly, 50,* 50–76.

Nideffer, R. (1976). Test of attention and interpersonal style. *Journal of Personality and Social Psychology, 34,* 394–404.

Ostrow, A. (1976). Goal setting behavior and need achievement in relation to competitive motor activity. *Research Quarterly, 47,* 174–183.

Pappo, M. (1972). Fear of success: A theoretical analysis and the construction and validation of a measuring instrument. *Dissertation abstracts international, 34,* 421B (University Microfilms No. 73-16, 235)

Raphaelson, A. (1957). The relationship between inaginative, direct, verbal, and physiological measures of anxiety in an achievement situation. *Journal of Abnormal and Social Psychology, 54,* 13–18.

Rupnow, A., & Ludwig, D. (1980). Psychometric notes on the reliability of the sport competition anxiety test: Form C. *Research Quarterly, 52.* 35–37.

Saad, S., Lenauer, M., Shaver, P. & Dunivant, N. (1978). Objective measurement of fear of success and fear of failure: A factor analytic approach. *Journal of Consulting and Clinical Psychology, 45,* 405–416.

Scanlan, T., & Ragan, J. (1978). Achievement motivation and competition: Perceptions and responses. *Medicine and Science in Sports, 10,* 276–281.

Singer, R., Harris, D., Kroll, W., Martens, R., & Sechrest, L. (1977). Psychological testing of athletes. *Journal of Physical Education and Recreation, 48,* 30–32.

Stadulis, R. (1976). Need achievement, competitive preference and evaluation seeking. In D. Landers & R. Christina (Eds.), *Psychology of motor behavior and sport* (pp. 113–122). Champaign, IL: Human Kinetics.

Tresemer, D. (1976a). The cumulative record of research on "fear of success." *Sex Roles, 2,* 211–216.

Tresemer, D. (1976b). Do women fear success? *Signs: Journal of Women in Culture and Society, 1,* 863–874.

Weinberg, R., & Jackson, A. (1979). Competition and extrinsic rewards: Effect on intrinsic motivation and attribution. *Research Quarterly, 50,* 494–502.

Zuckerman, M. (1979). Traits, states, situations and uncertainty. *Journal of Behavioral Assessment, 1,* 43–54.

Zuckerman, M., & Wheeler, L. (1975). To dispel fantasies about the fantasy-based measure of fear of success. *Psychological Bulletin,* 932–946.

6

RELATIONSHIPS AMONG SUCCESS/FAILURE, ATTRIBUTIONS, AND PERFORMANCE EXPECTANCIES IN COMPETITIVE SITUATIONS

J. Robert Grove
David Pargman

It has been theorized that a predictable relationship exists between the stability of causal attributions for success or failure and subsequent performance expectancies. The hypothesized relationship has been demonstrated in noncompetitive situations but not in competitive situations. Three studies are reported that addressed the connection between causal stability and expectancies in competitive settings. Results indicated a consistent relationship that was only partially predicted from theory and previous research. Potential explanations are offered for these findings, and implications are discussed within the limitations of the present paradigm.

Weiner and his colleagues (Weiner, 1972, 1974, 1979; Weiner et al., 1971) have suggested that a predictable relationship exists between causal attributions for immediate success or failure and expectancies for future success. This relationship is based on a theoretical connection between causal stability and expectancies for success. Specifically, it has been predicted that immediate success will lead to a realtively high expectancy for future success when the perceived cause of the outcome is considred stable over time rather than unstable over time. Similarly, immediate failure is predicted to lead to relatively low expectancies for future success when it is attributed to a stable rather than an unstable factor. Stated somewhat differently, attribution of outcomes to unstable factors is believed to maintain expectancies at a more intermediate level than is attribution of outcomes to stable factors. Figure 1 illustrates this relationship using unstable effort and stable ability as exemplary attributions.

Considerable evidence exists to support the proposed relationship between causal stability and expectancies both for cognitive and motor tasks (Fontaine, 1974; McCaughan, 1978; McMahan, 1973; Rosenbaum, 1973; Singer & McCaughan, 1978; Valle & Frieze, 1976). However, this research has been conducted in noncompetitive situations. There is little direct evidence that the predicted relationship between stability and expectancies would hold in situations involving interpersonal competition. Research on

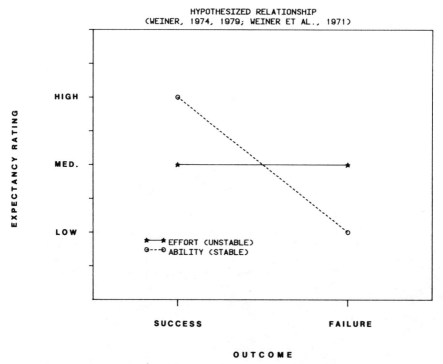

FIGURE 1. Hypothesized relationship between attributional stability and expectancies under conditions of success or failure.

attributions in competitive situations has tended to focus on the types of attributions made after successful or unsuccessful outcomes (for reviews, see Brawley & Roberts, 1984; Carron, 1980). This tendency to treat attributions as dependent measures has meant that the cognitive and behavioral *consequences* of different attributions have been largely ignored in the sport science literature. This oversight is potentially problematic because interpersonal competition can be distinguished from other types of achievement settings by the presence of rivalry and "multi-incentive" conditions (Atkinson & Raynor, 1978; Wankel, 1972). Thus, it is possible that a different relationship would exist between attributions and expectancies in such a situation.

The present paper reports three studies designed specifically to address the relationship between causal stability and expectancies for success in situations involving interpersonal competition. Unstable effort and stable ability were selected for examination because these attributions are commonly used in competitive situations and effective reactions are maximized when these causes are invoked (Frieze, 1976; Roberts & Pascuzzi, 1979; Weiner, Russell, & Lerman, 1978). It was assumed that an instructional set that emphasized one of these factors would induce subjects to attribute their outcomes primarily to that particular factor. Based on the work of Weiner and his colleagues, it was hypothesized that expectancies for success would be more intermediate when an unstable attribution was salient. More specifically, the following predictions were made (see Figure 1):

1. Given winning outcomes, expectancies for success will be higher when the instructional set emphasizes stable ability rather than unstable effort.
2. Given losing outcomes, expectancies for success will be lower when the instructional set emphasizes stable ability rather than unstable effort.

METHOD

Experiment 1

The Mehrabian Scale of Achieving Tendency (Mehrabian & Bank, 1978) was administered to 70 male undergraduates. A median split was then used to establish groups with relatively high or low achievement tendencies. Twenty subjects were randomly chosen from each group to take part in the experiment. These subjects reported for the experiment 1–3 weeks after completion of the Mehrabian scale and were randomly assigned to one of eight treatment conditions in a 2 (Task Orientation) × 2 (Competitive Outcome) × 2 (Achievement Tendency) design. They were informed that there were two phases to the study, and that during the first part they would be competing against each other in a best-three-out-of-five dart-tossing contest. During the second phase, the loser would ostensibly be required to perform some additional tasks while wearing headphones that would transmit "unpleasant" white noise. The winner would be free to leave early with full credit for experimental particpation. In actuality, there was no second phase of the study, and nobody was required to listen to the white noise. These procedures were used to give participants a motive for serious completion.

Subjects were then informed that they would be required to throw the darts with their nonpreferred hand. Pretesting indicated that the use of the nonpreferred hand increased the novelty of the experimental task and made the subsequent task orientation manipulation more believable. Different descriptions of the task were then provided. Half of the participants received an *Effort-oriented* instructional set and half received and *Ability-oriented*

instructional set. The specific wording of these instructional sets was as
follows (cf. Kukla, 1972; changes in parentheses):

> Since nobody used their opposite hand very much, this is a very pure task. It
> is pure in the sense that how well you do depends almost entirely on how
> much effort you put into it (on your natural eye-hand ability). Practically
> everyone who succeeds at this task does so because he works at it very hard
> (because he has the natural ability to do this sort of thing well). Failure is
> almost always related to a lack of effort (to a low level of natural ability).

Subjects then "competed" against each other in a best-out-of-five dart-
tossing contest. Each trial of competition was preceded by a rating of the
subject's expectancy for success on that particular trial. These ratings were
made on an 11-point scale labeled with "very sure I will win" at one end of
the scale, "very sure I will lose" at the other end of the scale, and "uncertain" at the midpoint. The numbers 0 through 10 appeared on the scale, with
higher numbers indicating a greater expectance for success. After making
expectancy ratings for a particular trial, the subjects were given 5 min to
practice before making a set of five performance throws at their target.[1]
their point totals for five throws were then ostensibly compared to determine who had won that trial. In actuality, whether a subject won or lost had
been randomly determined by a coin flip, and feedback was provided in
accordance with the condition to which the subject had been assigned.
Predetermined "Winners" were told after every trial that they had out-
scored their opponent and had won that trial. Predetermined "Losers" were
told repeatedly that they had scored fewer points and had lost. Thus, after
three trials the subjects believed that they had either won or lost the
best-of-five contest.

Experiments 2 and 3

The procedure for Experiments 2 and 3 was very similar to that used in
Experiment 1. However, the following changes were made prior to Experiment 2:

1. A stronger manipulation of achievement tendency was used in this
   experiment to provide a better test for the potential mediating influence of this variable. The manipulation was strengthened by admin-
   istering the Mehrabian scale to 220 male undergraduates and dividing the distribution into thirds. Subjects were then selected only from
   the upper and lower thirds of the distribution.

---

[1]The practice and performance data from these experiments have been reported elsewhere and are not reported here (see Grove, 1982; Grove & Pargman, 1984, in press).

2. A check on the adequacy of the attributional manipulation was employed. This manipulation check consisted of an open-ended question asking "What is the most important factor that distinguishes winners from losers on this task?" Only subjects who responded in accordance with their assigned attributional orientation were retained for purposes of analysis (final $N = 60$).

3. The expectancy scales were changed somewhat. The scales in Experiment 2 were anchored by statements "completely certain of winning" and "no chance at all of winning." The label at the midpoint of the scale was eliminated.

4. A premanipulation expectancy rating was obtained from each subject. This rating was used as a covariate to control for initial differences in expectancies concerning performance on the experimental task.

The following procedural changes were made for Experiment 3:

1. Female undergraduates (Final $N = 83$) were used as subjects and screened on the basis of a manipulation check similar to that used in Experiment 2.

2. An attempt was made to increase external validity by making the competition less artificial. Toward this end subjects were solicited on the basis of advertisements stating that participants would be competing for cash prizes range from $5 to $25. This format made it possible to eliminate the threat of white noise that was used to stimulate competition in the previous studies and provided a more realistic competitive atmosphere.

3. The attributional manipulations were strengthened by the use of a different cover story and subtle changes in wording (see Grove, 1982. for details). Unstable effort and stable ability remained, however, the factors that were stressed by the instructional sets.

4. In addition to manipulating attributional orientation and competitive outcome, the margin of victory/defeat was also manipulated. This manipulation was accomplished by providing subjects with written feedback concerning their performance. The written feedback indicated whether the subject had won or lost and presented a five-scale category scale indicating what the margin of victory or defeat had been. This scale ranged from "very small" through "moderate" to "very large." One of the extremes was circled in accordance with the subject's assigned condition (large margin vs. small margin).

5. A premanipulation expectancy rating was obtained as in Experiment 2 and used as a covariate in the analyses.

RESULTS

In the following presentation of results, no data from Trial 1 were included in any of the analyses because it was a preoutcome trial, and the predictions were based on the interactions of attributional orientation and outcome. The obtained results do not change if these data are included.

Experiment 1

The postoutcome ratings from Experiment 1 were analyzed using a four-way analysis of variance (ANOVA). Factors in this analysis were task orientation (ability, effort), competitive outcome (win, lose), achievement tendency (high, low), and trial (2,3). Contrary to the predictions, a significant interaction between task orientation and competitive outcome was *not* obtained. Instead, there was a tendency for a main effect of task orientation, $F(1, 32) = 2.91$, $p < .10$. An examination of the data indicated that expectancies tended to be higher under an effort orientation than under an ability orientation regardless of outcome (see Table 1). This trend is depicted graphically in Figure 2.

Experiment 2

The postoutcome expectancy ratings from Experiment 2 were analyzed using a four-way analysis of covariance (ANCOVA). Factors in this analysis were task orientation (ability, effort). competitive outcome (win lose), achievement tendency (high, low) and trial (2, 3, 4, 5). The premanipulation expectancy rating served as the covariate in this analysis. Again, the Task Orientation × Competitive Outcome interaction was not significant, and there was a trend for a main effect of task orientation, $F(1, 50) = 3.36, p <$

TABLE 1
Means for the Expectancy Ratings of Competitors Given Effort or Ability Orientations

Group	Experiment 1	Experiment 2	Experiment 3
Effort (overall mean)	7.77	6.37	6.18
Effort—win	8.13	7.49	7.03
Effort—lose	7.41	5.24	5.32
Ability (overall mean)	6.84	5.79	5.25
Ability—win	7.35	7.12	6.41
Ability—lose	6.32	4.45	4.09

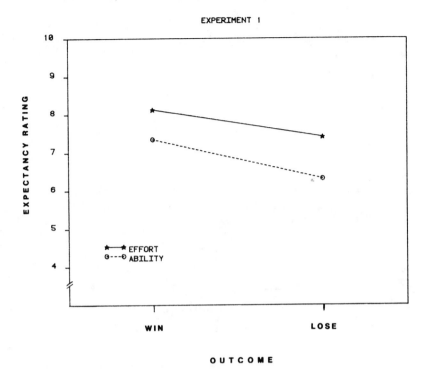

FIGURE 2. Mean expectancy ratings of effort-oriented and ability-oriented competitors under winning or losing conditions in Experiment 1.

.075. Examination of the data again indicated that expectancies tended to be higher under an effort orientation than under an ability orientation regardless of outcome (see Table 1). This trend is depicted graphically in Figure 3.

Experiment 3

The postoutcome expectancy ratings from Experiment 3 were analyzed using a four-way ANCOVA. Factors in this analysis were task orientation (ability, effort), competitive outcome (win, lose), outcome margin (small, large), and trial (2, 3, 4). The premanipulation expectancy rating was used as the covariate. This analysis again failed to detect a significant Orientation × Outcome interaction. There was, however, a significant main effect for task orientation, $F (1, 69) = 6.25, p < .025$. Examination of means indicated that, as in the previous studies, expectancies were higher under an effort orientation than under an ability orientation regardless of outcome (see Table 1). This effect is depicted graphically in Figure 4.

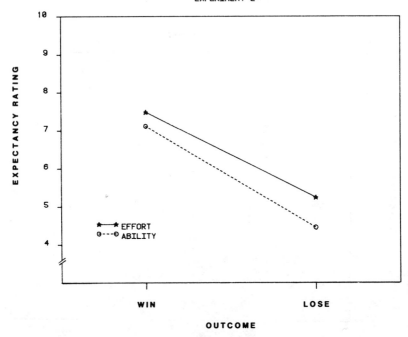

FIGURE 3. Mean expectancy ratings of effort-oriented and ability-oriented competitors under winning or losing conditions in Experiment 2.

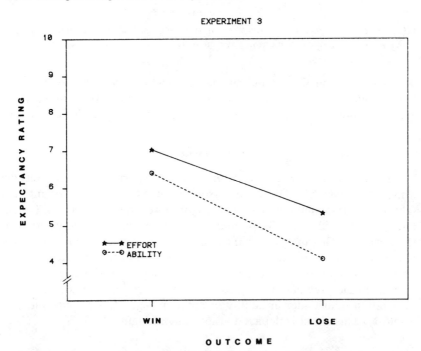

FIGURE 4. Mean expectancy ratings of effort-oriented and ability-oriented competitors under winning or losing conditions in Experiment 3.

DISCUSSION

Two aspects of the data deserve comment. First, it is evident that the findings from the experiments were very consistent. The same pattern of results emerged in all three studies, with the expectancies of effort-oriented competitors higher than those of ability-oriented competitors regardless of outcome. It should be noted that this pattern was unaffected by achievement tendencies or by manipulation of the margin of victory/defeat. It should also be noted that this consistent pattern emerged despite some variation in the experimental conditions across studies. These variations included the use of male subjects in Experiments 1 and 2, but female subjects in Experiment 3; a different number of competitive trials across the three experiments; and somewhat less artificiality in Experiment 3 than in the other two experiments.

The second interesting feature of the data concerns the extent to which the hypotheses were supported. These hypotheses were based on Weiner's (1972, 1974, 1979) theoretical model and on previous findings in noncompetitive situations. However, the present results only partially corroborated the theoretical model and its previous empirical support. Given failure, expectancies were maintained at a higher (more intermediate) level when the instructional set emphasized unstable effort. This finding was predicted. Given success, however, expectancies were again maintained at a high (*less* intermediate) level when the instructional set emphasized unstable effort. This finding was contrary to results from noncompetitive situations and contrary to our predictions.

Despite the fact that our predictions were only partially supported, one can derive a parsimonious explanation for the obtained results by focusing on the perceived controllability of the causal factors rather than their perceived stability. In addition to differing in stability, the causal factors of effort and ability differ in the degree to which they can be controlled by the individual. Personal control is more possible over effort than over ability. If one assumes that individuals will expect to do better under conditions where preceived control is high rather than low (cf. Abramson, Seligman, & Teasdale, 1978; Rotter, 1966), then the pattern of results obtained in these studies is understandable. As noted earlier, predictions based on perceived stability would lead one to anticipate a pattern of expectancies such as that depicted in Figure 1. Such a pattern was clearly not evident in the present studies. It is possible that the importance of perceived controllability could be enhanced in competitive situations due to the uncertain nature of the outcome and the high degree of ego involvement such situations entail. Such a process could account for the difference between the present findings and those from noncompetitive situations.

The implications of these results appear to depend on the theory of motivation under consideration. Some theories have argued that the maintenance of intermediate expectancies is beneficial from a motivational standpoint (Kukla, 1972; Weiner, 1972, 1974). If this argument is valid, the present results suggest that an effort orientation to competition may enhance motivation only under failure conditions. On the other hand, some theorists have proposed a more direct relationship between expectancies and motivation. Bandura's (1977) theory of self-efficacy, for example, links increases in expectancies to increases in the quality of performance. If this argument is valid, the present results suggest that an effort orientation to competition may enhance motivation under either success or failure conditions.

In conclusion, acknowledgment should be made of the limitations of the procedures used in these studies. First, rather than defining high and low achievers in terms of deviations from the normative means (Mahrabian & Bank, 1978), these groups were defined in a relative sense using either a median split or a one-third split. As a result, the groups may not have been extreme enough to provide an adequate test for the mediating influence of teh achievement tendency variable. Second, although attempts were made to enhance the realism of the competition in Experiment 3, it must be acknowledged that it was still not a "real-world" competition. Therefore one must be cautious in generalizing the present results beyond the laboratory. Finally, it should be noted that all three studies compared only two types of attributions and presented them so that ability was stable while effort was unstable. No provisions were made for the fact that ability may sometimes by perceived as unstable and effort may sometimes be perceived as stable (see, e.g., Roberts & Pascuzzi, 1979). Changing the attributions emphasized in the instructional sets and/or changing their dimensional properties could well have changed the results. The acknowledgment of these limitations not only helps to put the present results in proper perspective, but also suggests interesting directions for future research.

REFERENCES

Abramson, L.Y., Seligman, M.E.P., & Teasdale, J.D. (1978). Learned helplessness in humans: Critique and reformulation. *Journal of Abnormal Psychology, 87,* 49–74.

Atkinson, J.W., & Raynor, J.O. (1978). *Personality, motivation and achievement.* New York: Halsted Press.

Bandura, A. (1977). Self-efficacy: Toward a unifying theory of behavioral change. *Psychological Review, 84,* 191–215.

Brawley, L.R., & Roberts, G.C. (1984). Attributions in sports: research foundations, characteristics, and limitations. In J.M. SIlva & R.S. Weinberg (Eds.), *Psychological foundations of sport* (pp. 112–121). Champaign, IL: Human Kinetics.

Carron, A.V. (1980). *Social psychology of sport.* Ithaca, NY: Mouvement.

Fontaine, G. (1974). Social comparison and some detemrinants of expected personal control and expected performance in a novel task situation. *Journal of Personality and Social Psychology, 29,* 487–496.

Frieze, I.H. (1976). Causal attributions and information seeking to explain success and failure. *Journal of Research in Personality, 10,* 293–305.

Grove, J.R. (1982). Cognitive and behavioral consequences of attributional manipulation in a competitive situation. *Dissertation Abstracts International, 43,* 3409B.

Grove, J.R., & Pargman, D. (in press). Behavioral consequences of effort versus ability orientations to interpersonal competition. *Australian Journal of Science and Medicine in sport.*

Grove, J.R., & Pargman, D. (1984). Attributions and performance revisited: Further tests of theoretical predictions with competitive orientation as a manipulated variable. Manuscript submitted for publication.

Kukla, A. (1972). Attributional determinants of achievement-related behaviour. *Journal of Personality and Social Psychology, 21,* 166–174.

McCaughan, L.R. (1978). Stability/instability and change of expectancy: A test for the cognitive determinants of psychomotor performance. *Perceptual and Motor Skills, 46,* 219–225.

McMahan, L. (1973). Relations between causal attributions and expectancy of success. *Journal of Personality and Social Psychology, 28,* 108–114.

Mehrabian, A., & Bank, I. (1978). A questionnaire measure of individual differences in achieving tendency. *Educational and Psychological Measurement, 38,* 475–478.

Roberts, G.C. & Pascuzzi, D. (1979). Causal attribution in sport: Some theoretical implications. *Journal of Sport Psychology, 1,* 203–211.

Rosenbaum, R. (1973). A dimensional analysis of the perceived causes of success and failure. *Dissertation Abstracts International, 33,* 5040B.

Rotter, J.B. (1966). Generalized expectancies for internal versus external control of reinforcement. *Psychological Monographs, 80* (1, Whole No. 609).

Singer, R.N., & McCaughn, L.R. (1978). Motivational effects of attributions, expectancy, and achievement motivation during the learning of a novel motor task. *Journal of Motor Behaviour, 10,* 245–253.

Valle, V.A., & Frieze, I.H. (1976). Stability of causal attributions as a mediator in changing expectations of success. *Journal of Personality and Social Psychology, 33,* 579–587.

Wankel, L.M. (1972). Competition in motor performance: An experimental analysis of motivation components. *Journal of Experimental Social Psychology, 8,* 427–437.

Weiner, B. (1972). *Theories of motivation: From mechanism to cognition.* Chicago: Markham.

Weiner, B. (Ed.). (1974). *Achievement motivation and attribution theory.* Morristown, NJ: General Learning Press.

Weiner, B. (1979). A theory of motivation for some classroom experiences. *Journal of Educational Psychology, 71,* 3–25.

Weiner, B., Frieze, I., Kukla, A., Reed, L., Rest, S., & Rosenbaum, R. (1971). Perceiving the causes of success and failure. In E.E. Jones et al. (Eds.), *Attribution: Perceiving the causes of behaviour.* Morristown, NJ: General Learning Press.

Weiner, B., Russell, D., & Lerman, D. (1978). Affective consequences of causal ascriptions. In J.H. Harbey, W. Ickes, & R.F. Kidd (Eds.), *New directions in attribution research* (Vol. 2, pp. 210–218). Hillsdale, NJ: Erlbaum.

7

MOOD ALTERATION WITH SWIMMING:
A REEXAMINATION

Bonnie G. Berger

David R. Owen

Two studies tested the relationship between swimming, an aerobic activity, and mood. College students, voluntarily enrolled in beginning or intermediate swimming or control classes, completed the Profile of Mood States (POMS) before and after class during the fall (N = 100) and summer (N = 78) terms. As predicted, results of a four-way multivariate analysis of variance in the first study conducted during a 14-week semester indicated that swimmers felt significantly less tense, depressed, angry, and confused and more vigorous after class than before. Novice and intermediate swimmers changed significantly more than did the controls on all of these scales. There were no gender differences in amount of mood change associated with swimming despite different social connotations of exercise for women and men. However, in contrast to the literature, women were significantly less tense, depressed, angry, and confused than men. Results of the second study conducted during a 5-week summer session failed to replicate those of the first. The mood-enhancing effects of swimming seemed to be sensitive to environmental conditions. It is now important to determine which exercise parameters are most conducive to consistent mood benefits.

Jogging is associated with a variety of desirable psychological changes. For example, some report decreases in anxiety and depression (e.g., Berger, 1982a, 1984a; Folkins & Sime, 1981; Morgan, 1979; Wood, 1977), and others cite enhanced self-concept and self-awareness (Berger, 1982b; 1984c; Sonstroem, 1982). Based on the mood-enhancing benefits of jogging psychotherapists are using running as a therapeutic technique and report success in treating clients who are clinically anxious or depressed (Blue, 1979; Greist et al., 1979; Rindskopf & Gratch, 1982; Sacks & Sachs, 1981). Surprisingly little research concerning the psychological effects of other types of exercise has been reported (e.g., Brown, Ramirez, & Taub, 1978; Dishman & Gettman, 1981). Thus, we decided to investigate the influence of swimming, another aerobic activity, on mood.

The relationship between swimming and mood has widespread implications. Sedentary members of the American population may be encouraged to exercise more regularly and thus promote their own health (Brandt, 1982) if it can be demonstrated that exercise produces immediate psychological benefits as well as the more long-term physical benefits. If the psychological benefits of swimming are similar to those of jogging, people who find running to be boring, or physically difficult (the arthritic, obese, and physically handicapped). can obtain psychological effects by swimming. Finally, psychotherapists who employ running as a therapeutic modality may present clients with an alternative activity.

Two studies were conducted to illuminate the following unresolved issues concerning the relationship between exercise and mood:

1. Does exercise cause or is it associated with mood benefits (Jasnoski, Holmes, Solomon, & Aguiar, 1981)?
2. Is exercise effective in altering the psychological states of "normal" adults (Berger, 1984a)?
3. What exercise parameters are most likely to enhance psychological well-being (Berger, 1984b)?

HYPOTHESIZED MOOD CHANGES BEFORE AND AFTER EXERCISE

Swimming and Mood

Two studies, differing in exercise frequency and duration, focused on short-term influences of swimming on participants' moods. The first study was conducted during a 14-week fall semester; the second one, during a 5-week summer term. Otherwise, the experimental procedures in the two studies were similar. Due to the unexpected results of the second study, we recapitulate the results of the first study (Berger & Owen, 1983) and include a new multivariate analysis which confirms the initially reported results.

Four hypotheses were examined in each study. First, we hypothesized greater mood changes as measured before and after class for swimmers than for control students who attended a lecture.

Second, because of the task similarities between swimming and jogging, we hypothesized that their psychological effects would be comparable. Both swimming and jogging are aerobic, require little monitoring of the environment, are rhythmical and repetitive in nature, and do not require the manipulation of an implement or ball. Based on the results of several studies testing runners (Morgan, 1979, 1980; Wilson, Morley, & Bird, 1980), swimmers were hypothesized to be (1) less tense or anxious, (2) less depressed, (3) less angry, (4) less confused, but (5) more vigorous after swimming than before. Although some runners have decreased in fatigue when measured at the beinning and end of long-term exercise programs (Morgan, 1979, 1980), we did not propose a directional hypothesis about fatigue for swimmers tested immediately before and after a single swimming session.

The third hypothesis was that the mood benefits of swimming would be greater for intermediates than for beginners. Swimming, in contrast to running, is composed of new, complex motor patterns that require time and practice to acquire. Intermediate swimmers who have mastered a variety of swimming strokes can exercise continuously for a longer time than beginners. This would be a major advantage if Carmack and Martens (1979) are correct in suggesting that continuous exercise for over 40 min is more conducive to psychological benefits. Berger (1982b, 1984b) modified their recommendation and suggested that three 20-min sessions per week at 70% – 85% of maximal heart rate would produce the mood benefits.

Gender and Mood

Since physical activity appears to have different meanings for women and men in American society (Berger, 1984c; Rindskopf & Gratch, 1982; Sage, 1980), it seemed possible that men and women would also differ in their psychological responses to exercise. Reports indicate that women are more anxious and depressed than men (e.g., Justice & McBee, 1978; King & Buchwald, 1982; Scarf, 1980), which further supported the inclusion of gender as a quasi-independent variable because running is more likely to reduce anxiety and depression among those who score in the clinical range of the scales (Brown et al., 1978; Morgan, Roberts, Brand, & Feinerman, 1970; Wood, 1977). So, the final hypothesis was that pre- to postexercise mood changes would differ in amount, especially for anxiety and depression, but would be in the same direction for men and women swimmers.

STUDY 1

Method

Subjects

The subjects were female and male college students ($N = 100$) who ranged in age between 17 and 50 years (mean = 22.3 years) and were voluntarily enrolled in one of six classes. There were two beginning (ns = 17, 8) and two intermediate (ns = 19, 14) swimming classes. Students attending lecture classes in the Departments of Health Science ($n = 22$) or Physical Education ($n = 20$) served as controls. Some students were excluded from the study: five beginning and four intermediate swimmers had language problems; five members of the varsity swim team were excluded; and three beginners and nine intermediates either dropped the course or chose not to participate in the study.

Equivalence of the two beginning, two intermediate, and two control classes was investigated. An analysis of variance (ANOVA) confirmed that ages were comparable across the beginners, intermediates, and controls ($p > .32$). The three groups also were comparable ($p > .19$) on the Lie Scale (Eysenck & Eysenck, 1968), a measure of social desirablility response set. There were no differences among the three groups on the pretest Profile of Mood States (POMS) scores (women, $p > .93$, and men, $p > .95$).

Procedure

The four swimming classes, taught by the first investigator, met in 40-min sessions twice a week during a 14-week semester. Control classes met for 50 min, three times a week, and were taught by female faculty members who were not associated with the study.

The POMS (McNair, Lorr, & Droppleman, 1971) was selected for these studies because it measures state, rather than trait, characteristics which are hypothesized to fluctuate as a result of exercise: (1) Anxiety–Tension, (2) Depression–Dejection, (3) Anger–Hostility, (4) Vigor–Activity, (5) Fatigue–Inertia, and (6) Confusion–Bewilderment. Swimmers and controls completed the POMS before and after class on one occasion during the 13th week of swimming. Early in the semester, students also completed the Lie Scale of the Eysenck Personality Inventory for a measure of social desirability.

Design

A four-factor multivariate analysis of variance (MANOVA) was employed to investigate the effects of swimming skill level, the particular class, and gender on the six POMS subscales with repeated measures before and after an instructional period. Specifically, a 3 (level: beginners, intermediates, and controls) × 2 (number of classes at each level) × 2 (gender) × 2 (pre-, postinstruction) MANOVA was calculated on the vector of six mood scores. The level factor was conceived as two independent a priori 1 df contrasts: (1) all swimmers versus controls and (2) beginning swimmers versus intermediate swimmers. Two classes were nested in each of three levels of instruction.

In addition, a multivariate profile analysis was employed to examine the equivalence of the effects on the six mood scales (Harris, 1975). For this analysis, five pairs of difference scores were employed (e.g., for pretest scores, Difference 1 = Tension − Depression, Difference 2 = Depression − Anger, etc., and similarly for posttest scores). The BMDP4V program facilitated analyses (Davidson & Toporek, 1981).

Results

The research questions were organized around two issues: changes in mood following swimming, and gender differences in both mood and mood change. Results of the MANOVA to examine the effect of swimming on mood appear in Table 1. Figure 1 shows the before-and-after POMS scores

TABLE 1
MANOVA Results: Study 1(Fall)

Source	T^2	Λ	df_h	df_e	F	m	n	P
Between-Subject Effects								
LEVELS		(.8496)	(2)	(88)	(1.17)	(12)	(166)	(.3052)
Swimmers-vs.-controls	12.94		1	88	2.03	6	83	.0702
Beginner-vs.-intermed	3.68		1	88	.58	6	83	.7459
Class in Levels		.8499	3	88	.77	18	235	.7300
Gender	12.98		1	88	2.04	6	83	.0693
Levels × Gender		(.8830)	(2)	(88)	(.89)	(12)	(166)	(.5601)
Swimmers-vs.-controls × Gender	3.81		1	88	.60	6	83	.7301
Beginner-vs.-intermed × Gender	7.06		1	88	1.11	6	83	.3639
Class × Gender in Levels		.7810	3	88	1.19	18	235	.2673
Within-Subject Effects								
PRE-POST	30.23		1	88	4.75	6	83	.0003
Pre-post × Levels		(.8210)	(2)	(88)	(1.43)	(12)	(166)	(.1551)
Pre-post × Swimmers-vs.-controls	15.13		1	88	2.38	6	83	.0361
Pre-post × Beginner-vs.-intermed	2.62		1	88	.41	6	83	.8696
Pre-post × Class in Levels		.7959	3	88	1.10	18	235	.3543
Pre-post × Gender	4.60		1	88	.72	6	83	.6324
Pre-post × Gender × Levels		(.9077)	(2)	(88)	(.69)	(12)	(166)	(.7629)
Pre-post × Gender × Swimmers-vs.-controls	6.45		1	88	1.01	6	83	.4222
Pre-post × Gender × beginner-vs.-intermed	2.71		1	88	.43	6	83	.8597
Pre-post × Class × Gender in Levels		.7631	3	88	1.31	18	235	.1813

Note. When hypothesis degrees of freedom (df_h) is 1, Hotelling's T^2 is reported together with its exact $F(m,n)$ distribution equivalent. When df_h is 2, Wilk's Λ is reported together with its exact $F(m,n)$ distribution equivalent. When df_h is 3, Wilk's Λ is reported together with Rao's approximation to the $F(m,n)$ distribution.

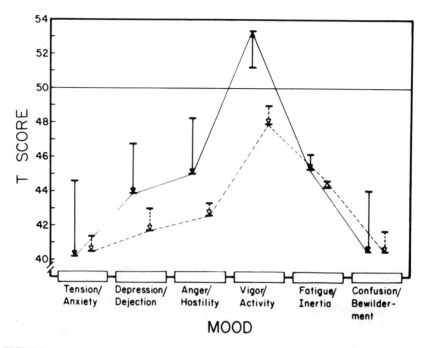

FIGURE 1. Study 1 (Fall): Mean T scores before and after class for the swimmers ($n = 58$) and controls ($n = 42$) on the Profile of Mood States ($\rightarrow$ swimmers' direction of change; ---$\triangleright$ lecture- controls' direction of change).

of the four swimming classes and two control classes. Although the controls appeared lower than the swimmers on many POMS scales, the preclass scores of beginners, intermediates, and controls were not significantly different (women, $p > .93$; men, $p < .95$). Although both swimmers and controls scored below the means for college students for all scales except Vigor, scores that fall within one standard deviation of the mean can be considered within the normal range.

Pre- to Postinstructional Effect

Our hypothesis that swimmers would report greater mood benefits than controls was tested by the pre-post swimmers-vs.-control effect. This interaction was significant ($p < .04$), but the profile analysis on difference scores also was significant ($TA^2 = 14.10$; $F(5, 84) = 2.69$; $p < .03$) which suggested the wisdom of examining a simple pre-post $\times$ swimmers-vs.-control interaction for each mood scale separately (Keppel, 1982). From these simple interactions, it is clear that swimmers reported significantly greater pre- to postclass changes than controls on Depression ($p < .05$), Anger ($p < .002$), Vigor ($p < .04$), and Confusion ($p < .05$), with a trend on Tension ($p < .06$). No difference between the swimming and control classes was observed for Fatigue ($p > .65$).

The second hypothesis was that swimmers would be less anxious, depressed, and angry, but more vigorous after swimming than before. Results of the six simple, simple pre-post effects (each mood separately using only beginning and intermediate swimmers together) indicated significant differences in the hypothesized direction (one-tailed tests) on Tension ($p < .0002$), Depression ($p < .0003$), Anger ($p < .001$), Vigor ($p < .05$), and Confusion ($p < .0002$). The two-tailed test on Fatigue was not significant ($p < .44$). As expected, none of the corresponding pre- to postclass changes for control subjects were significant for any mood scale ($ps > .24$ each).

The hypothesized interaction between mood change and swimming skill level was not significant ($p > .87$; see Table 1). Furthermore, the profile analysis on difference scores was not significant ($T^2 = 2.22$, $F(5, 84) = .42$, $p > .83$). There was, therefore, no support for our hypothesis that the intermediate swimmers would report greater mood change than beginners.

Gender Effect

We found no evidence to indicate that the size of the hypothesized pre- to postclass mood changes differed between women and men. As reported in Table 1, the pre-post × gender effect was not significant ($p > .63$), and it did not interact significantly with any other effects ($ps > .18$ in each).

A related question concerned a possible main effect for gender, which approached significance ($p < .07$). Consequently, the six simple effects (univariate tests) were examined. Women, in comparison to men, were significantly less tense (mean for women = 40.41, mean for men = 43.43; $p < .03$), less angry (mean for women = 42.89, mean for men = 47.77; $p < .009$), less confused (mean for women = 40.01, mean for men = 43.94; $p < .003$), and possibly less depressed (mean for women = 42.96, mean for men = 43.94; $p < .07$). Gender differences in Vigor ($p > .82$) and Fatigue ($p > .30$) were not significant.

It should be noted that women swimmers did not significantly differ from their control counterparts on average mood scores ($p > .14$). Thus, these swimmers were not an unusual group of Brooklyn College women. Nor were the men unusually high on Tension, Anger, Confusion, or Depression; the women scored considerably below the college student norms (McNair et al., 1971).

Discussion

Swimmers in this study were significantly less tense, less depressed, less angry, less confused, and more vigorous after exercising than before, suggesting that the psychological concomitants of swimming are similar to those of running (Berger, 1982a; Dienstbier et al., 1981; Folkins & Sime, 1981; Morgan, 1979). These mood-enhancing effects were significant on five of the six POMS subscales and were in the directions hypothesized. The lack of a pre- to postclass change among members of the control groups supported the likelihood that the swimming classes caused, or were associated with, the observed changes. Note, however, that these results are for people who elected to swim and may not pertain to individuals who do not "enjoy" swimming. Refer to the General Discussion for a more complete discussion.

Since all mood scores, except those for Vigor, were below the mean (see Figure 1), both the swimming and control subjects in the first study exhibited the same *"iceberg" profile* which Morgan (1980) reported for "highly successful" world-class athletes. However, the various configurations of mood scores may be an artifact of the test itself, or of the instructional set, rather than a description of an elite, unusually well-adjusted group of people such as the Olympic athletes. One reason for the low POMS scores in this study may have been the instructions for students to indicate how they felt "right now" rather than the more usual "how you have been feeling during the past week including today" (Spielberger, Gorsuch, & Luchener, 1970, pp. 5, 19−20). Why people who indicate how they feel "right now" tend to have lower scores on the POMS than when they average their feelings over the past week is uncertain. Since Morgan employed the "past week" instruction set, it is difficult to compare his results with ours. Before the practical meaning of these scores can be interpreted, additional POMS norms for college students and new norms for the "right now" instructional set need to be established.

STUDY 2

Because of the complex, practical limitations of field studies and the similar mood changes in beginners and intermediates in the first study, a second study was conducted during the summer of 1981. The timing of instruction constituted the major planned difference between the two studies. The fall study had been conducted during a 14-week semester, but the summer study was concentrated into a 5-week period. Although the total amount of instructional class time in the fall and summer swimming classes was comparable swimming duration and frequency varied. Students swam twice a week in 40 min sessions in the fall. They swam four times a week (Monday through Thursday) in 55-min sessions in the summer.

Method

Subjects

The subjects were 78 female and male college students whose mean age was 23.9 years (range = 18−59 years) and who were enrolled voluntarily in one of five classes during the summer of 1981. As in the first study, there were two beginning swimming classes (*ns* = 16, 11) and two lecture control classes (*ns* = 22,9). However, college budgetary considerations permitted the scheduling of only one intermediate swimming class (*n* = 20). All classes were coeducational and contained unequal numbers of women and men. Some students were excluded from the study: two beginners had language problems, and six beginners dropped the course.

An ANOVA on ages was not significant across groups ($p > .07$), nor was the ANOVA on Lie Scores ($p > .62$). Results of simple, simple effects comparing the pretest POMS scores for the three levels indicated no significant differences for the women ($p > .95$) or for the men ($p > .88$).

Procedure

Again, the first investigator taught the three swimming classes; a male faculty member in the Health Science Department taught the two lecture control classes. All classes met 4 days a week during the 5-week summer school session. During the first week of the term, the investigator met with each class, explained the nature of the study, and solicited informed consent forms. Swimmers and controls completed the Lie Scale before class and the POMS before and after class on one occasion during the fourth week of class. (Refer to the Procedure section of the first study for a description of the POMS and Lie Scale.)

Design

The design in this second study was similar to that in the first, but it was incomplete with only one intermediate swimming class. Again, a four-factor MANOVA was employed to investigate the influence of swimming skill level, the particular class, and gender on mood as measured before and after swimming. The Design section of Study 1 contains additional information.

Results

A 3 × 2 × 2 × 2 MANOVA was performed on the summer school data with the questions organized as in the first study. In contrast to the results of the fall semester, none of the hypotheses were confirmed for the summer schools tudents (see Table 2). Figure 2 portrays the T scores of swimmers and controls on the POMS subscales. In contrast to the swimmers in the first study, these swimmers were low on Vigor and high on Fatigue. Supporting

TABLE 2
MANOVA Results: Study 2(Summer)

Source	T^2	Λ	df_h	df_e	F	m	n	P
	Between-Subject Effects							
LEVELS		(.6884)	(2)	(68)	(2.16)	(12)	(126)	(.0177)
Swimmers-vs.-controls	148.11		1	68	22.87	6	63	.0000
Beginner-vs.-intermed	280.84		1	68	43.37	6	63	.0000
Class in Levels		.8104	2	68	1.16	12	126	.3162
Gender	4.49		1	68	.69	6	63	.6554
Levels × Gender		(.8383)	(2)	(68)	(.97)	(12)	(126)	(.4829)
Swimmers-vs.-controls × Gender	10.56		1	68	1.63	6	63	.1536
Beginner-vs.-intermed × Gender	2.81		1	68	.43	6	63	.8532
Class × Gender in Levels		.8439	2	68	.93	12	126	.5193
	Within-Subject Effects							
PRE-POST	4.34		1	68	.67	6	63	.6741
Pre-post × Levels		(.8779)	(2)	(68)	(.71)	(12)	(126)	(.7429)
Pre-post × Swimmers-vs.-controls	2.40		1	68	.37	6	63	.8952
Pre-post × Beginner-vs.-intermed	3.55		1	68	.55	6	63	.7693
Pre-post × Class in Levels		.8905	2	68	.63	12	126	.8162
Pre-post × Gender	3.30		1	68	.51	6	63	.7993
Pre-post × Gender × Levels		(.8357)	(2)	(68)	(.99)	(12)	(126)	(.4663)
Pre-post × Gender × Swimmers-vs.-controls	4.03		1	68	.62	6	63	.7112
Pre-post × Gender × beginner-vs.-intermed	6.31		1	68	.97	6	63	.4505
Pre-post × Class × Gender in Levels		.8193	2	68	1.10	12	126	.3656

Note. See Table 1 Note.

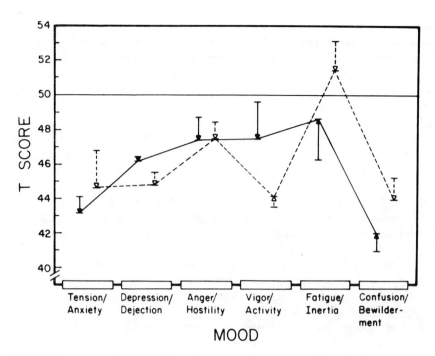

FIGURE 2. Study 2 (Summer): Mean T scores before and after class for the swimmers (n = 47) and controls (n = 31) on the Profile of Mood States. ($\rightarrow$ swimmers' direction of change; ---$\triangleright$ lecture-controls' direction of change).

the need for new norms on the POMS, all subjects were below the mean on Tension, Depression, Anger, and Confusion.

Mean mood scores of students in the fall and summer studies initially were the same; in the summer, however, students' moods did not shift after exercising. The only significant effects were for levels (T^2 = .69, $F(12, 126)$ = 2.16, $p < .02$; swimmers vs. controls, T^2 = 148.11, $F(6, 63)$ = 22.87, $p < .0001$; beginners vs. intermediates, T^2 = 280.84, $F(6, 63)$ = 43.37, $p < .001$) and were not related to the hypotheses. There was no gender effect on mood. Mean scores for women and men, respectively, were as follows: Tension = 44.53, 44.41; Depression = 44.81, 46.72; Anger = 47.81, 48.70; Vigor = 45.60, 47.22; Fatigue = 48.36, 50.14; and Confusion = 42.19, 43.13.

Discussion

In contrast to the significant, hypothesized results in the fall study, the lack of significance in the summer study emphasized the fragile nature of the relationship between swimming and mood elevation, and possibly also of running and mood. The mood-enhancing capabilities of exercise may have been accepted too uncritically and too quickly. Of course, an explanation for a failure to replicate the fall results is speculative. However, there were major differences between the summer and fall studies: (1) extreme heat during the summer, (2) a 4-day rather than a 2-day per week schedule, and (3) a 55-min rather than 40-min instructional session. Actual swimming times in the summer and fall studies were 40 and 25 min, respectively. There probably was little experimenter difference between the two studies, because the first investigator taught both fall and summer classes.

The pool environment may have offset any mood benefits that occurred during the summer Classes met in an old, small pool because the main modern college pool was closed for repair. The uncontrollably high air temperature, which rose to 106° on several occasions including the day of testing, is the factor most likely to have obviated the psychological benefits of swimming. Anticipating a need for strenuous exertion (Berger, 1984b), the investigator required all swimmers to swim long distances on the day of testing despite the heat. This was probably counterproductive to mood enhancement.

The intense summer schedule may have tired students sufficiently to reduce any mood-enhancing effects of exercise. The summer classes met 4 days a week rather than twice a week as in the fall. Exercise physiologists recommend that athletes in some sports exercise on alternate days (Sharkey, 1979). The "need for recovery" may also apply to lesser skilled individuals, such as our swimmers. In addition to the physical consequences, swimming 4 consecutive days may have had a psychological effect. Students might regard indoor summer classes as a "chore" rather than a "treat." A difference in the perception of pleasure could have diminished many mood-enhancing properties of swimming.

Students in the fall semester swam for 25-min sessions during a 14-week period whereas summer school students swam for 40 min during the 5 weeks. Runners who exercise more than 30 min have reported more psychological benefits than those who exercise less (Carmack & Martens, 1979). However, this may be true only for highly conditioned individuals. Since the summer session was only 5 weeks and students completed the POMS at the beginning of the fourth week, they may not have been as physically fit as students in the fall semester who completed the inventory at the end of their third month of swimming. The suggested 40 min of exertion for runners may be inappropriate for swimmers if mood enhancement is destroyed by fatigue. Clearly the parameters of exercise intensity, duration, and frequency that enhance mood (Berger, 1982b) require additional investigation.

GENERAL DISCUSSION

Many factors influence mood, and exercise probably is one of these (e.g., Berger, 1982a, Sacks & Sachs, 1981). However, the two studies reported herein emphasize the complexity of the relationship between mood and swimming. Rather than continue to correlate exercise with mood change, future studies might employ an interactive perspective as suggested by Duda (1982). Mood changes probably accompany swimming; however, these changes seem to interact with, or be affected by, environmental conditions.

Given the conflicting results of our two studies, interrelationships between mood factors and situational exercise variables need to be specifically examined. Exercise frequency, rhythm, duration, repetition, and intensity; the pleasantness of the activity; and the differing requirements of open and closed sports seem likely to influence the mood benefits of exercise. Running and swimming are, under certain conditions, associated with mood enhancement. It is now important to determine which parameters are most conducive to mood changes.

Mood Enhancement in Swimmers

Results of the first study indicated that (1) swimmers did "feel better" after swimming than before, (2) the mood-enhancing results of swimming occurred in a "normal" population, (3) swimming enhanced the moods of beginners and intermediates, and (4) there were gender differences in mood although gender did not influence the amount of change resulting from swimming. As hypothesized, mood-enhancing qualities of swimming seen in the first study were quite similar to those previously reported for running (Berger, 1982a, 1984a; Folkins & Sime, 1981; Morgan, 1979; Sacks & Sachs, 1981).

It seems that psychological benefits comparable to those of running will occur if swimming is conducted on alternate days for 25 min or less, as was done in the fall study. Results of the summer study suggest that for swimming to be effective, conditions need to be pleasurable. Under these conditions, injured runners, people who dislike running, individuals whose health precludes running (the arthritic, obese, and physically handicapped), and others can anticipate psychological benefits if they swim regularly. Psychotherapists who employ running as a therapeutic technique can now tentatively include swimming for novices and for clients who already know how to swim. Since the mood changes occurred in a class situation, therapists probably should advise their clients to enroll in an instructional class. The psychological benefits of swimming alone or at a beach are not known.

Mood Enhancement in a "Normal" Population

Investigators have observed large mood changes among runners who were initially clinically anxious and depressed (Blue, 1979; Brown et al., 1978; Greist et al., 1979). The extent of mood change among runners initially in the "normal" population is more controversial, with some reporting only minimal changes (Dishman & Gettman, 1981; Morgan et al., 1970), while others find significant mood change (Wilson, Berger, & Bird, 1981). Our fall swimmers were well within the "normal" range (McNair et al., 1971), and they showed significant mood changes. Thus, it seems that people who are not particularly anxious, depressed, angry, confused, or low in vigor can reap psychological benefits correlated with swimming.

An Associative Relationship

The promising results of the first study must be tempered by the negative, but important, results of the second. The mood-enhancing properties of swimming seem to be negated by adverse pool conditions and/or the duration and frequency of swimming sessions. Diversion, relaxation, increase in self-perceived abilities, or having a pleasant experience seem to influence the psychological benefits of swimming. This is consistent with suggestions from other investigators (e.g., Bahrke & Morgan, 1978; Jasnoski et al., 1981; Wilson et al., 1981). Of course, associative and causal explanations need not be mutually exclusive. Dienstbier and associates (1981) have produced substantial evidence of a causal relationship between running and stress tolerance.

The significant mood changes reported by beginning swimmers in the first study are somewhat at variance with the suggestion that at least 20 continuous min of vigorous exercise is necessary to produce psychological benefit (Berger, 1984b; Carmack & Martens, 1979; Morgan, 1979). Our results seem consistent with those of deVries (1981), who produced evidence that rhythmic exercise for 5–30 min at 30%–60% of maximum intensity is most effective in reducing tension measured at a neuromuscular level. Perhaps the beginning swimmers were exercising more vigorously than expected, or possibly the 20-min recommendation for runners should not be extrapolated to swimmers. Of course, swimming may be associated with the fluctuations in mood rather than causing them (Bahrke & Morgan, 1978; Wilson et al., 1981). A second possibility is that any initial difference in amount of pre- to postclass change between beginners and intermediates may have disappeared by the third month of instruction. Measuring mood on several occasions during an instructional sequence would provide some important, missing information.

Gender Differences

Despite the different meanings and implications of exercise for women and men (Berger, 1984c; Rindskopf & Gratch, 1982; Sage, 1980), gender was not related to mood change in swimming. However, the significant differences between women and men on four of the six POMS scores in the fall study were noteworthy. Contrary to other evidence that women tend to be more anxious and depressed than men (Justice & McBee, 1978; King & Buchwald, 1982; McNair et al., 1971; Scarf, 1980), the women in the fall study were significantly less tense or anxious, less depressed, less angry, and less confused than both the male swimmers and controls. There were no gender differences in the summer study. These results are the opposite of those of King and Buchwald (1982), who reported that women, and sometimes men, disclose *more* depressive symptoms when the examiner is of the same rather than opposite gender. The depression and anxiety scores of the women swimmers, tested by a women instructor, were similar to those of men in the summer study and were significantly lower than the men's in the fall study. Until it is clear that there are no gender differences in mood-enhancing effects of various types of exercise, investigators should continue to explore the possible influence of gender.

ACKNOWLEDGMENT

This research was supported by Professional Staff Congress–Board of Higher Education Research Award No. 13388 from the City University of New York to the first author.

REFERENCES

Bahrke, M.S., & Morgan, W.P. (1978). Anxiety reduction following exercise and meditation. *Cognitive Therapy and Research, 2*, 323–334.

Berger, B.G. (1982a). Facts or fancy: Mood alteration through exercise. *Journal of Physical Education, Recreations, and Dance, 53*(9), 47–48.

Berger, B.G. (1982b). Psychological effects of running: Implications for personal significance and self-direction. In J.T. Partington, T. Orlick, & J.H. Salmela (Eds.), *Sport in perspective* (pp. 140–144). Ottawa: Sport in Perspective, Inc., and the Coaching Association of Canada.

Berger, B.G. (1984a). Running away from anxiety and depression: A female as well as male race. In M. Sachs & G. Buffone (Eds.), *Running as therapy: An integrated approach* (pp. 138–171). Lincoln: University of Nebraska Press.

Berger, B.G. (1984b). Running strategies for women and men. In M. Sachs & G. Buffone (Eds.), *Running as therapy: An integrated approach* (pp. 23–62). Lincoln: University of Nebraska Press.

Berger, B.G. (1984c). Running toward psychological well-being: Special considerations for the female client. In M. Sachs & G. Buffone (Eds.), *Running as therapy: An integrated approach* (pp. 172–197). Lincoln: University of Nebraska Press.

Berger, B.G., & Owen, D.R. (1983). Mood alteration with swimming: Swimmers really do "feel better." *Psychosomatic Medicine, 45*(5), 425–433.

Blue, F.R. (1979). Aerobic running as treatment for moderate depression. *Journal of Perceptual and Motor Skills, 48*, 228.

Brandt, E.N. (1982). Prevention policy and practice in the 1980s. *American Psychologist, 37*, 1038–1042.

Brown, R.S., Ramirez, D.E., & Taub, J.M. (1978). The prescription of exercise for depression. *The Physician and Sportsmedicine, 6*(12), 34–37, 40–41, 44–45.

Carmack, M.A., & Martens, R. (1979). Measuring commitment to running: A survey of runners' attitudes and mental states. *Journal of Sport Psychology, 1*, 25–42.

Davidson, M., & Toporek, J. (1981). General univariate and multivariate analysis of variance and covariance, including repeated measures (URWAS). In W.J. Dixon (Ed.), *BMDP statistical software* (pp. 67–72). Berkeley: University of California Press.

deVries, H.A. (1981). Tranquilizer effect of exercise: A critical review. *The Physician and Sportsmedicine, 9*(11), 46–49, 52–53, 55.

Dienstbier, R.A., Crabbe, J., Johnson, G.D., Thorland, W., Jorgensen, J.A., Sadar, M.M., & LaValle, D.C. (1981). Exercise and stress tolerance. In M. Sacks & M. Sachs (Eds.), *The psychology of running* (pp. 192–211). Champaign, IL: Human Kinetics.

Dishman, R.K., & Gettman, L.R. (1981). Psychological vigor and self-perceptions of increased strength. *Medicine and Science in Sports and Exercise, 13*(2), 73 (Abstract)

Duda, J.L. (1982). Toward a phenomenology of children in sport: New directions in sport psychology research. In L.L. Gedvilas (Ed.,), *Proceedings of the National Associations for Physical Education in Higher Education* (Vol. III, pp. 38–48). Champaign, IL: Human Kinetics.

Eysenck, H.J. & Eysenck, S.B. (1968). *Eysenck Personality manual.* San Diego: Education and Industrial Testing Service.

Folkins, C.H., & Sime, W.E. (1981). Physical fitness training and mental health. *American Psychologist, 36*, 373–389.

Greist, J.H., Klein, M.H., Eischens, R.R., Faris, J., Gurman, A.S., & Morgan, W.P. (1979). Running as treatment for depression. *Comprehensive Psychiatry, 20*, 41–54.

Harris, R.J. (1975). *A primer of multivariate statistics.* New York: Academic Press.

Jasnoski, M.L., Holmes, D.S., Solomon, S., & Aguiar, C. (1981). Exercise, changes in aerobic capacity, and changes in self-perceptions: An experimental investigation. *Journal of Research in Personality, 15*, 460–466.

Justice, D., & McBee, G.W. (1978). Sex differences in psychological distress and social functioning. *Psychological Reports, 43*, 659–662.

Keppel, G. (1982). *Design and analysis: A researcher's handbook* (2nd ed., pp. 209–242). Englewood Cliffs, NJ: Prentice-Hall.

King, D.A., & Buchwald, R.M. (1982). Sex differences in subclinical depression: Administration of the Beck Depression Inventory in public and private disclosure situations. *Journal of Social Psychology, 5*, 963–969.

McNair, D.M., Lorr, M. & Droppleman, L.F. (1971). *Profile of Mood State manual.* San Diego: Educational and Industrial Testing Service.

Morgan, W.P. (1979). Anxiety reduction following acute physical activity. *Psychiatric Annals, 9,* 141–147.

Morgan, W.P. (1980, July), Test of champions: The iceberg profile. *Psychology Today,* pp. 92–99, 101, 109.

Morgan, W.P., Roberts, J.A., Brand, F.R., & Feinerman, A.D. (1970). Psychological effect of chronic physical activity. *Medicine and Science in Sports, 2,* 213–217.

Rindskopf, K.D., & Gratch, S.E. (1982, April). *Women and exercise: A therapeutic approach.* Paper presented at the Midwest Symposium on Exercise and Mental Health, Lake Forest, College, IL.

Sacks, M.H., & Sachs, M.L. (Eds.). (1981). *The Psychology of running.* Champaign, IL: Human Kinetics.

Sage, G.H. (1980). Orientations toward sport of male and female intercollegiate athletes. *Journal of Sport Psychology, 2,* 355–362.

Scarf, M. (1980), *Unfinished business: Pressure points in the lives of women.* New York: Doubleday.

Sharkey, B.J. (1979). *Physiology of fitness.* Champaign, IL: Human Kinetics.

Sonstroem, R.J. (1982). Exercise and self-esteem: Recommendations for expository research. *Quest, 33,* 124–139.

Spielberger, C.D., Gorsuch, R.L., & Lushene, R.E. (1970). *STAI manual.* Palo Alto, CA: Consulting Psychologists Press.

Wilson, V.E., Berger, B.G., & Bird, E.I. (1981). Effects of running and of an exercise class on anxiety. *Perpetual and Motor SKi8lls, 53,* 472–474.

Wilson, V.E., Morley, N.C., & Bird, E.I. (1980). Mood profiles of marathon runners, joggers, and non-exercisers. *Perceptual and Motor Skills, 50,* 117–118.

Wood, D.T. (1977). The relationship between state anxiety and acute physical activity. *American Corrective Therapy Journal, 31,* 67–69.

8

A CROSS-CULTURAL ANALYSIS OF ACHIEVEMENT MOTIVATION IN SPORT AND THE CLASSROOM

Joan L. Duda

The purpose of the present study was to analyze the goals and achievement orientations held by male and female members of two different cultures (Anglo and Navajo Indian) in two distinct achievement-oriented situations (sport and the classroom). The present investigation was based on a recent conceptualization of achievement motivation which attempts to more sensitively account for cultural, sex-linked, and contextual variations in this construct. Results suggest that there are cultural and sex differences in the goals or definitions of success and failure manifested in athletic and academic settings. Present findings also indicate that there are situational, cultural, and sex-linked differences in achievement orientations or the preferred means of meeting the goals of achievement behavior. Specifically, it was found that an emphasis on social comparison or mastery-based means to goal attainment varied as a function of social group membership and situational factors.

A substantial amount of literature in the social sciences has focused on examining achievement motivation among different social groups within various situations. The major theoretical perspectives on achievement motivation which have guided these investigations (see Atkinson, 1964; McClelland, 1961; Weiner, 1974) have recently been criticized for their failure to account for cultural, sex, and contextual differences. In the view of Maehr and others (Frieze, Francis, & Hanusa, 1983; Maehr, 1974a, 1974b; Maehr & Nicholls, 1980; Parsons & Goff, 1980), previous theoretical approaches to the motivation to achieve are viewed as ethnocentric and skewed to the perspective of white, middle-class, American males. Specifically, as purported by Maehr and Nicholls (1980), the conception of achievement which is assumed in these theories does not consider cultural and situational variations in achievement goals and the preferred means to attain these goals.

Recent work among American college students (Frieze et al., 1983; Parsons & Goff, 1980) and several comparative studies (Allison & Duda, 1982; Duda, 1980; Duda & Allison, 1981; Fyans, Salili, Maehr, & Desai, 1980) have supported Maehr and Nicholls' contention that achievement motivation is contextually and culturally influenced. Support for this new perspective on achievement motivation is also found in the sport world, where it has been suggested that athletic outcomes and goals have different meanings to different individuals (Ewing, 1981; Kimiecik, Allison, & Duda, 1984; Roberts & Duda, in press; Spink & Roberts, 1980).

Based on more recent reformulations of achievement motivation theory (Maehr & Nicholls, 1980; Nicholls, 1980), the present research proposes a new conceptualization with attempts to more sensitively account for social group and situational variations in the motivation to achieve. This new perspective (Duda, 1981, 1983) emphasizes the complexity and multidimensionality of achievement motivation. In particular, it is assumed that there are two important components to understanding the motivation to achieve of a specific group of people in a specific setting.

First, as can be seen in Figure 1, this approach maintains that we need to examine the subjective definitions of success and failure held by different individuals in different situations. These conceptions of success and failure are held to be the focus of achievement-oriented behavior—that is, in an achievement setting, a person will behave in a manner which will secure subjectively defined success and/or avoid subjectively defined failure. Importantly, it is suggested that definitions of success and failure can be primarily equated to process (behaviors) or product (outcome) criteria and predominantly based on ability or effort.

Second, this new approach to the study of achievement motivation maintains that we need to examine the means to goal attainment or "how" individuals want to achieve subjective success and/or avoid subjective failure. These processes are labeled "achievement orientations," and there are two major types. In one, labeled "ego-involvement," judgments of subjective success and/or failure are based on social comparison. That is, in an ego-involved situation, success means being better than and failure means being worse than significant others with respect to valued goals. The second achievement orientation is termed "task-involvement." In this case, goal attainment is mastery based. When an individual is task-involved, perceptions of subjective success and/or failure are made in respect to the person's own capabilities or the requirements of the activity. It is assumed in this conceptualization of achievement motivation that ego-involved or task-involved achievement orientations can be defined in reference to the individual or the group.

In the present study, this new approach to the study of achievement motivation is employed to examine possible cultural and sex-linked variations in subjective definitions of success and failure and preferred achievement orientations between Navajo and Anglo adolescents. The Navajo Indian culture was selected as the comparative group in the present research

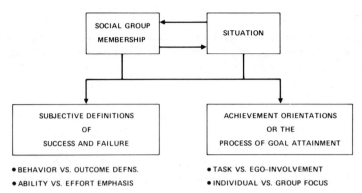

FIGURE 1. Conceptualization (Duda, 1981) of major components of the motivation to achieve.

for several important theoretical and methodological reasons. Residing predominantly on the Navajo Reservation in the southwestern part of the United States, the Navajo people have kept themselves, geographically and culturally, rather separate from mainstream society. Although the Anglos and Navajos do interact in the schools, sport arenas, cities, and border towns, the Navajo culture has remained relatively distinct in value orientation from the Anglo society (Childress, 1976). Based on past field work (Allison, 1979, 1980; Allison & Duda, 1982; Duda, 1980) as well as extensive anthropological literature on the Navajo (Adams, 1963; Allison, 1979, 1980; Bryde, 1971; Childress, 1967; Kluchhohn & Leighton, 1966; Kluckhohn & Strodtbeck, 1961; Ladd, 1957; Leighton & Kluckhohn, 1942; Reichard, 1950; Shepardson & Hammond, 1970; Vogt & Albert, 1966; Witherspoon, 1977), I believe that the Navajo's orientation to achievement would be different than the perspective held by Anglo individuals. Since previous theoretical approaches to achievement motivation have been criticized as being ethnocentric and skewed to mainstream ideology (Maehr, 1974a; Maehr & Nicholls, 1980), data collected from the Navajo would serve as a methodological negative case (Blumer, 1962; Denzin, 1978) to challenge past perspectives on achievement motivation (Atkinson, 1964; McClelland, 1961; Weiner, 1974).

Similar to other minorities in this country, the Navajo hae been labeled as lower in the motivation to achieve in predominantly mainstream school systems (Case, 1971; Lloyd, 1962; McDonald, 1973) and "noncompetitive" in sport settings (Allison, 1980; Blanchard, 1974). After reviewing past anthropological work on the Navajo, Allison and Duda (1982) pointed out several key dimensions that might suggest the particular form that achievement motivation might take in Navajo society.

First, in contrast to the mainstream culture (and previous perspectives on achievement motivation), the individual is secondary in importance to the family, peer group, and community in Navajo society (Allison, 1980; Bryde, 1971; Kluckhohn & Leighton, 1966; Ladd, 1957; Vogt & Albert, 1966). That is, group solidarity is fostered and valued in this culture—a Navajo should not single himself or herself out from the group. Consequently, the preferred achievement orientations among Navajo adolescents in the present study should be more likely to be group-based rather than individualistic in emphasis.

A second major dimension of Navajo society which might influence the particular form achievement motivation might take in this culture is the Navajo orientation toward time. As suggested by Vogt and Albert (1966) and others (Graves, 1970; Kluckhohn & Strodtbeck, 1961), the Navajo seem to have a present-time emphasis rather than the strong future-time orientation which typifies Anglo society (Hall, 1977) and past theories of achievement motivation (Parsons & Goff, 1980).

A third dimension of Navajo society which might have an impact on the particular form of achievement motivation in this culture is the Navajo's orientation toward competition. In general, the Navajo tend to be more cooperative in their day-to-day activities—competition between individuals does not seem to be valued or preferred (Allison, 1980; Kluckhohn & Strodtbeck, 1961). Again, this philosophy is quite distinct from the value system assumed in past work on achievement motivation (Atkinson, 1964; McClelland, 1961; Weiner, 1974) and fostered in mainstream society.

Based on these three dimensions, it was believed that the definitions of success and failure and preferred achievement orientations held by Navajo subjects would be different from those stressed by Anglo subjects. Possible distinctions in motivational perspective were investigated in two specific achievement settings—sport and the classroom.

Although the majority of work on achievement motivation has focused on the classroom (Alschuler, 1973; McClelland, 1972; Nicholls, 1980; Weiner, 1979), several studies have investigated the role of achievement in athletic situations. For example, research has indicated that male athletes (Ogilvie & Tutko, 1971; Willis, 1968) and female athletes (Berlin, 1974; Duda, 1978; Duquin, 1978) are motivated by the need to achieve. Recent studies have also suggested that the athletic realm is a salient achievement setting for members of the Navajo culture (Allison, 1979, 1980; Blanchard, 1974).

Similar to the academic context, the sport setting is characteristic of those situations considered achievement-oriented (Maehr, 1974a). Thus, in the sport world, individuals are held to be directed toward goals in a competitive situation which entail some standard of excellence. Previous perspectives on achievement motivation, however, have not considered that achievement goals and the preferred means to meet those goals can vary as a function of the situation (Maehr, 1974a; Maehr & Nicholls, 1980). Consequently, in the present study, it was deemed crucial to determine the definitions of success and failure and preferred achievement orientations held by male and female Navajo and Anglo adolescents in sport and the classroom setting.

METHOD

Subjects

The subjects were 92 male and 96 female Navajo high school students and 36 male and 56 female Anglo high school students from a large public school district in northwest New Mexico. The subjects averaged 17.2 years in age and were predominantly from the 11th and 12th grades of the two high schools. An athlete subsample of 36 male and 35 female Navajos and 21 male and 23 female Anglos was drawn from members of boys' and girls' varsity sport teams.

Procedure

After providing their informed consent to participate in this study, all students in the sample were administered a questionnaire tapping pertinent demographic information (age, sex, race/ethnicity, grade in school), their subjective definitions of success and failure, and preferred achievement orientations in the classroom. At a different time, the athlete subsample was administered a similar questionnaire focused on the sport context. All questionnaires were administered in a group setting. After instructions were explicitly stated, the experimenter read each item on the questionnaire orally while requesting the subjects to read along with her and then write down their responses.

Both the sport and classroom inventories were divided into four parts. The first section assessed demographic information. Part Two focused on the subject's subjective definitions of success and failure in sport or the classroom. Subjects were asked to respond to a series of open-ended questions (e.g., "Think of sometime that you personally believed that you were a success in sport—what was success in this situation?") requesting them to describe a personal success and failure in an athletic or academic context. These subjective definitions were categorized as reflecting either process (behaviors) or product (outcomes) criteria (see Duda 1980, 1981) by two trained coders who were blind to the sex and ethnicity of the questionnaire respondent. Interrater reliability was .81 in this investigation.

The third part of the questionnaire determined the subject's specific emphasis on either ability-based or effort-based goals in a success and failure situation in sport or the classroom. Similar to a procedure used by Nicholls (1976), subjects were asked in a forced-choice format, given that they do well (or poorly) in sport/school, would they prefer to be someone who does well (or poorly) because of having (or not having) ability or trying (or not trying) hard.

Part Four of each questionnaire assessed the preferred achievement orientations of subjects in sport or the classroom. Specifically, this section determined the subject's orientation to task-involved and ego-involved goals which are focused on either the individual or group in both success and failure situations. The subject was presented with several hypothetical situations involving an individual in an achievement-oriented sport or classroom setting. In each situation, the individual does (or does not) achieve an individual (or group) task-involved or ego-involved goal. To determine the respondent's preference for each type of achievement orientation, he or she was asked, "Would you like this person really to be you?" The subject was requested to indicate his or her preference on a 9-point Likert-type scale which ranged from a low point of "not at all" to a high point of "very much so."

RESULTS

Definitions of Success and Failure

The definitions of success and failure in sport/the classroom were categorized with respect to a conceptualization previously suggested by Duda (1980, 1981). Specifically, athletic and academic success and failure were classified as a(n)

1. Behavior—response referred to an action or something the person has done or is currently doing which is oriented to the individual (e.g., practices hard, messes around) or other people (e.g., talks back to the coach, helps her friends), or
2. Outcome—response referred to some consequence or product, symbolic or material, which is in the possession of the individual (e.g., grades, money, win) or group (e.g., team loss) or to some social consequence which is individual-oriented (e.g., respect, disapproval) or focused on the group (e.g., team becomes famous).

As can be seen in Tables 1 and 2, there was a tendency for Navajo athletes to equate success, χ^2 (3) = 13.2, $p < .05$, *and failure,* χ^2 (3) =14.1, $p < .05$, to behaviors or process criteria (e.g., practicing, not trying) more than Anglo athletes. Anglo sport participants and Navajo male athletes, however, were more likely to emphasize outcome or product-oriented definitions of athletic success and failure (e.g., winning, losing).

In the classroom, as seen in Table 3, all subjects predominantly defined success with respect to outcomes (e.g., high grades), χ^2 (3) = 7.23, $p < .10$, although this trend was slightly more pronounced for Anglos. As illustrated in Table 4, Anglo students were more likely to equate academic failure to outcomes (e.g., poor grades) while Navajo students tended to define classroom failure with respect to behaviors (e.g., doesn't do the homework, does not study), χ^2 (3) = 8.21, $p < .05$.

Emphasis on Ability or Effort in Success and Failure

In choosing whether one would like to be an athlete who succeeds in sport because of ability or because he or she tried hard, a significant difference emerged between the groups, χ^2 (3) = 23.9, $p < .001$. Anglo

TABLE 1
Definitions of Success in Sport

Group	Behaviors (%)	Outcomes (%)
Navajo males	37.5	62.5
Navajo females	54.5	45.5
Anglo males	0.0	100.0
Anglo females	16.7	83.3

TABLE 2
Definitions of Failure in Sport

Group	Behaviors (%)	Outcomes (%)
Navajo males	44.4	55.6
Navajo females	66.3	33.7
Anglo males	0.0	100.0
Anglo females	25.5	74.5

TABLE 3
Definitions of Success in the Classroom

Group	Behaviors (%)	Outcomes (%)
Navajo males	23.0	77.0
Navajo females	36.9	63.1
Anglo males	11.0	89.0
Anglo females	8.6	91.4

TABLE 4
Definitions of Failure in the Classroom

Group	Behaviors (%)	Outcomes (%)
Navajo males	67.7	32.3
Navajo females	51.1	48.9
Anglo males	11.1	88.9
Anglo females	26.5	73.5

males strongly preferred to be the athlete who is successful in sports as a result of ability in comparison to Navajo males and females and Anglo females. These results are illustrated in Table 5.

In the case of sport failure, as illustrated in Table 6, Navajo and Anglo males placed an emphasis on low effort rather than low ability. Navajo females and, in particular, Anglo females preferred to be the athlete who failed because of a lack of ability, $\chi^2 (3) = 13.65$, $p < .003$.

As seen in Table 7, there was a significant difference in whether Navajo and Anglo males and females preferred to be someone who succeeds in school because of being smart (ability) or trying hard, $\chi^2 (3) = 10.2$, $p < .02$. All groups predominantly emphasized effort as a preferred cause of academic success, but this trend was not as strong in Anglo females.

There was a significant difference between groups in preferring to be a student who encounters failure in school because of ability or effort, $\chi^2 (3) = 26.5$, $p < .001$. As seen in Table 8, Navajo males and females preferred to be someone who experienced academic failure because he or she did not try hard. Anglo males and females expressed a greater preference for not being smart in accounting for their classroom failures.

TABLE 5
Athlete Preference in Sport Success

Group	Ability (%)	Try Hard (%)
Navajo males	10.7	89.3
Navajo females	15.9	84.1
Anglo males	77.8	22.2
Anglo females	14.3	85.7

TABLE 6
Athlete Preference in Sport Failure

Group	Low Ability (%)	Does not Try Hard (%)
Navajo males	33.9	66.1
Navajo females	55.8	44.2
Anglo males	11.1	88.9
Anglo females	85.7	14.3

TABLE 7
Student Preference in Academic Success

Group	Smart (%)	Try Hard (%)
Navajo males	14.3	85.7
Navajo females	12.1	87.9
Anglo males	13.8	86.2
Anglo females	28.7	71.3

TABLE 8
Student Preference in Academic Failure

Group	Not Smart (%)	Does Not Try Hard (%)
Navajo males	28.6	71.4
Navajo females	29.7	70.3
Anglo males	67.9	32.1
Anglo females	57.0	43.0

Achievement Orientations

To analyze the data obtained from the classroom and sport question-
naires, a $2 \times 2 \times 2 \times 2 \times 2$ analysis of variance (ANOVA) was performed in
each case with sex (male/female), culture (Anglo/Navajo), orientation
(ego/task), emphasis (individual/group) and outcome (success/failure) as
factors and a measure of preference as the dependent variable. Post hoc
Newman-Keuls tests were utilized where appropriate. The criterion level of
significance was $p < .05$ for all analyses.

Cultural, sex, and situational differences in achievement orientations
emerged in the present study. For purposes of brevity, only the major
findings are discussed here (see Duda, 1981, for Complete ANOVA results). Anglo students significantly placed more emphasis on classroom task-
involved success than Anglos. In sport, females significantly indicated the
least preference for athletic success that focused on the individual and was
ego-involved. Males significantly indicated the least preference for individual, ego-involved sport failure.

To further highlight such variations, an achievement orientation profile
was determined for each social group. These profiles graphically illustrate
the emphasis placed on each achievement orientation (individual/group,
task/ego-involved) by Navajo and Anglo males and females in success and
failure conditions in an athletic and academic context.

As can be seen in Figure 2, it is interesting to note that, regardless of
achievement orientation, Anglos seem to have a greater preference for

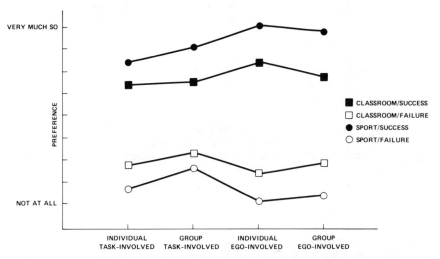

FIGURE 2. Achievement orientation profile of Anglo males in sport and the classroom.

success in sport than success in the classroom. Moreover, Anglo males seem to have the least preference for failure when it occurs in an athletic in comparison to an academic context. These results reinforce the work of Coleman (1961) and Eitzen (1976), who point out the importance of athletic participation in the Anglo male's status system in high school. In the classroom and particularly in sport, the Anglo male's emphasis on an ego-involved achievement orientation reflecting on the individual is evident in both success and failure situations.

The motivation profile for Anglo females can be seen in Figure 3. In striking contrast to the pattern found for Anglo males, Anglo females seem to hold less preference for classroom failure than failure in sport. It seems that, to Anglo females, failure in the classroom, regardless if task- or ego-involved or defined in terms of the individual or group, is an experience to be avoided. Failure in the sex-inappropriate achievement realm of athletics, however, does not appear to be as salient as classroom failure to Anglo females.

In the perspective of Anglo females, success in sport seems to be an important achievement experience. As shown in Figure 3, Anglo females seem to hold a strong preference for athletic success particularly when this success is *not* attained through an individual-oriented, ego-involved process. Thus, these data point to the tendency for Anglo females (in contrast to Anglo males) to shy away from individual competition, particularly in the sex-inappropriate context of athletics (Helmreich & Spence, 1978; Horner,

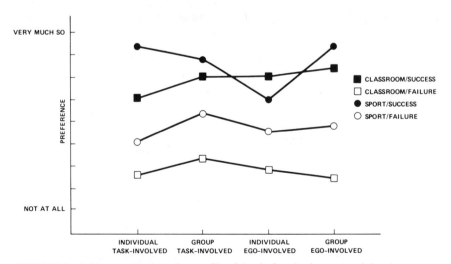

FIGURE 3. Achievement orientation profile of Anglo females in sport and the classroom.

1970). It seems though, that it is accepted for Anglo females to be ego-involved in academic and athletic settings if that competition involves the group (Parsons & Goff, 1980; Veroff, 1977). In the more sex-appropriate situation (i.e., the classroom in comparison to sport), however, Anglo females seem to be more willing to engage in individual, ego-involved achievement pursuits.

The motivation profile for Navajo males can be seen in Figure 4. In comparing the different emphases placed on the various achievement orientations in sport and the classroom, what is most striking for this particular social group is the finding that, to Navajo males, athletic and academic success (as well as failure) seem to be similar in saliency.

The motivation profile of Navajo females, as shown in Figure 5, is similar to the pattern found for Anglo females. Like Anglo females, Navajo females seem to hold less preference for failure in the sex-appropriate context of school in comparison to failure in the sex-inappropriate sport situation. Comparable to the perspective indicated by Anglo females, however, sport success appears to be a salient experience to Navajo females. In contrast to the competitive structure which is manifested in athletics, though, Navajo females seem to prefer sport success which is mastery based.

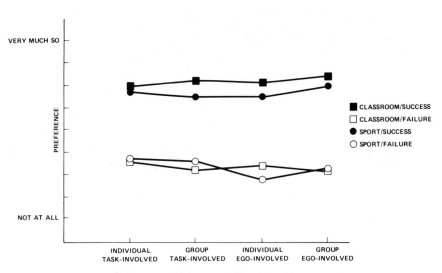

FIGURE 4. Achievement orientation profile of Navajo males in sport and the classroom.

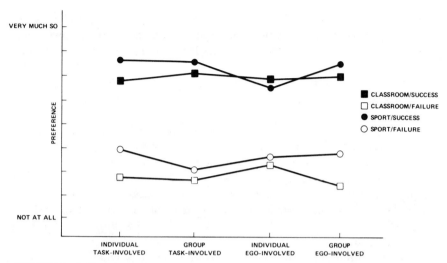

FIGURE 5. Achievement orientation profile of Navajo females in sport and the classroom.

DISCUSSION

The purpose of this study was to analyze the perspective on achievement motivation held by male and female adolescent members of two distinct cultures—Navajo and Anglo. Besides examining cultural and sex-linked variations in the motivation to achieve, the present study also focused on situational differences. A major thrust of this research entailed a comparison of the motivational perspective maintained by individuals in a sport setting with the motivational perspective emphasized in a classroom context.

The present work was based on a recent conceptualization of achievement motivation (Duda, 1981), which assumes that achievement goals and the preferred means to attain those goals vary as a function of social group membership and situational factors. Specifically, this approach argues that there are two important components to achievement motivation which must be considered if we are to understand the achievement-oriented behavior of certain people in certain settings: (1) definitions of success and failure, and (2) preferred achievement orientations or means to goal attainment.

First, it is crucial to determine subjective definitions of success and failure. Conceptions of success and failure are assumed to be the goals of behavior manifested in a particular situation. When subjectively defining success and/or failure, an individual can equate these concepts to behaviors and process criteria *or* outcomes and products. Further, it is also important to consider that people tend to differentially base their subjective definitions of success and failure on ability or effort.

Variations in personal conceptions of success and failure were found in the present study. Specifically, in an athletic and academic situation, Anglo adolescents were more likely to define achievement goals with respect to outcomes or products such as wins/losses, grades, etc. Consistent with past work (Veroff, 1977), this was particularly true for Anglo males in the sport context. Navajo high school students, however, were more likely to equate particular behaviors (such as studying or not practicing) to achievement goals than Anglo students. An emphasis on process criteria was slightly more evident for Navajo males and females in athletic and academic failure situations.

The tendency for Navajo students to equate failure to behaviors is consistent with past research on the Navajo (Allison & Duda, 1982, Duda, 1980) and previous anthropological work which found the Navajo value system to be based on "negative prescriptions" or what people should not do (Ladd, 1957). That is, when regarding someone as a failure in the Navajo perspective, it is the actions of the person that have the most impact.

The present findings also suggest that subjective definitions of success and failure may be differentially based on ability or effort. In the sport setting, Anglo males preferred ability-based athletic success while Anglo females and Navajo males and females tended to emphasize sport success which reflected effort. When encountering failure in sport, though, Anglo males predominantly preferred to be the athlete who failed because of not trying hard. Navajo males and females, and particularly Anglo females, were more likely to claim that they prefer athletic failure attributed to a lack of ability.

These findings, in the case of Anglo athletes, support previous research which suggests that mainstream males and females differ in their attributions for sport success and failure. In general, Anglo males are more likely to attribute athletic success to their competence and attribute athletic failure to a lack of effort (see Ewing, 1981). According to Weiner (1979), this attribution pattern should accentuate positive affect and enhance expectancies of future athletic success. In the sex-inappropriate realm of athletics, though, Anglo females tend to attribute their successes to effort or external causes.

Reinforcing the position of Weiner and colleagues (Weiner & Kukla, 1970) and in contrast to the results reported by Nicholls (1976), all students tended to prefer academic success that was effort-based. This trend, however, was not as strong for Anglo females. In the academic failure condition, Anglo males and females were more likely to prefer to be a student who failed in the classroom because of a lack of ability than Navajo males and females. The results from the classroom suggest that, particularly for Anglo students, effort is an important means to achievement in the high school classroom (Covington & Omelich, 1979; Maehr & Nicholls, 1980; Weiner & Kukla, 1970). As reported by Covington and Omelich (1979), teachers and other significant others in mainstream school systems frequently reinforce and punish on the basis of effort.

The second important component in this new conceptualization of achievement motivation (Duda, 1981) holds that it is necessary to examine the means to goal attainment or "how" individuals want to achieve subjective success and/or avoid subjective failure in a specific context. In particular, we need to consider whether people prefer an individual or group-directed task-involved or ego-involved orientation to achievement. Task-involvement entails processing success and/or failure experiences as a function of mastery information (e.g., personal standards, the requirements of the task). An ego-involved achievement orientation means that judgments of goal attainment are based on social comparison.

The results of this study suggest that an emphasis on an individual or group, task- or ego-involved achievement orientation is dependent on social group membership and situational factors. In a classroom situation, for example, Anglo students preferred ego-involved success more than academic success that was task-involved. Navajo males and females, however, placed more emphasis on task-involved classroom success than Anglos. Sex differences in achievement orientations were also revealed in the present data. For example, in sport, females placed the least preference on athletic success which was oriented to the individual and ego-involved. Males, particularly Anglo males, indicated the least preference for individual, ego-involved sport failure.

Taking into consideration that there are cultural, sex-linked, and situational variations in goals and the preferred means to goal attainment, future work will need to determine how to best maximize motivation in achievement contexts such as sport. In the view of Brophy (1978), one of the ways that social psychological research can contribute to the improvement of athletic (or academic) performance is by providing information about how learners and performers might be instructed and reinforced in a manner that meets their individual needs. In maximizing athletic settings, for example, one could group individuals according to their preferred achievement goals and orientations or identify ways to structure heterogeneous sport contexts "so that diverse needs are met effectively" (Brophy, 1978, p. 135).

In summary, the present findings indicate that the construct of achievement motivation needs to be expanded. In future work in this area, it will be important to consider that the motivation to achieve entails distinct conceptions of success and failure and different achievement orientations or means to goal attainment. With this in mind, our theoretical understanding of behavior in achievement settings such as sport will be enhanced. Further, a theory of achievement motivation will evolve which is more sensitive to the personal values of individuals and the meaning of achievement strivings in varied settings. It is to be hoped that the approach forwarded in this preliminary work will be developed so as to lead to quality and equality in motivation and enjoyment in sport and the classroom.

ACKNOWLEDGMENT

This research has been supported by grants from the Sigma Xi Scientific Research Society and the Graduate College at the University of Illinois, Urbana-Champaign.

REFERENCES

Adams, W. (1963). *Shonto: A study of the role of the trader in a modern Navajo community.* Washington, DC: U. S. Government Printing Office.

Allison, M.T. (1979). Competition and cooperation: A socio-cultural perspective. In A.T. Cheska (Ed.), *Play as context* (pp. 92–100). West Point, N.Y.: Leisure Press.

Allison, M.T. *A structural analysis of Navajo basketball.* Unpublished doctoral dissertation, University of Illinois at Urbana-Champaign, 1980.

Allison, M.T., & Duda, J.L. (1982). Socio-cultural influences on definitions of achievement: The case of the Navajo Indian. In J.W. Loy (Ed.), *Paradoxes of play* (pp. 188–197). West Point, NY: Leisure Press.

Alschuler, A.S. (1973). *Developing achievement motivation in adolescents: Education for human growth.* Englewood Cliffs, NJ: Educational Technology Publications.

Atkinson, J.W. (Ed.) (1964). *An introduction to motivation.* Princeton: Van Nostrand.

Berlin, P. (1974). The woman athlete. In P. Berlin, J. Felshin, & E. Gerber (Eds.), *The American woman in sport* (pp. 283–400). Reading, MA: Addison-Wesley.

Blanchard, K. (1974). Basketball and the culture change process: The Rimrock Navajo case. *Council on Anthropology and Education Quarterly, 5*(4), 8–13.

Blumer, H. (1962). Society as symbolic interactionism. In A. Rose (Ed.), *Human behavior and social processes* (pp. 179–192). Boston: Houghton Mifflin.

Brophy, J.E. (1978). Interactions between learner characteristics and optimal instruction. In D. Bar-Tal & L. Saxe (Eds.), *Social psychology of education: Theory and research* (pp. 121–143). Washington, DC: Hemisphere.

Bryde, J. (1971). *Modern Indian psychology.* Vermillion, SD: University of South Dakota Press.

Case, C. (1971). Navajo education: Is there hope? *Educational Leadership, 10,* 7–12.

Childress, S. (1976). *Variations in value orientation of Navajo Indians.* Unpublished doctoral dissertation, Eastern New Mexico University.

Coleman, J.S. (1961). *The adolescent society.* New York: Free Press.

Covington, M.V., & Omelich, C.L. (1979). Effort: The double-edged sword in school achievement. *Journal of Educational Psychology, 71*(5), 169–182.

Denzin, N. (1978). *The research act.* New York: McGraw-Hill.

Duda, J.L. (1978). *Fear of success in selected women athletes and non-athletes.* Unpublished master's thesis, Purdue University.

Duda, J.L. (1980). Achievement motivation among Navajo Indians: A conceptual analysis with preliminary data. *Ethos, 8*(4), 316–331.

Duda, J.L. (1981). *A cross-cultural analysis of achievement motivation in sport and the classroom.* Unpublished doctoral dissertation, University of Illinois, Urbana-Champaign.

Duda, J.L. (1983). Goals and achievement orientations of Anglo and Mexican-American adolescents in sport and the classroom. *International Review of Sport Sociology, 4*(18): 63–80.

Duda, J.L., & Allison, M.T. (1981, April). *Variations in achievement values: Race, sex, and situational influences.* Paper presented at the annual meeting of the Association for the Anthropological Study of Play, Fort Worth, TX.

Duquin, M.E. (1978). Attributions made by children in coeducational sport settings. In D.M. Landers & R. Christina (Eds.), *Psychology of motor behavior and sport—1977* (pp. 462–469). Champaign, IL: Human Kinetics.

Eitzen, D.S. (1976). Sport and social status in American public secondary education. *Review of Sport and Leisure, 1,* 139–155.

Ewing, M.E. (1981). *Achievement orientations and sport behavior of males and females.* Unpublished doctoral dissertation, University of Illinois, Urbana-Champaign.

Frieze, I.H., Francis, W.D., & Hanusa, B.H. (1983). Defining success in classroom settings. In J. Levine & M. Wang (Eds.), *Teacher and student perceptions: Implications for learning* (pp. 3–28). Hillsdale, NJ: Erlbaum.

Fyans, L., Salili, F., Maehr, M., & Desai, K.D. (1980). *Cultural variations in the meaning of achievement.* Unpublished manuscript, University of Illinois, Urbana-Champaign.

Graves, T.D. (1970). The personal adjustment of Navajo Indian migrants to Denver, Colorado. *American Anthropology, 72,* 35–54.

Hall, E.T. (1977). *Beyond culture.* New York: Anchor Books.

Helmreich, R., & Spence, J.T. (1978). Sex roles and achievement. In D.M. Landers & R. Christina (Eds.), *Psychology of motor behavior and sport—1977* (pp. 147–162). Champaign, IL: Human Kinetics.

Horner, M. (1970). Femininity and successful achievement: A basic inconsistency. In J.M. Bardwick (Ed.), *Feminine personality and conflict* (pp. 212–218). Los Angeles: Brooks Cole.

Kimiecik, J.C., Alison, M.T., & Duda, J.L. (1984, July). *Performance satisfaction, game outcome, and perceived competence: The competitive sport experiences of Boys' Club Youth.* Paper presented at the 1984 Olympic Congress, Children in Sport interdisciplinary session, Eugene, OR.

Kluckhohn, C., & Leighton, C. (1966). *The Navajo.* Philadelphia: Octagon Press.

Kluckhohn, F., & Strodtbeck, F.L. (1961). *Variations in value orientations.* Evanston, IL: Row, Peterson.

Ladd, J. (1957). *The structure of a moral code.* Cambridge, MA: Harvard University Press.

Leighton, C., & Kluckhohn, C. (1974). *Children of the people.* Philadelphia: Octagon Press.

Lloyd, D. (1962). Comparison of standardized test results of Indians and non-Indians in an integrated school system. *Journal of American Indian Education, 1*(1), 217–225.

Maehr, M.L. (1974a). Culture and achievement motivation. *American Psychologist, 29*(12), 887–896.

Maehr, M.L. (1974b). *Sociocultural origins of achievement.* Monterey, CA: Brooks/Cole.

Maehr, M.L., & Nicholls, J.G. (1980). Culture and achievement motivation: A second look. In N. Warren (Ed.), *Studies in cross-cultural psychology* (Vol. 3, pp. 221–265). New York: Academic Press.

McClelland, D.C. (1972). What is the effect of achievement motivation training in the schools? *Teaching Record, 74*(2), 129–145.

McClelland, D.C. 1961. *The Achieving Society*. New York: Free Press.

McDonald, P. (1973). Unique problems of education on the Navajo Reservation. *Colorado Journal of Educational Research, 12*(3), 6–7.

Nicholls, J.G. (1976). Effort is virtuous, but it's better to have ability: Evaluative responses to perceptions of effort and ability. *Journal of Research in Personality, 10,* 306–315.

Nicholls, J.G. (1979). Quality and equality in intellectual development: The role of motivation in education. *American Psychologist, 34,* 1071–1084.

Nicholls, J.G. (1980, July). *Striving to demonstrate and develop ability: A theory of achievement motivation*. Paper presented at Attributional Approaches to Human Motivation symposium, Center for Interdisciplinary Research, University of Bielefeld, West Germany.

Ogilvie, B., & Tutko, T. (1971). If you want to build character, try something else. *Psychology Today, 5,* 15–19.

Parsons, J.E., & Goff, S.B. (1980). Achievement motivation and values: An alternative perspective. In L.J. Fyans (Ed.), *Achievement motivation: Recent trends in theory and research* (pp. 215–237). New York: Plenum.

Reichard, G. (1950). *Navajo religion*. Princeton, NJ: Princeton University Press.

Roberts, G.C., & Duda, J.L. (in press). Understanding motivation in sport: Role of perceived competence. *Journal of Sport Psychology*.

Shepardson, M., & Hammond, D. (1970). *The Navajo mountain community*. Los Angeles: University of California Press.

Spink, K., & Roberts, G.C. (1980). Ambiguity of outcome and causal attributions. *Journal of Sport Psychology, 2,* 237–244.

Veroff, J. (1977). Process vs. impact in men's and women's achievement. *Psychology of Women Quarterly, 1,* 283–293.

Vogt, E., & Albert, E. (1966). *People of Rimrock: A study of values in five cultures*. Cambridge, MA: Harvard University Press.

Weiner, B. (Ed.) (1974). *Achievement motivation and attribution theory*. Morristown, NJ: General Learning Press.

Weiner, B. (1979). A theory of motivation for some classroom experiences. *Journal of Educational Psychology, 71,* 3–25.

Weiner, B., & Kukla, A. (1970). An attributional analysis of achievement motivation. *Journal of Personality and Social Psychology, 15,* 1–20.

Willis, J.D. (1968). *Achievement motivation, success, and competitiveness in college wrestling*. Unpublished doctoral dissertation, Ohio State University.

Witherspoon, G. (1977). *Language and art in the Navajo universe*. Ann Arbor: University of Michigan Press.

PART II

Sociology

9

RECIPROCITY AND CHILDHOOD SOCIALIZATION INTO SPORT

Cynthia A. Hasbrook

The purposes of this study were to determine (a) if a reciprocal intepretation of the childhood socialization into sport process could be supported by empirical data, and (b) if gender differences in the socialization process were present and influenced the directionality of the process. A 50-item, fixed-alternative questionnaire with a test-retest reliability of r= .952 was administered to a stratified random sample of 526 high school students. Only those questionnaires (N=340) completed by white children whose fathers and mothers were both present in the home through the children's 11th birthdays were retained for analysis. The resulting sample consisted of 199 females (80 athletes and 119 nonathletes) and 141 males (80 athletes and 61 nonathletes). Partial correlational techniques were utilized to determine the extent to which male and female athletes' and nonathletes' sport interest and ability may have elicited parental encouragement to participate in sport, thereby supporting a reciprocal interpretation of the socialization process. Results indicated that the data supported a reciprocal interpretation of the socialization into sport process. There did not appear to be distinct gender differences in the directionality of the process. Caution in the interpretation of ex post facto, correlational data was stressed, and several methodological suggestions were made with respect to future socialization in sport research.

The pursuit of scientific knowledge is often directed toward the parsimonius description and explanation of what was previously considered complex phenomena (Zetterberg, 1965). Yet the pursuit of scientific knowledge with respect to the process of childhood socialization appears to be taking a different and perhaps more fruitful approach. Specifically, research in one major area of childhood socialization, namely parent-child interaction, is portraying the process as more, rather than less, complex (Bell, 1979).

Although childhood socialization was initially conceptualized as a two-way or reciprocal process (Bandura, 1969; Bell, 1968), researchers lacked methods to identify and control for what has been termed "child effects," or those aspects of a child's behavior and/or appearance that elicit certain responses from adults (Bell & Harper, 1977; Yarrow, Waxler, & Scott, 1971). Consequently, childhood socialization has traditionally been investigated as a unidirectional or one-way process, and attention directed toward the assessment of parents' effects on children. More recently, however, investigators have begun utilizing techniques that have enabled them to examine the "reciprocalness" of the childhood socialization process (Bates, 1975, 1976; Bell, 1981; Buss, 1981; Keller, 1981; Keller & Bell, 1979; Lytton, 1982). Results from these studies and others suggest that in addition to the role parents play in socializing their children, children influence their own socialization via their behaviors and appearances. For example, Anderson (1982) found that handicapped children who were attractive, competent, or socially skilled elicited more positive responses from adults than did those who were not. Buss (1981) reported that parent—child interactions involving highly physically active children were marked by more strife and conflict than parent—child interactions involving more quiescent, less active children in the case of father—daughter, mother—daughter, and mother—son interactions, but not in the case of father—son interaction. Father—son interaction was marked by considerably less strife and conflict, suggesting that there may be gender differences associated with reciprocity and childhood socialization. Finally, Bates (1975) found that male college students assigned to teach young boys various basketball moves were more positive toward those boys who imitated their moves than toward those who did not. These studies have also posed new questions regarding the specific nature of the socialization process. Are parent or child effects greater (Lytton, 1982)? Is the directionality of the socialization process (one-way or two-way) dependent upon the particular situational context under investigation (Lytton, 1982)? Are there gender differences in the socialization process, and if so, do these differences determine whether the process is unidirectional or bidirectional (Buss, 1981)?

Within the sociology of sport research, the process of socialization into sport has also, until recently, been examined from a unidirectional perspective as is most readily demonstrated by the work of Greendorfer (1977), Kenyon (1970), Kenyon and Knoop (1978), Kenyon and McPherson (1974), McPherson (1972), and Spreitzer and Snyder (1976). Much of this research has been based on Sewell's (1963) social role—social system theoretical model. Briefly, this model portrays the socializee as having no active role in his or her socialization. Rather, the socializee has been portrayed as being socialized by significant others found within several social systems. Such significant others have typically included parents, siblings, peers, teachers, and coaches, and social systems have included the home, school, and/or community.

The research conducted using this social role—social system approach has produced results that account for anywhere between 17% and 47% of the variance in male sport participation and 27%—55% of the variance in female sport participation (Greendorfer & Lewko, 1978; Hasbrook, 1982;

Hasbrook, Greendorfer, & McMullen, 1981;Kenyon & Knoop, 1978; Spreitzer & Snyder, 1976). Thus, a significant proportion of the variance in sport participation has been left unaccounted for. For this reason, as well as others (see Theberge, 1984), it appears that the social role–social system model should not be the only and may perhaps not be the strongest theoretical approach worth pursuing with respect to an understanding and explanation of the socialization into sport process.

More recently, a different theoretical approach to the study of socialization into sport has been taken. It has been suggested that the socialization into sport process may be reciprocal—that one might intuitively expect a child who exhibits a high degree of interest and/or ability in sport to elicit more parental encouragment of sport participation than would a child who was not interested and/or skilled in sport (Hasbrook, 1982). I found initial support for this contention, and Snyder and Purdy (1982) also found support for the notion that the sport socialization process between parents and their children is often bidirectional. Thus, the general childhood socialization literature and the more specific socialization into sport literature indicate that there is reason to suspect that childhood socialization into sport may be a reciprocal rather than unidirectional process.

Given that childhood socialization into sport may be reciprocal, it was the purpose of this study to determine if (a) a reciprocal interpretation of the childhood socialization into sport process could be supported by empirical data, and (b) given that sport is still considered by many to be a gender-role–appropriate activity for males and a gender-role–inappropriate activity for females, and given the question raised in the general socialization literature as to whether there are gender differences which may influence the directionality of the socialization process, might there be gender differences in the socialization into sport process which may influence the directional nature (i.e., unidirectional or bidirectional) of the process?

METHOD

Subjects

A stratified random sample of 526 students attending a large suburban high school located in the central coast region of California was administered a questionnaire in May 1982. Of the 526 questionnaires returned, 186 were eliminated to control for cultural and/or racial differences and variation in parental influence. Only those questionnaires ($N=340$) completed by white children whose fathers and mothers were both present in the home through the children's 11th birthdays were retained for analysis. The resulting sample consisted of 199 females, of which 80 were athletes and 119 were nonathletes, and 141 males, of which 80 were athletes and 61 were nonathletes. Subjects were classified as athletes if they had been or were currently members of any varsity or junior varsity high school sport team. Subjects having never participated in an interscholastic sport were categorized as nonathletes.[1]

Questionnaire

To examine the potential "reciprocalness" of the childhood socialization into sport process, data from a 50-item, fixed-alternative questionnaire on childhood and adolescent sport involvement were analyzed. The test—retest reliability of the questionnaire was $r = .952$.

Four variables were selected from the available data and examined in relation to one another. The first variable, childhood socialization into sport, was defined as the degree to which a child participates in sport (Greendorfer, 1977; Greendorfer & Lewko, 1978; Hasbrook, 1982; Hasbrook, Greendorfer, & McMullen, 1981; Lewko & Ewing, 1980). For the purposes of this study, degree of childhood sport participation was measured by a single question which asked subjects to recall "how much" they participated in sport as children. The question was assessed on a 5-point Likert scale ranging from "not at all" (1) to "very much" (5).

The three remaining variables were selected because of their noted predictive power of childhood sport participation (Greendorfer, 1977; Greendorfer & Lewko, 1978; Hasbrook, 1982; Spreitzer & Snyder, 1976). These variables included the child's (socializee's) (a) interest in sport, (b) ability in sport, and (c) parental encouragement of sport participation. Childhood interest in sport was measured by a single question which asked subjects to recall how interested they were in sport as children. Childhood ability in sport was also measured by a single question which asked subjects to recall how "good" they were in sport as children. Each of these questions was assessed on a 5-point Likert scale ranging from "not at all" (1) to "very much" (5). Parental encouragement of childhood sport participation was a constructed variable consisting of responses to eight questions which asked subjects to recall as children how much their mothers and fathers (a) played with them in sport activities, (b) hinted that they should participate in sport,

[1]The designation "nonathletes" is not meant to connote individuals who do not participate in sporting activities, but is meant to distinguish those with a lower degree of sport participation from those with a higher degree ("athletes"). The data collected and analyzed in this study indicate that such a classification successfully distinguishes between subjects with higher and lower degrees of sport participation (see degree of sport participation means for athletes and nonathletes in Table 1).

(c) spent time teaching them sport skills, and (d) gave them sport equipment. Each of these questions was also assessed on a 5-point Likert scale. Responses to these eight questions were summed for each subject to ascertain subjects' degree of parental encouragement to participate in sport.

RESULTS AND DISCUSSION

Presented in Table 1 are the means and standard deviations for each of the four variables across all sample groups (i.e., male athletes, male nonathletes, female athletes, female nonathletes). The male athlete group reported the highest degrees of childhood sport participation, interest, ability, and parental encouragement of sport participation, followed respectively by the female athlete, male nonathlete, and female nonathlete groups. Other researchers have also found male athletes to report the greatest degrees of sport participation and perceived ability in contrast to female athletes and male and female nonathletes (Greendorfer, 1980; Greendorger & Lewko, 1978; Lewko & Ewing, 1980). There are few data reported in the literature regarding differences among male and female athletes' and nonathletes' perceptions of parental encouragement. In contrast to the findings reported in this study, Lewko and Ewing (1980) reported that female athletes perceived a greater degree of parental influence/encouragement than did male athletes. Unfortunately, Lewko and Ewing did not indicate how parental influence/encouragement was operationalized, and without this informa-

TABLE 1
Variable Means and Standard Deviations by Sample Group

	Male Athletes (*N*=80)	Male Nonathletes (*N*=61)	Female Athletes (*N*=80)	Female Nonathletes (*N*=19)
Childhood sport participation	4.107 1.006	3.549 1.119	3.933 .946	3.177 1.023
Childhood interest in sport	4.274 1.176	3.690 1.316	4.178 .943	3.305 1.189
Childhood ability in sport	4.012 1.024	3.620 .947	3.944 .952	3.284 1.155
Childhood parental encouragement	35.272 15.153	21.211 9.720	29.433 10.655	17.638 8.219

Note. Means are represented by the upper number of each pair, and standard deviations are represented by the lower number of each pair.

tion their findings cannot be accurately compared with those from other studies that may or may not have measured parental encouragement in a similar manner.

To determine if and how childhood sport participation, interest, ability, and parental encouragement of such participation were related, Pearson product-moment correlation coefficients were calculated between pairs of these four variables for each of the sample groups. As may be ascertained from an inspection of the intercorrelation matrix presented in Table 2, all variables were significantly and positively related to each other among all sample groups with a few interesting exceptions. Parental encouragement of childhood sport participation, although reported to be greatest among the male athlete group, did not appear to be related to male athletes' childhood interest, ability, or degree of sport participation as it generally was among the other sample groups. Examination of the standard deviations with respect to these variables among the male athlete group indicated that they were similar in size to those of the other sample groups (see Table 1). Therefore, the weak, nonsignificant relationships found here cannot be explained as statistically due to small variances within the variables. Further, it appears unlikely that these results are simple idiosyncratic to the sample, because prior research has reported similar results (Hasbrook, 1982).

TABLE 2
Intercorrelation Matrix of Variables for All Samples Groups

	1	2	3	4
1	1.0000	.7347*	.6665*	.5432*
	1.0000	.4924*	.5086*	.1450
2	.6243*	1.0000	.6515*	.4818*
	.6916*	1.0000	.3975	.1329
3	.2318	.4103*	1.0000	.5000*
	.5192*	.5679*	1.0000	−.0627
4	.3905*	.3804*	.2322	1.0000
	.5003*	.4442*	.3743*	1.0000

Note. 1=degree of childhood sport participation; 2=degree of childhood interest in sport; 3=degree of childhood ability in sport; 4=degree of parental encouragement of childhood sport participation.

The figures in the upper half of the matrix represent correlations among athletes. The figures in the lower half represent correlations among nonathletes. The top figures of each pair of correlations represent correlations among females. The bottom figures of each pair represent correlations among males.

*Significant at $p < .01$.

One possible explanation for the lack of a relationship between parental encouragement of childhood sport participation and childhood sport participation among male athletes comes from preliminary research findings reported by Horn and Hasbrook (1983). (Because the findings are preliminary, caution is warranted in their interpretation and application.) In an investigation of sources of perceived athletic competence among male and female youth soccer players, Horn and Hasbrook found that boys with high perceived athletic ability most often identified internal sources of information (i.e., their own evaluation of their athletic abilities) rather than external sources of information (i.e., significant others' evaluation of their athletic abilities) as most important to their beliefs about their athletic abilities and pursuance of sport participation. Such findings when applied to the results of this study suggest that although males may receive more parental encouragment to participate in sport than do females, their participation is not contingent upon such an external source but rather is contingent upon an internal source—their own evaluation of their ability. This explanation is further supported by the strong relationship reported between ability and sport participation among the male athlete group in this study ($r+$ .5086) and by other research that reports perceived ability to be a strong predictor of childhood athletic participation (Spreitzer & Snyder, 1976).

The correlational data discussed above suggest differences in the role parental encouragement plays in the childhood socialization into sport process. Although it appears that females' and male nonathletes' sport ability, interest, and degree of sport participation are somehow linked to the degree to which their parents encourage their sport participation, no such linkage is evident among male athletes. These differences, though not appearing to be gender differences, were more closely examined with respect to the notion of reciprocity.

To examine the possible reciprocity of the childhood socialization into sport process and to examine differences in the role parental encouragement may play in the process, the extent to which male and female athletes' and nonathletes' sport interest and ability may have elicited parental encouragement to participate in sport was examined. Partial correlation, a statistical technique employed to determine the relationship between two variables while controlling for the influence of a third variable, was utilized (Kenny, 1979; Kerlinger & Pedhauzer, 1973). Controlling for ability, interest, and then the two in combination, the relationship between parental encouragement of sport participation and degree of childhood sport participation was compared with the zero-order correlation coefficient between parental encouragement and childhood participation among all four sample groups.

Presented in Table 3 are the zero-order and partial-order correlation coefficients for each sample group. These correlation coefficients indicate

TABLE 3
Zero-order and Partial-Order Correlations for All Sample Groups

Group	N	$r_{1,4}$	$r_{1,4.2}$	$r_{1,4.3}$	$r_{1,4.2,3}$
Female athletes	80	.5432*	.3183* $(F=2.9124*)$	.3258* $(F=2.7799*)$	.2158* $(F=6.3371*)$
Female nonathletes	119	.3905*	.2118* $(F=3.4037*)$	.3558* $(F=1.2045*)$	.2128* $(F=3.3736*)$
Male athletes	80	.1450	.0922 $(F=2472)$	.2058 $(F=.4963)$	.1556 $(F=.8682)$
Male nonathletes	61	.5003*	.2983* $(F=.2809)$	.3860* $(F=.1677)$	.2730 $(F=.3355)$

Note. 1=degree of childhood sport participation; 2=degree of childhood interest in sport; 3=degree of childhood ability in sport; 4=degree of parental encouragement of childhood sport participation. F=test for significant difference between zero order and partial-order correlations.

*$p < .01$

that when ability and/or interest in sport is/are controlled among female athletes and male and female nonathletes, the relationship between degree of childhood sport participation and parental encouragement of such participation is substantially reduced.[2] Such reduction in these correlation coefficients among the female athlete and male and female nonathlete groups suggest that the reciprocal model does fit the data. Parents' encouragement (or lack thereof) of their children's sport participation may *in part* be due to their children's demonstrated ability/interest (or lack thereof) in sport. "In part" is emphasized because parents own initial interest and/or participation in sport has been demonstrated to play a role in the socialization process (Greendorfer, 1974; Orlick, 1972; Sage, 1980; Spreitzer & Snyder, 1976) and can be considered as parental encouragement which is not elicited by children's sport interest and/or ability. It should also be noted that such an interpretation offered here is based upon "one's conception of the underlying reality behind the data" (Blalock, 1971, p. 467).

Unfortunately, a reciprocal interpretation is somewhat more complicated when the correlation coefficients among the male athlete sample are considered. When ability and/or interest is/are controlled among the male athlete group, the already weak relationship between degree of childhood sport participation and parental encouragement is not significantly reduced.

[2]Because of the small sample size associated with the male nonathlete group (N-61), the differences between the zero-order and partial-order correlation coefficients were not statistically significant. However, they varied enough in magnitude to be considered substantively different.

Because the relationship is not significantly reduced, one might argue that these findings indicate that the socialization into sport process for male athletes is not reciprocal. In other words, parental encouragement of male athletes' childhood sport participation would be interpreted as unidirectional and not elicited by these children's demonstration of interest and/or ability in sport. There is indeed a body of research that lends support to such a contention. The gender-role socialization literature indicates that parents encourage physical activity in their sons while failing to encourage such activity in their daughters via the types of toys they give to members of each gender and by the type of play they allow and encourage their sons and daughters to engage in (Langlois & Downs, 1980; Rheingold & Cook, 1975; Tauber, 1979). In addition, findings from play research suggest that learning to be an athlete is an important aspect of the male gender-role socialization process carried out by parents (Kleiber, Barnett, & Wade, 1978). It has also been proposed that although male sport socialization is institutionalized within this society, sport has not yet become a cultural expectation for females (Greendorfer, 1983). Hence, it could be argued that the socialization into sport process is not reciprocal for males because sport is consonant with the male gender-role, and parents may automatically expect and therefore encourage their sons to participate in sport regardless of their sons' interest and/or ability levels. In contrast, because sport is less consonant with the female gender-role, parents may not automatically expect and consequently fail to encourage their daughers to participate in sport unless their daughters first demonstrate an ability or interest in sport which in turn elicits parental encouragement. However, this explanation of a unidirectional interpretation of the data for male athletes appears to be problematic.

If the unidirectional gender-role socialization argument is valid, then the findings should also suggest that the socialization process for male *nonathletes* is unidirectional. Yet, as previously discussed, the findings with respect to male nonathletes are supportive of a reciprocal interpretation. Therefore, an alternative and reciprocal interpretation of the results with respect to the male athlete sample is offered.

The lack of a significant reduction in the strength of the relationship between parental encouragement of childhood sport participation and actual childhood sport participation when controlling ability and/or interest is not necessarily due to unidirectional causation but may be due to the suppressing effect of ability. A closer examination of the partial-order correlation coefficients generated for the male athlete group indicates that when ability is controlled, the relationship between participation and parental encouragement increases, thereby demonstrating the suppressing effect of ability. This may be the case because, as mentioned previously, males with high perceived ability (male athletes) do not view their beliefs about their ability or sport participation as contingent upon parental encouragement. Consequently, when that high perceived ability is partialled out of the relationship, the relationship becomes stronger. Thus, the absence of a reduction in the zero-order correlation coefficient between participation and parental encouragement when controlling ability does not negate the possibility that the small relationship that does exist between these two variables may in part be due to a reciprocal interaction between child and parent.

CONCLUSION AND RECOMMENDATIONS

This study has attempted to demonstrate via the analysis of empirical data that a reciprocal interpretation of the socialization into sport process is not only plausible but possible. In addition, findings from this study indicate that there do not appear to be gender differences in the directionality of the process.

Unfortunately, this study, as well as most (if not all) of the previously published socialization into sport studies, was ex post facto and correlational in nature. Consequently, causation, be it reciprocal or unidirectional, was not *directly* demonstrated in this study nor has it been in others. If researchers are to better understand and explain the socialization into sport process, future studies must incorporate methodologies that can aid in directly demonstrating the directionality of causation within the socialization into sport process. Four such methodologies—longitudinal studies, triangulation of data, path analytic techniques, and observational studies—are now briefly discussed.

Longitudinal studies, which obtain measures of children's sport interest, ability, participation, and parental encouragement of sport participation through early, mid-, and late childhood, need to be conducted. Such studies will eliminate the problem created by "static" data (i.e., data collected at a single moment in time). Static data do not allow for the direct determination of a causal chain or temporal ordering of variables such as those involved in studies of childhood socialization into sport (e.g., children's sport interest, ability, participation, parental encouragement of sport participation).

The method of triangulation (Denzin, 1978), or the collection of data on the same variables via the utilization of multiple methodologies, needs to be incorporated within socialization into sport studies. Researchers should measure children's, parents', and objective observers' perceptions of children's sport interest, ability, participation, and parental encouragement, rather than relying on a single method of data collection such as the self-administered questionnaire that measures only the perceptions and recall of the socializee.

More sophisticated statistical techniques need to be incorporated within studies. Path analytic methods relying on structural equation procedures can be employed so that we may more accurately depict the directionality of the socialization into sport process (Bielby & Hauser, 1977; Blalock, 1971; Duncan, 1975). There currently exists at least one computer program, "LISREL" (Jöreskog & Sörbom, 1978), which has been specifically designed to accommodate reciprocal causation and "latent" or constuct variables such as sport participation, parental encouragement, ability, and interest.

Finally, observational studies of adult−child interaction in controlled laboratory and perhaps field settings need to be conducted. Such studies will allow us to directly observe if children with demonstrated ability and/or interest in sport elicit greater degrees of adult encouragement to participate in sport than do children with lower degees of ability and/or interest in sport.

REFERENCES

Anderson, C.W. (1982). Parent−child relationships: A context for reciprocal developmental influence. *Counseling Psychologist, 9,* 35−44.

Bandura, A. (1969). Social learning theory of identificatory process. In D. Goslin (Ed.), *Handbook of socialization theory and research* (pp. 213−262). Chicago: Rand McNally.

Bates, J.E. (1975). Effects of a child's imitation versus nonimitation on adults' verbal and nonverbal positivity. *Journal of Personality and Social Psychology, 31,* 840−851.

Bates, J.E. (1976). Effects of children's nonverbal behavior upon adults. *Child Development, 47,* 1079−1088.

Bell, R.Q. (1968). A reinterpretation of the direction of effects in studies of socialization. *Psychological Review, 75,* 81−95.

Bell, R.Q. (1979). Parent, child, and reciprocal influences. *American Psychologist, 34,* 821−826.

Bell, R.Q. (1981). Parent, child, and reciprocal influences: New experimental approaches. *Journal of Abnormal Child Psychology, 9,* 299−302.

Bell, R.Q., & Harper, L.V. (1977). *Child effects on adults.* New York: Wiley.

Bielby, W.T., & Hauser, R.M. (1977). Structural equation models. *Annual Review of Sociology, 3,* 137−161.

Blalock, H.M., Jr. (1971). *Causal models in the social sciences.* Chicago: Aldine-Atherton.

Buss, D.M. (1981). Predicting parent-child interactions from children's activity level. *Developmental Psychology, 17,* 59−65.

Denzin, N. (1978). *The research act.* New York: McGraw-Hill.

Duncan, O.D. (1975). *Introduction to structural equation models.* New York: Academic Press.

Greendorfer, S.L. (1974). *The nature of female socialization into sport: A study of selected college women's sport participation.* Unpublished doctoral dissertation, University of Wisconsin, Madison.

Greendorfer, S.L. (1977). Role of socializing agents in female sport involvement. *Research Quarterly, 48,* 304−310.

Greendorfer, S.L. (1980). Gender differences in physical activity. *Motor Skills: Theory into Practice, 4,* 83−90.

Greendorfer, S.L. (1983). Shaping the female athlete: The impact of the family. In M.A. Boutilier & L. SanGiovanni (Eds.), *The sporting woman* (pp. 135–156). Champaign, IL: Human Kinetics.

Greendorfer, S.L., & Lewko, J.H. (1978). Role of family members in sport socialization of children. *Research Quarterly, 49,* 146–152.

Hasbrook, C.A. (1982). The theoretical notion of reciprocity and childhood socialization into sport. In A.O. Dunleavy, A.W. Miracle, & C.R. Rees (Eds.), *Studies in the sociology of sport* (pp. 139–151). Fort Worth: Texas Christian University.

Hasbrook, C.A., Greendorfer, S.L., & McMullen, J.A. (1981). Implications of social class background on female athletes and nonathletes. In S.L. Greendorfer & A. Yiannakis (Eds.), *Sociology of sport: Diverse perspectives* (pp. 95–107). West Point, NY: Leisure Press.

Horn, T., & Hasbrook, C.A. (1983, October). *Kids, coaches and sport.* Paper presented at the meeting of the Wisconsin Association for Health, Physical Education and Recreation, Milwaukee.

Jöreskog, K. G., & Sörbom, D. (1978). *Lisrel IV: Analysis of inner structural relationships by the method of maximum likelihood.* Chicago: National Educational Resources.

Keller, B.B. (1981). The study of reciprocal influences through experimental modification of social interaction between functional adult-child pairs. *Journal of Abnormal Psychology, 9,* 311–319.

Keller, B.B., & Bell, R.Q. (1979). Child effects on adults' method of eliciting altruistic behavior. *Child Development, 50,* 1004–1009.

Kenny, D.A. (1979). *Correlation and causality.* New York: Wiley.

Kenyon, G.S. (1970). The use of path analysis in sport sociology with reference to involvement socialization. *International Review of Sport Sociology, 5,* 191–203.

Kenyon,G.S., & Knoop, J.C. (1978, August). *The variability and cross-cultural invariance of a reduced social role–social system model of sport socialization.* Paper presented at the IX World Congress of the International Sociological Association, Uppsala, Sweden.

Kenyon, G.S., & McPherson, B.D. (1974). An approach to the study of socialization. *International Review of Sport Sociology, 9,* 127–138.

Kerlinger, F.N., & Pedhauzer, E.J. (1973). *Multiple regression in behavioral research.* New York: Holt, Rinehart & Winston.

Kleiber, D.A., Barnett, L.A., & Wade, M.G. (1978, October). *Playfulness and the family context.* Paper presented at Society of Park and Recreational Educators Research Symposium of the National Recreation and Park Association, Miami.

Langlois, J.H., & Downs, A.C. (1980). Mothers, fathers, and peers as socialization agents of sex-typed play behaviors in young children. *Child Development, 51,* 1237–1247.

Lewko, J.H., & Ewing, M.E. (1980). Sex differences and parental influence via sport involvement of children. *Journal of Sport Psychology, 2,* 62–68

Lytton, H. (1982. Two-way influence processes between parents and child—When, where, and how? *Canadian Journal of Behavioral Science, 14,* 259–275.

McPherson, B.D. (1972). *Socialization into the role of sport consumer: The construction and testing of a theory and causal model.* Unpublished doctoral dissertation, University of Wisconsin.

Orlick, T.D. (1972). Family sports environment and early sports participation. In I.D. Williams & L.M. Wankel (Eds.), *Proceedings of the Fourth Canadian Psychomotor Learning and Sport Psychology Symposium* (pp. 503–513). Ottawa: Fitness and Amateur Sport Directorate.

Rheingold, H.L., & Cook, K.V. (1975). The contents of boys' and girls' rooms as an index of parents' behavior. *Child Development, 46,* 459–463.

Sage, G.H. (1980). Parental influence and socialization into sport for male and female intercollegiate athletes. *Journal of Sport and Social Issues, 4,* 1–12.

Sewell, W.H. (1963). Some recent developments in socialization theory and research. *Annals of the American Academy of Political Science, 349,* 163–181.

Snyder, E.E., & Purdy, D.A. (1982). Socialization into sport: Parent and child reverse and reciprocal effects. *Research Quarterly for Exercise and Sport, 53*(3), 263–266.

Spreitzer, E., & Snyder, E.E. (1976). Socialization into sport: An exploratory path analysis. *Research Quarterly, 47,* 238–245.

Tauber, M.A. (1979). Parental socialization techniques and sex differences in children's play. *Child Development, 50,* 225–234.

Theberge, N. (1984). On the need for a more adequate theory of sport participation. *Sociology of Sport Journal, 1*(1), 26–33.

Yarrow, M.R., Waxler, C.Z., & Scott, P. (1971). Child effects on adult behavior. *Developmental Psychology, 5,* 300–311.

Zetterberg, H.I. (1965). *On theory and verification in sociology* (3rd ed.). Totowa, NJ: Bedminister Press.

10

CAUSAL FACTORS OF DEVIANT BEHAVIOR AMONG YOUTH SPORT PARTICIPANTS AND NONPARTICIPANTS

Douglas Hastad

Jeffrey O. Segrave

Robert Pangrazi

Gene Peterson

Although several studies have indicated a negative relationship between participation in sport and deviancy, data have almost exclusively been derived from samples of high school students, with little or no attention being paid to younger populations. Consequently, the purpose of this study was to analyze the relationship between youth sport participation and deviant behavior among a sample of elementary school children. The study also sought to evaluate the relative contribution of 10 sociopsychological variables in the etiology of deviant behavior among male and female youth sport participants and nonparticipants. Data were collected from responses to self-report questionnaires administered to a total sample of 381 (186 boys and 195 girls) sixth-grade students. Of the 381 respondents, 278 (145 boys and 133 girls) were classified as youth sport participants. Overall the results indicated that participants report less involvement in deviant behavior than nonparticipants, although few of the differences were statistically significant. A similar pattern was also found to persist in the etiology of deviant behavior among male and female youth sport participants and nonparticipants.

The relationship between sport and deviance has been a topic of discussion for years. Only recently, however, have efforts been made to empirically assess the relationship (see Segrave, 1983, for a review). Although attention has variously been paid to the effect that the institution of play facilities has on delinquency and to the relationship between participation in Outward Bound and delinquency, recent interest has focused in particular on the association between interscholastic athletic participation and juvenile delinquency. Several studies have demonstrated that interscholastic athletes report significantly less delinquency than comparable nonathletes (Buhrman, 1977; Buhrman & Bratton, 1978; Landers & Landers, 1977; Schafer, 1969; Segrave & Chu, 1978; Segrave & Hastad, 1982; Segrave & Hastad, 1984). The negative relationship between interscholastic athletic participation and delinquency has also been found to occur regardless of gender and socioeconomic status. Furthermore, two studies by Buhrman (1977) and Buhrman and Bratton (1978) have indicated that, as a group, high school athletes exhibit different characteristics than deviants. Buhrman and Bratton, in fact, concluded that "the profiles of deviants and athletes are almost diametrically opposed to one another" (1978, p. 33).

In an attempt to extend the scope of the research on athletics and delinquency, Segrave and Hastad (1984) sought to empirically locate some of the factors underlying the negative relationship between participation in interscholastic athletics and delinquent behavior. Specifically, Segrave and Hastad evaluated the relative contribution of 12 sociopsychological variables in the etiology of delinquent behavior among male and female athletes and nonathletes. Although the overall results indicated that a similar pattern occurred, they reported that among both males and females, the delinquent behavior of athletes as opposed to nonathletes was more influenced by lack of attachment to school and perceptions of limited opportunities, and that the delinquency of nonathletes was more affected by delinquent associates and negative value orientations.

Although several investigations have provided some insight into the relationship between sport and deviance, data have almost exclusively been derived from samples of high school students, with little or no attention being paid to younger populations. Given the increase in serious crime by preteenage children (e.g., Fritsch, 1981) and the burgeoning interest and emphasis on organized programs of sport for young children, it would appear both timely and fitting to extend the research on sport and deviance to include pre-adolescent populations. It is therefore the purpose of this investigation to analyze the relationship between youth sport participation and deviant behavior. Furthermore, in an effort to identify some of the factors underlying the relationship, the study seeks to evaluate the relative contribution of 10 sociopsychological variables in the etiology of deviant behavior among male and female youth sport participants and nonparticipants.

SOCIOPSYCHOLOGICAL VARIABLES

The sociopsychological variables treated in this study revolve around the influences of family status, school, peer associations, perceptions of self, personal values, and boredom on deviant behavior. Specifically, the 10 independent factors are socioeconomic status, family status, boredom, self-concept, concept of physical self, attachment to school, attitude toward physical education, peer status, deviant associates, and personal values.

The 10 variables considered in this study were chosen in order to focus the reader's attention on the relevance of several key factors in the search for the causes of deviant behavior. Any study of deviancy reveals the complexity of the issues and it was not practically possible to operationalize all the variables which have been found to be of significance in the etiology of deviant behavior. While our selection is incomplete, it is not dissimilar to the cluster of variables used in other multivariate analyses of deviancy (e.g., Johnson, 1979), and it does include many of the variables considered most relevant.

Socioeconomic Status

Official records (Federal Bureau of Investigation, 1979) demonstrate that delinquency and social class are inversely related. Hirschi (1969), however, has concluded that "careful quantitative research shows again and again that the relationship between socioeconomic status and the commission of delinquent acts is small, or nonexistent" (p. 69). Although socioeconomic status itself may be a poor predictor of delinquency, theories relative to delinquent behavior and social class should not be ignored (Johnson, 1979). This would be true regarding the association between sport participation and delinquency, since several investigations have shown that athletics may be more effective in reducing delinquent behavior among youth from lower socioeconomic groups (Schafer, 1969; Segrave & Chu, 1978).

Family Status

The empirical evidence is fairly consistent in showing that deviants, more so than nondeviants, are more likely to be from homes in which one or both parents are absent because of death, divorce, or desertion (Glueck & Glueck, 1950; Toby, 1957). However, Nye (1958) found greater deviancy among youth from intact homes rather than from broken homes, indicating the significance of the quality of family relationship, not necessarily the presence of parents in the home. No investigations were found that evaluated the association between youth sport participation and family status.

Boredom

Several theorists have posited that acts of delinquent behavior are often prompted out of sheer boredom (Bordua, 1960; Clinard & Wade, 1964). On the other hand, Schafer (1969) has stated that athletes "are less likely to be bored and thereby susceptible to delinquency than comparable nonathletes, since sports take up so much after school time" (p. 42).

Self-Concept

Several theorists (see Reckless, 1961) have argued that individuals with an inadequate self-concept are likely to be directed toward delinquent behavior, while individuals with a good self-concept are likely to refrain from delinquency. In a study of high school girls, Buhrman and Bratton (1978) found that self-image was negatively related to deviant behavior and positively related to participation in athletics.

Concept of Physical Self

Snyder and Kivilin (1975) compared athletes to nonathletes on self-report measures of psychological well-being and body image and found that athletes demonstrated more positive self-perceptions than nonathletes. Identifying the concept of physical self as a separate factor in deviancy causation in an investigation devoid of a population comprised of athletes would be gratuitous in light of the similar variable, self-concept.

Attachment to School

Several studies have indicated that students who display negative school-related attitudes are more apt to report delinquent behavior than individuals who like school (see Gibbons, 1976). The strength of the bond between students and their school environment has been shown to be an important deterrent to delinquent involvement. Research has indicated that athletes, due possibly to special treatment from teachers and enhancement of chances for upward mobility, are more likely to view school as a positive rather than negative experience (Phillips & Schafer, 1971). The social restraints associated with athletic participation tend to constrain athletes toward conformity behavior (Matza, 1964; Schafer, 1969).

Attitude toward Physical Education

A recent investigation has suggested that "children are primarily involved in those activities for which they hold the most positive attitudes" (Smoll, Schutz, & Keeney, 1976, p. 801). If the bond between student and school acts as a deterrent to delinquency, then a positive attitude toward physical education would not only support that bond, but also, because of its close relationship to youth sport, would appear to be an important additional factor in the prevention of deviant behavior.

Peer Status

Selected theoretical orientations have focused emphasis on some form of "status deprivation" as the motivational source of delinquent behavior (Bordua, 1960; Cloward & Ohlin, 1960; Cohen, 1958). Buhrman (1977) reported that the interscholastic athlete retained high positive status among peers as well as teachers. The nonathlete, on the other hand, had little status with peers in school. In a later study, Buhrman and Bratton (1978) found that both athletes and deviants enjoyed high peer status, although deviants, unlike athletes, were "also disliked by a sizeable number" (p. 34).

Deviant Associates

Empirical investigations have shown strong support for the direct association between deviant associates and deviant behavior (Johnson, 1979). In fact, Johnson concluded that "as to the inferred effects of delinquent associates, they appear to be the most clearly substantiated of all delinquent predictors considered." Matza (1964) and Schafer (1969) have suggested that the relationship between athletic participation and delinquency is likely to be negative because athletes are typically subjected to strong conforming influences within the school and the community. Support for the hypothesis was found by Rehberg and Schafer (1968), who demonstrated that athletes, more so than nonathletes, tended to associate with friends who were more positive in attitudes, aspirations, and behavior.

Personal Values

It has generally been argued that conventional value orientations tend to inhibit delinquent behavior while subterranean value attachments are apt to induce delinquency (Cernkovich, 1978; Hirschi, 1969). Several theoretical statements have maintained that athletes are usually constrained by conventional values from engaging in delinquent behavior. Ferdinand (1966), for example, has argued that "any anti-social tendencies that exist incipiently in the athletic cliques are counterbalanced . . . with rather powerful forces of a conventional sort" (p. 125).

This brief overview indicates that socioeconomic status, family status, self-concept, concept of physical self, attachment to school, attitude toward physical education, and peer status are negatively related to deviant behavior, and boredom, deviant associates, and personal values are positively related to deviant behavior.

METHODS

The data collected in this study comprised responses to anonymous self-report questionnaires administered to a total sample of 381 sixth-grade students (186 boys and 195 girls) from six different elementary schools in the same suburban Southwest school district. For the purpose of this study, the students from the six schools were treated as a single sample. Subjects were asked to complete a Personal Value/Behavior Survey during the spring of 1981. Minor language modifications were made in order to meet the reading level of the sample population. The survey was administered by qualified personnel and was completed during regularly scheduled physical education classes. Testing protocol consisted of using an overhead projector and having test administrators display each survey item separately onto a large screen or available wall space. Overlays were designed so letters and words were legible and easy for the child to distinguish. To assure proper interpretation of each item the test administrator read aloud each question and response options. Students in the sample ranged from 11 to 13 years of age.

Of the 381 in the total sample, 278 (145 boys and 133 girls) were classified as youth sport participants. These students reported active involvement in at least one organized sport during the past year. Of the 278 participants, 35% participated in one sport, 24% participated in two sports, 20% participated in three sports, and 21% participated in four or more sports. The organized youth sport programs readily available to children in this sample were baseball, basketball, football, gymnastics, ice hockey, soccer, softball, swimming, track and field, and wrestling.

Operationalization of Variables

The independent factors were defined and operationalized as described in the following paragraphs.

Socioeconomic status was defined as the relative prestige of the father's or guardian's occupation. Subjects' social status position was determined by Duncan's Socioeconomic's Index (Miller, 1977). High scale scores reflected high socioeconomic status.

Family status was defined as the presence or absence of parents in the home. Based on responses to one question, subjects were dichotomized into two groups—those from an intact home and those from a broken home.

Boredom was defined as an individual's awareness that there is "nothing much to do." The two-item index was taken from Hirschi (1969). High scale scores indicated feelings of boredom.

Self-concept was defined as an individual's feeling toward himself or herself. Semantic differential scales were used to differentiate between the child's feeling of physical self and self-concept. The instrument use was based on a semantic differential technique developed by Osgood, Suci, and Tannenbaum (1957) and consisted of bipolar adjectives such as "good-bad" and "healthy-sick." Separate scores were derived for physical self and self-concept, with each being treated as a separate variable. High scale scores indicated a positive self-image.

Attachment to school was defined as an individual's current feelings toward school and teachers. The three-item index employed was derived from questions developed by Hirschi (1969) and Johnson (1979). High scale scores represented strong attachment to school.

Attitude toward physical education was defined as the child's current feeling toward physical education class and the physical education specialist.

The three-item index utilized was similar to that used to determine attachment to school. Wording was changed to make each item germane to the physical education environment. High scale scores indicated a positive attitude toward physical education.

Deviant associates was defined as the reported activities relative to delinquent behavior of an individual's best friends. The five items used were taken from a questionnaire developed by Segrave and Hastad (1982) and were altered so that each was presented in a forced choice (yes/no) manner. High scale scores reflected deviant involvement among the respondent's best friends.

Peer status was defined as an individual's perception of his or her position in the school with respect to the degree of deference or popularity accorded to him or her. The two items were taken from Spreitzer and Pugh (1978) and Hirschi (1969). High scale scores indicated high perceived peer status.

Personal values were defined as attitudes about the acceptability of certain illegal activities. The five items used were Likert scales in form and were taken from Johnson (1979). High scale scores indicated a positive attitude toward illegal behavior.

The dependent variable, deviant behavior, was defined as "behavior which violates institutional expectations, that is, expectations which are shared and recognized as legitimate within a social system" (Cohen, 1959, p. 462). Deviant behavior was measured from responses to 12 questions on self-reported acts of deviancy, and was categorized as drug related (alcohol, tobacco, etc.), school related (cheating on tests, breaking school rules, etc.), nonschool related (running away from home, loitering, etc.), and serious deviance (vandalism, trouble with the police, etc.). A composite score of deviant behavior was also calculated. Analysis was based on frequency of deviant behavior. The frequency index was derived by adding the number of times a subject reported having committed each of the 12 acts of deviance within the past year. Of the 381 subjects, 58 (15%) reported no involvement in deviant behavior.

Statistical Analyses

In the first phase of the data analysis we used an independent samples t test. In the second phase we employed simple bivariate correlational procedures to determine relationships between the selected independent factors and deviant behavior. In the final phase stepwise regression analysis was used to evaluate the relative contribution of the 10 sociopsychological variables in the etiology of deviant behavior among male and female youth sport participants and nonparticipants. In each case, the criterion, or alpha level, of significance was $p < .05$.

RESULTS AND DISCUSSION

The data in Table 1 present a comparison of deviant behavior among youth sport participants and nonparticipants. These data indicate that, overall, participants report less involvement in deviant behavior than nonparticipants, although the differences are statistically significant only for the items regarding drug-related and serious deviance.

The data in Tables 2 and 3 show the relationship between youth sport participation and deviant behavior when the sample is classified by gender. Once again, these data show that, among both boys and girls, youth sport participants report less deviant behavior then nonparticipants, although the only statistically significant relationship occurs among boys for serious deviance. In each case, however, with the exception of nonschool-related deviance among girls, the means are consistently lower for all types of deviant behavior among youth sport participants than nonparticipants.

Although the results reported in Tables 2 and 3 are not all statistically significant, the data do support the findings of previous studies which have consistently shown that individuals involved in sport report less deviance than those who are not (Buhrman, 1977; Buhrman & Bratton, 1978; Landers & Landers, 1977; Schafer, 1969; Segrave & Chu, 1978; Segrave & Hastad, 1982; Segrave & Hastad, 1984). These results further confirm that the negative relationship between participation in sport and deviance occurs among both males and females (Segrave & Hastad, 1982, 1984), although the results of the present study are more pronounced among males than females. Similar to the results reported in numerous other studies (e.g.,

TABLE 1
Youth Sport Participants (N=278) and Nonparticipants
(N=103) Self-Reported Deviant Behavior (Total Sample)

Deviant Behavior	Mean		Standard Deviation		t value	p
	YSP	NP	YSP	NP		
Drug related	2.32	2.49	.66	.76	−2.03	.043*
School related	5.71	5.93	1.52	1.50	−1.12	.262
Nonschool related	7.27	7.38	1.85	1.87	−0.49	.623
Serious deviance	4.61	4.88	1.07	1.16	−2.15	.032*
Composite deviance	15.31	15.78	3.47	3.31	−1.17	.242

df = 379
*p < .05.

TABLE 2
Youth Sport Participants (*N*=145) and Nonparticipants
(*N*=41) Self-Reported Deviant Behavior (Boys)

Deviant Behavior	Mean		Standard Deviation		*t* value	*p*
	YSP	NP	YSP	NP		
Drug related	2.34	2.56	.71	.89	−1.62	.107
School related	6.01	6.49	1.58	1.43	−1.76	.080
Nonschool related	7.61	8.19	2.18	2.35	−1.48	.140
Serious deviance	4.74	5.27	1.25	1.38	−2.35	.020*
Composite deviance	15.97	17.74	3.89	2.71	−1.88	.062

df = 184
*p < .05.

TABLE 3
Youth Sport Participants (*N*=133) and Nonparticipants
(*N*=62) Self-Reported Deviant Behavior (Girls)

Deviant Behavior	Mean		Standard Deviation		*t* value	*p*
	YSP	NP	YSP	NP		
Drug related	2.30	2.44	.60	.67	−1.40	.162
School related	5.39	5.53	1.40	1.43	−0.62	.539
Nonschool related	6.90	6.84	1.30	1.23	0.32	.747
Serious deviance	4.47	4.63	.82	.91	−1.19	.236
Composite deviance	14.60	14.81	2.81	2.68	−0.48	.629

df=193

Jensen & Eve, 1976; Johnson, 1979), our data also indicate that, overall, boys report more involvement in deviant behavior than girls.

The bivariate correlations in Table 4 depict the association between 10 sociopsychological variables and self-reported deviant behavior for the subjects by youth sport participation and gender. In general, the correlations are in the direction predicted by theory, except for attachment to school and attachment to physical education, which are positively associated with deviant behavior rather than negatively as theory posits. It is possible that for many younger children, even deviant or potentially deviant youth, school has yet to become a negative experience. The fact that attachment to physical education is positively related to deviant behavior among both youth sport participants and nonparticipants lends some credence to Yiannakis's (1980) contention that the relatively threat-free environment of physical education classes may be attractive to deviants and sport participants alike.

The data in Table 4 also reveal that the bivariate associations between family status and deviant behavior among youth sport participants and nonparticipants are in the opposite direction. This relationship is particularly marked for boys. It is possible that sport may serve as an opportunity for youth from single-parent homes to become exposed to what might be perceived as conforming standards. As such, single parents may purposefully enroll their child in organized sport to provide exposure to social patterns that are purported to mold normative character.

Limiting the analysis to bivariate associations, however, failed to determine which of the 10 sociopsychological variables account for the greatest amount of unique variance in deviant behavior among male and female youth sport participants and nonparticipants. Stepwise regression with forward inclusion was used to facilitate this comparative analysis.

Overall, the data in Tables 5, 6, and 7 indicate that the 10 sociopsychological variables taken collectively account for a substantial amount of

TABLE 4
Pearson Product-Moment Correlations of 10 Sociopsychological Variables with Deviant Behavior by Youth Sport Participation and Gender

Independent Variables	Total Sample		Boys		Girls	
	YSP (N=278)	NP (N=103)	YSP (N=145)	NP (N=41)	YSP (N=133)	NP (N=62)
Ses	−.120*	−.090	−.125	−.108	−.113	−.011
FamSt	.099*	−.176*	.199*	−.272*	−.020	−.126
Boredom	.145*	.049	.190	−.007	.060	.192
SelfCon	−.105*	−.069	−.032	−.096	−.245**	−.072
PhySelf	−.126*	.038	−.087	−.000	−.226**	−.015
AtchSchl	.265***	.220*	.197**	.143	.300***	.177
AttPe	.123*	.055	.084	.072	.163*	.148
PeerSt	−.079	−.064	−.008	−.074	−.231**	−.317**
DevAsso	.610***	.542***	.583***	.485***	.624***	.538***
PerVals	.517***	.383***	.567***	.387**	.414***	.262*

*$p < .05$.
**$p < .01$.
***$p < .001$.

TABLE 5
Rank Orderings of the Causal Variables According to Total Standardized
Effects on Deviant Behavior for Youth Sport Participants and Nonparticipants

Participants ($N=278$)		Nonparticipants ($N=103$)	
Causal Variables	**Beta**	**Causal Variables**	**Beta**
1. DevAsso	.47	1. DevAsso	.48
2. PerVals	.32	2. PerVals	.23
3. PhySelf	−.11	3. FamSt	−.21
4. PeerSt	−.06	4. SelfCon	−.19
5. Boredom	.04	5. PhySelf	.14
6. SelfCon	−.07	6. AtchSchl	.12
7. Ses	−.03	7. AttPe	.11
8. AtchSchl	.02	8. Boredom	.07
9. AttPe	.01	9. Ses	−.05
		10. PeerSt	−.04
Multiple R	.68	Multiple R	.66
R^2	.47	R^2	.44
Adjusted R^2	.45	Adjusted R^2	.38
SE	2.58	SE	2.61

Note. Table includes only effects with $p<.05$.

TABLE 6
Rank Orderings of the Causal Variables According to Total Standardized
Effects on Deviant Behavior for Youth Sport Participants and
Nonparticipants by Gender (Boys $N=186$)

Participants ($N=145$)		Nonparticipants ($N=41$)	
Causal Variables	**Beta**	**Causal Variables**	**Beta**
1. DevAsso	.41	1. DevAsso	.54
2. PerVals	.42	2. FamSt	−.44
3. PeerSt	−.22	3. PeerSt	−.29
4. FamSt	.10	4. PerVals	.27
5. AtchSchl	.10	5. PhySelf	.35
6. Boredom	.06	6. SelfCon	−.35
7. AttPe	.03	7. AttPe	.12
8. SelfCon	−.17	8. Boredom	.07
9. PhySelf	−.17	9. AtchSchl	.05
		10. Ses	.02
Multiple R	.71	Multiple R	.73
R^2	.50	R^2	.54
Adjusted R^2	.47	Adjusted R^2	.38
SE	2.83	SE	2.91

Note. Table includes only effects with $p<.05$.

TABLE 7
Rank Orderings of the Causal Variables According to Total Standardized
Effects on Deviant Behavior for Youth Sport Participants and
Nonparticipants by Gender (Girls $N=195$)

Participants ($N=133$)		Nonparticipants ($N=62$)	
Causal Variables	Beta	Causal Variables	Beta
1. DevAsso	.45	1. DevAsso	.42
2. PerVals	.26	2. PeerSt	$-.37$
3. AtchSchl	.19	3. FamSt	$-.23$
4. PeerSt	$-.14$	4. Boredom	.22
5. PhySelf	$-.13$	5. AtchSchl	.20
6. Ses	$-.06$	6. AttPe	$-.12$
7. AttPe	$-.06$	7. Pervals	.09
8. FamSt	$-.05$	8. SelfCon	$-.15$
9. SelfCon	.04	9. PhySelf	.08
10. Boredom	$-.01$	10. Ses	$-.05$
Multiple R	.70	Multiple R	.68
R^2	.50	R^2	.47
Adjusted R^2	.46	Adjusted R^2	.36
SE	2.07	SE	2.11

Note. Table includes only effects with $p<.05$.

variance in the self-reported deviant behavior of youth sport participants (47%) and nonparticipants (44%), male youth sport participants (50%) and male nonparticipants (54%), and female youth sport participants (50%) and female nonparticipants (47%). These results compare most favorably with the results of other studies which have attempted to explain deviance on the basis of multivariate analyses (e.g., Cernkovich, 1978; Johnson, 1979).

The results presented in Tables 5, 6, and 7 also indicate that a similar pattern occurs in the etiology of deviant behavior among youth sport participants and nonparticipants. The two variables of delinquent associates and personal values variously account for the greatest amount of the explained variance in deviant behavior among male and female youth sport participants and nonparticipants. Segrave and Hastad (1984) reported similar results indicating that delinquent associates, attachment to school, and value orientations were the most powerful predictors of delinquent behavior among athletes and nonathletes. Numerous other studies have also attested to the efficiency of delinquent associates and delinquent values in the etiology of male and female delinquency (e.g., Conger, 1976; Johnson, 1979; Liska, 1973). Although the general pattern remains similar, there are several differences in the hierarchical ordering of the variables and the respective magnitudes of the coefficients which suggest that certain variables have greater influence than others in the etiology of deviant behavior among youth sport participants and nonparticipants.

From the data presented in Table 5, it appears that the deviant behavior of youth sport participants is more influenced by values conducive to deviant behavior than of nonparticipants. Among youth sport participants, personal values ranks second with a beta coefficient of .32; among nonparticipants the beta is only .23. The salient role that personal values plays in accounting for deviant behavior among youth sport participants may be a result of inappropriate attitudes and norms learned in the sport situation. Several studies have alluded to the possibility that deviant behavior is learned in athletics because of cheating (Lueschen, 1976) and physical aggression (Vaz, 1976). Coaches may implicitly or explicitly endorse rule infractions or physically violent play. Segrave and Hastad (1984) reported that among their sample of adolescents, delinquent values played a more profound role in the etiology of delinquency among nonathletes compared to athletes. Since the present sample is comprised of pre-adolescents it may be that the age factor is significant. Younger children may not have internalized the conventional values associated with athletics, or it may be that these children are ultimately weeded out of sport.

On the other hand self-concept and family status display greater relevance to deviant behavior among nonparticipants than participants. Among nonparticipants family status and self-concept rank third and fourth, respectively, with corresponding beta values of –.21 and –.19. Among youth sport participants self-concept ranks sixth with a beta of –.07, while family status did not achieve statistical significance and was excluded from the regression equation. The fact that self-concept plays a more profound role in the etiology of deviant behavior among nonparticipants compared to participants suggests that participation in sport may indeed nurture a child's feelings of self-worth and act as an insulator against delinquency. Studies by Schendal (1965), Buhrman (1977), and Buhrman and Bratton (1978) have all reported that athletes tend to have a more positive self-image than comparable nonathetes or deviants.

The impact of family status on the deviant behavior of nonparticipants is particularly marked. Although research suggests that delinquents are more likely to come from broken homes (cf. Toby, 1957), our data show the alternative to be the case among the present sample. It may be as Nye (1958) has posited that the quality of the family relationship is more significant than the lack of one parent in the etiology of deviance. Whether or not participation in sport satisfies this quest for quality is of course questionable and unanswerable from our data. However, our data do show that coming from a single-parent home is not a significant factor in the etiology of deviant behavior among the present sample.

The data in Table 6 indicate that a similar pattern persists in the etiology of deviant behavior among male youth sport participants and non-participants as evidenced between participants and nonparticipants. The deviant behavior of male participants as opposed to male nonparticipants is more influenced by personal values, and the deviant behavior of male nonparticipants is more influenced than male participants by family status and self-concept. The impact that personal values have on deviant behavior among male youth sport participants may be indicative of the attraction that sport has for boys. Boys in particular may be drawn to sport by the physicalness and often unsportsmanlike behavior expressed in "big-time" play.

Table 7 presents a comparison of the relative importance of the causal variables in the etiology of deviant behavior among female youth sport participants and nonparticipants. Once again the overall pattern remains similar with personal values being particularly influential in the etiology of deviant behavior among female participants, and family status and self-concept having particular relevance to deviant behavior among female nonparticipants. The data in Table 7 also show, however, that peer status and boredom play a more significant role in the etiology of deviant behavior among female nonparticipants than among participants. These findings suggest that as a source of deviant behavior, lack of peer status would appear to be less efficacious to athletes. Several studies have indicated that athletic achievement is highly valued in the status system of school children (Buhrman, 1977; Buhrman & Bratton, 1978), and in a study conducted to ascertain the relationship between athletic participation and deviant behavior among high school girls, Buhrman (1977) reported that athletes tend to enjoy high positive peer status compared to deviants who received little status. Our data likewise suggest that among girls, the status accrued through participation in youth sports may act as an insulator against deviant behavior. Furthermore, these results lend some support to Hirschi's (1969) contention that children involved in sport may not have the time to become involved in deviant behavior. It would seem that this hypothesis only holds true for girls, though. Segrave and Hastad (1984) reported a similar finding among their sample of high school athletes and nonathletes.

CONCLUSIONS

Within the scope and limitations of this study, it appears that little difference exists in the deviant behavior of youth sport participants and nonparticipants, although participants consistently report less involvement than nonparticipants. Few of the results, however, attain statistical significance. Furthermore, it seems that a similar pattern persists in the etiology of deviant behavior among both male and female youth sport participants and nonparticipants. The most powerful predictors of deviant behavior among all four samples are the variables delinquent associates and personal values. In all cases, delinquent associates is the most salient variable in explaining deviant behavior among the present sample.

Although our data show that the negative relationship between athletics and delinquency reported in other studies occurs among a sample of pre-adolescent children, the distinction is clearly less marked in the present study. Most of the results obtained from samples of high school children indicate that athletes report significantly less delinquency than comparable nonathletes (see Segrave, 1983, for a review). Few of the results in this study were statistically significant, with the exception of serious deviance. Segrave (1983) suggested that the overall relationship between athletics and delinquency is in part a function of the seriousness of the offense. Segrave and Chu (1978) and Segrave and Hastad (1982) reported that delinquent behavior among athletes decreased when the type of offense was classified as more serious; that is, athletes committed offenses of a less serious nature. Most of the behaviors defined as deviant in this study may be considered innocuous, except those classified as serious which involve criminally chargeable acts including vandalism and trouble with the police. In this respect, our data suggest a pattern consistent with previous research. The negative relationship between serious deviance and youth sport participation, however, was not statistically significant among the present sample of girls.

While a similar pattern occurs in the etiology of deviant behavior among all samples, our data also indicate that values conducive to deviant behavior is a more salient factor in the explanation of deviant behavior among youth sport participants than nonparticipants. This finding runs counter to previous empirical (Segrave & Hastad, 1984) and theoretical (Schafer, 1969) research, which suggests that athletes are more likely to be insulated from deviant behavior because they are exposed to norms and values which stress conventional behavior and oppose rebellious or illegal behavior. Several explanation for our results, however, seem possible. First, it may be that younger children, both boys and girls, are attracted to sport because it may appear to condone unsportsmanlike behaviors and attitudes. Or it may be that antisocial attitudes are learned in sport. It is also possible that young children have yet to internalize the conventional norms typically associated with participation in sports. It is also plausible that those children with deviant values have yet to be weeded out of organized sport. Coaches of younger children are less likely to weed out deviant or potentially deviant children than coaches at the interscholastic level. Finally, it may be that at a younger age, even deviant and deviant-prone children remain attracted to organized sport and have not yet self-selected themselves out of organized programs—an interpretation often espoused to account for the negative association between athletics and deviant behavior (see Segrave, 1983, for a review). The fact that attachment to school does not apear to play a substantial role in the etiology of deviant behavior among either youth sport participants or nonparticipants in this study provides some support for this position and suggests that institutionalized forms such as school and organized sport may yet to have assumed negative connotations among young children, even deviants. Numerous studies have found that delinquency is associated with negative school-related attitudes (see Gibbons, 1976, or Schafer & Polk, 1967, for a summary). The data in the present study show that attachment to school is positively related to deviant behavior among particpants and nonparticipants.

Our results also show that family status and self-concept are more instrumental in explaining deviant behavior among nonparticipants than participants. Among female nonparticipants, peer status and boredom were also found to be particularly salient. With the exception of family status, these findings conform to theory and suggest that sport participants may be insulated against deviant behavior as a result of the time, status, and self-image that participation encourages.

As a final note, we recognize that we have not grounded this research within a theoretical framework. Nor have we taken into consideration numerous other variables which are likely to prove significant in the relationship between youth sport participation and deviant behavior such as scholastic success or parental love/concern. We also caution that the small number of nonparticipants compared to participants renders our interpretations as only tentative. Notwithstanding these limitations, the results of this study provide further empirical data in the quest to more fully comprehend the relationship between sport participation and deviance.

ACKNOWLEDGMENT

Partial funding for this investigation was obtained through grants from the Graduate School, Northern Illinois University, and Skidmore College.

REFERENCES

Bordua, D. (1960). *Sociological theories and their implications for juvenile delinquency.* Washington, DC: U.S. Government Printing Office.

Buhrman, H. G. (1977). Athletics and deviance: An examination of the relationship between athletic participation and deviant behavior of high school girls. *Review of Sport and Leisure, 2,* 17–35.

Buhrman, H. D., & Bratton, R. (1978). Athletic participation and status of Alberta high school girls. *International Review of Sport Sociology, 12,* 57–67.

Cernkovich, S. A. (1978). Evaluating two models of delinquency causation: Structural theory and control theory. *Criminology, 16,* 335–352.

Clinard, M., & Wade, A. (1964). Juvenile delinquency. In R. S. Cavan (Ed.), *Readings in juvenile delinquency* (pp. 220–226). New York: Lippincott.

Cloward, R. A., & Ohlin, L. E. (1960). *Delinquency and opportunity: A theory of delinquent gangs.* New York: Free Press.

Cohen, A. K. (1958). *Delinquent boys: The culture of the gang.* Glencoe, IL: Free Press.

Cohen, A. K. (1959). The study of social disorganization and deviant behavior. In R. K. Merton, L. Broom, & L. Cottrell (Eds.), *Sociology today* (p. 461–484). New York: Basic Books.

Conger, R. D. (1976). Social control and social learning models of delinquent behavior: A synthesis. *Criminology, 14,* 17–40.

Federal Bureau of Investigation. (1979). *Uniform crime reports, 1978.* Washington, DC: Author.

Ferdinand, T. N. (1966). *Typologies of delinquency.* New York: Random House.

Fritsch, J. (1981, July 19). Crimes committed by children soars in Cook County. *Chicago Tribune,* p.3.

Gibbons, D. C. (1976). *Delinquent behavior.* Englewood Cliffs, NJ: Prentice-Hall.

Glueck, S., & Glueck, E. (1950). *Unraveling juvenile delinquency.* New York: The Commonwealth Fund.

Hirschi, T. (1969). *Causes of Delinquency.* Berkeley: University of California Press.

Jensen, G. F., & Eve, R. (1976). Sex differences in delinquency: An examination of popular sociological explanations. *Criminology, 13,* 427–448.

Johnson, R. E. (1979). *Juvenile delinquency and its origins: An integrated theoretical approach.* New York: Cambridge University Press.

Landers, D. M., & Landers, D. M. (1977). Socialization via interscholastic athletics: Its effect on delinquency. *Sociology of Education, 51,* 299–303.

Liska, A. E. (1973). Delinquency involvement and delinquent peers. *Sociology and Social Research, 58,* 23–36.

Lueschen, G. (1976). Cheating in sport. In D. M. Landers (Ed.), *Social problems in athletics* (pp. 67–77). Urbana-Champaign: University of Illinois Press.

Matza, D. (1964). Position and behavior patterns of youth. In R. E. L. Faris (Ed.), *Handbook of modern sociology* (pp. 191–216). Chicago: Rand McNally.

Miller, D. C. (1977). *Handbook of research design and social measurement* (3rd ed.). New York: David McKay.

Osgood, C., Suci, G., & Tannenbaum, P. (1957). *The measurement of meaning.* Urbana: University of Illinois Press.

Nye, F. I. (1958). *Family relationships and delinquent behavior.* New York: Wiley.

Phillips, J. C., & Schafer, W. E. (1971). Consequences of participation in interscholastic sports: A review and prospectus. *Pacific Sociological Review, 14,* 328–338.

Reckless, W. (1961). *The crime problem.* Englewood Cliffs, NJ: Prentice-Hall.

Rehberg, R. A., & Schafer, W. E. (1968). Participation in interscholastic athletics and college expectations. *American Journal of Sociology, 73,* 732–740.

Schafer, W. E. (1969). Participation in interscholastic athletics and delinquency: A preliminary study. *Social Problems, 17,* 40–47.

Schafer, W. E., & Polk, K. (1967). Delinquency and the schools. In President's Commission on Law Enforcement and Administration of Justice, *Task Force Report: Juvenile Delinquency and Youth Crime* (Appendix M, pp. 222–277). Washington, DC: U.S. Government Printing Office.

Schendal, J. (1965). Psychological differences between athletes and nonparticipants in athletics at three educational levels. *Research Quarterly, 36,* 52–67.

Segrave, J. O. (1983). Sport and juvenile delinquency. In R. Terjung (Ed.), *Exercise and Sport Sciences Reviews* (Vol. 11, pp. 181–209). Philadelphia: Franklin Institute Press.

Segrave, J. O., & Chu, D. B. (1978). Athletics and juvenile delinquency. *Review of Sport and Leisure, 3,* 1–24.

Segrave, J. O., & Hastad, D. N. (1982). Delinquent behavior and interscholastic athletic participation. *Journal of Sport Behavior, 5,* 96–111.

Segrave, J. O., & Hastad, D. N. (1984). Interscholastic athletic participation and delinquent behavior: An empirical assessment of relevant variables. *Sport Sociology Journal, 1,* 117–138.

Smoll, F., Schutz, R., & Kenney, J. (1976). Relationships among children's attitudes, involvement, and proficiency in physical activity. *Research Quarterly, 47,* 797–803.

Snyder, E., & Kivilin, J. (1975). Women athletes and aspects of psychological well-being and body image. *Research Quarterly, 46,* 191–199.

Spreitzer, E., & Pugh, M. (1973). Interscholastic athletics and educational expectations. *Sociology of Education, 46,* 171–182.

Toby, J. (1957). The differential impact of family disorganization. *American Scociological Review, 22,* 502–512.

Vaz, E. (1976). The culture of young hockey players: Some initial observations. In A. Yiannakis, T. Mctyre, M. Melnick, & D. Hart (Eds.), *Sport sociology: Contemporary themes* (pp. 211–215). Dubuque, IA: Kendall Hunt.

Yiannakis, A. (1980). Sport and deviancy: A review and reappraisal. *Motor Skills: Theory into Practice 4,* 59–64.

11

FEMALE SPORT RETIREMENT: DESCRIPTIVE PATTERNS AND RESEARCH IMPLICATIONS

Susan L. Greendorfer

Elaine M. Blinde

A 16-page questionnaire designed to tap several sport retirement concepts was mailed to 1,656 female former intercollegiate athletes in the Big Ten Conference. Although only descriptive data pertaining to sport role commitment, educational preparation, adjustment to sport retirement, postcareer sport participation, and reasons for sport participation are reported here, the data clearly indicated that sport retirement did not represent termination of a sport role for the majority of athletes in this study. The data also demonstrated that the process was not traumatic and did not require substantial adjustment. An additional finding suggested the possibility of anticipatory socialization, as a pattern of shifting priorities was found—increasing interest in education and social life concurrent with a declining commitment toward sport. Such findings seem to challenge existing conceptual notions pertaining to sport retirement, and discussion focuses on issues related to generalizability of current theoretical perspectives.

Prior to 1970 the topic of sport retirement generated little interest from sociologists of sport. Since that time, however, several theoretical discussions and empirical studies have appeared in the literature (cf. Hill & Lowe, 1974; McPherson, 1977; Rosenberg, 1980, 1981, 1982). This research attention has focused solely on former male athletes, usually those in professional spectator sports such as baseball, soccer, football, and boxing (Haerle, 1975; Lerch, 1981; Mihovilovic, 1968; Reynolds, 1981). As a consequence, the sport retirement process has been depicted as traumatic, causing varying degrees of disruption and psychosocial difficulty for the retiring athlete (Hare, 1971; Mihovilovic, 1968). Typical themes receiving attention in empirical or conceptual studies pertain to (a) perceptions of failure, loss of status, or downward mobility (Ball, 1976; Weinberg & Arond, 1952); (b) alcoholism and drug use among former athletes (Hill & Lowe, 1974); and (c) psychosocial adjustment patterns (Haerle, 1975; Lerch, 1981; McPherson, 1977).

Although most researchers have not considered the male professional athlete as a selective sample frame, it is entirely possible that patterns obtained from this group may not be generalizable. Moreover, there could be methodological and conceptual ramifications of viewing sport from such a "narrow" perspective. The process of leaving sport applies to thousands of individuals—males and females—who engage in sport within the institutionalized setting of the American educational system. Thus, the conceptualization and design of research topics pertaining to sport retirement could be analyzed from the perspective of many athletic competitors (i.e., former college athletes) rather than the few (i.e., former professional athletes) who represent less than 2% of all sport competitors (Eitzen & Sage, 1982).

Equally worthy of consideration is the applicability of the sport retirement process to females as well as males. All too often sociologists of sport have ignored the fact that females have been socialized into sport and compete at top interscholastic and intercollegiate (as well as professional) levels. Similar to their male counterparts, they also may be forced into involuntary retirement at an early age by either expending eligibility or injury. Yet very little is known about the sport retirement experience of females. Not only are empirical data lacking, but females have been systematically ignored in theoretical conceptualizations pertaining to sport phenomena.

PROBLEM

The literature on sport retirement has been dominated by two major assumptions: (1) sport retirement is a termination—perhaps a rather abrupt one, and (2) sport retirement requires considerable psychosocial adjustment to role withdrawal. These assumptions are derived from notions pertaining to "old age" retirement, and, as such, are viewed as inherent in the sport retirement process. Although useful for drawing analogies or parallels, these assumptions have essentially limited conceptualization to two primary orientations: social gerontology and thanatology. Theoretical perspectives from social gerontology emphasize the finality of activity and focus on psychological adjustment to occupational disengagement or "old age" retirement. Typical orientations emanating from social gerontology are represented by disengagement, activity or substitution, subculture, continuity, social breakdown, and exchange theories (Rosenberg, 1981; Snyder 1981). The second orientation emanates from a thanatological perspective and equates disengagement from sport with death and dying. From this perspective termination from a sport role is viewed as a form of social death, one which results in loss of social function, social isolation, or ostracism. Subsequent deep feelings of loss and disillusionment require considerable psychosocial adjustment.

These notions represent the assumptions underlying most sport retirement research, and they implicitly suggest that the process is a system-induced termination created by involuntary factors. It was with this orientation that the present study was undertaken. In order to broaden considerations pertaining to sport retirement and to consider whether existing orientations adequately capture the nature and dynamics of the experience, data were collected on female former intercollegiate athletes.

METHOD

Subjects

Generalizations about sport retirement traditionally emanate from empirical findings obtained from male athletes in professional sports. Yet, any test of the generalizability of conceptual notions pertaining to the retirement process should include females as well as other levels of competition. (It should be noted, however, that the effects of sex and level were not separated in this study.) Our subjects consisted of female former intercollegiate athletes in the Big Ten Conference who competed in various individual and team sports between 1976 and 1982.

Our letter to each Big Ten University requested lists of names and addresses of all female athletes who completed eligibility between 1976 and 1980. Initially, two schools refused to participate in the study because of the inadequacy of available records. Three other universities never sent eligibility lists after agreeing to do so. Although eligibility lists were received from five athletic departments in the Big Ten, the completeness of such lists is suspect. For example, in some instances only campus addresses were available; in others, only lists of letter winners were available. In addition, names of athletes during certain years or in specific sports were missing. Upon examination of the data, it was found that not all athletes surveyed had completed their eligibility between the years of 1976 and 1980. Thus, due to record-keeping inadequacies, subjects included in the sample may not be totally representative of former female athletes in the Big Ten Conference.

Questionnaire

A 16-page questionnaire consisting of fixed-alternative and open-ended items was mailed to 1656 female former athletes from the Big Ten Conference. The questionnaire was designed to tap several concepts, and items served as operational indicators of the following sport retirement concepts: degree of commitment to a sport role, educational and occupational preparation, psychological adjustment to sport retirement, achievement motivation, postcareer sport participation, and social interests. Specific questions dealt with past and current sport involvement, current occupational and social activities, academic interests while in college, reasons for sport participation, self-concept, achievement motivation, attitudes toward sport, and feelings about having left sport.

RESULTS AND DISCUSSION

Usable questionnaires were received from 697 former athletes, representing a response rate of 42%. This low response rate suggests that caution be exercised in interpreting the findings from this study. However, it should be noted that this return rate is actually higher than that obtained in other sport retirement studies (McPherson, 1980).

We found discrepancies between the data from this study and existing theoretical notions. Essentially, these data lead us to question several assumptions that underlie existing research on this topic. Although considered separately, each issue revolves around the definition and conceptualization of "retirement." Three issues become of critical importance: (1) who is the sport retiree; (2) is sport retirement a termination; and (3) how traumatic is the process for the majority of athletes. Therefore, the remainder of this paper is devoted to a discussion of the descriptive data pertaining to these three issues.

Who Is the Sport Retiree?

The question of who is the sport retiree has never been addressed in the sport retirement literature. Although rather simplistic in tone, it includes a wealth of conceptual issues that are worthy of research attention. It would seem that a critical factor is whether departure from sport is voluntary or involuntary. The degree to which an individual feels prepared to move into new roles may determine the nature of withdrawal from the current role. Obviously, those forced to surrender the role of "athlete" may have totally different experiences than those who willingly relinquish the role. Yet, existing research has been preoccupied with involuntary retirees, unintentionally focusing attention on only one type of sport retiree.

In contrast to this perspective, one of the more prominent findings rendered by our frequency data was the existence of two distinct groups of sport retirees. Four hundred and thirty-one athletes (62%) expended eligibility or were forced to end their intercollegiate careers because of injury. In comparison, 265 (38%) of the athletes ended their careers prematurely, for reasons other than injury. That is, they still had eligibility remaining. The numerical size of this second category of "retirees" was totally unanticipated, creating a void in the data relative to reasons for premature departure. Although several athletes had indicated that they had quit the team, there may be other reasons for premature departure, such as being cut from the team or losing a scholarship.

This perfunctory descriptive finding suggests that there may be some shortcomings in conceptualization about sport retirement. Although several factors could contribute to leaving sport, only nominal attention has been given to voluntary sport retirement (McPherson, 1977). Conceptually, voluntary retirement has never been an issue when considering the professional athlete. Perhaps this oversight represents another limitation in our research. It would seem that once the topic is broadened to include other levels of sport competition, it becomes necessary to distinguish between "dropouts" and "retirees."

As a second consideration, a host of system-induced factors could contribute to involuntary retirement—expended eligibility, injury, or being cut from a team, to name a few. A critical question, then, is whether each factor encompasses similar experiences. Theoretically, expended eligibility suggests anticipatory socialization, whereas being cut or injury would have different implications.

Is Sport Retirement a Termination?

Although retirement may be viewed as a process, event, social role, or phase of life, traditionally sport retirement conveys the notion of termination (perhaps rather abruptly) of activity. From this perspective retirement could be viewed as an event—a rite of passage, symbolizing separation from an old position (Atchley, 1976). Previous research on sport retirement has assumed that such separation consists of activity withdrawal as well as role withdrawal. Consequently, sport participation/involvement patterns following "retirement" have rarely been examined. A critical aspect of sport retirement research, then, would be to empirically examine the extent to which an athlete actually withdraws from sport.

Data from our study clearly indicated that retirement from the role of intercollegiate athlete did not mark the end of involvement with sport per se. Rather, sport remained an important element in the lives of these former athletes. Interestingly, 75% of these "retired" athletes indicated current involvement in sport as a participant or a coach. As the following percentages suggest, several were involved in more than one form: 92% (of this 75%) reported present involvement in informal sport, 57% (of this 75%) were currently participating in an organized league, and 28% were currently coaching. In addition to actual participation patterns, 55% of all respondents indicated that they continued to follow their former sport "regularly" or "religiously" through the media. (One of the more interesting findings relative to postcareer sport involvement is the fact that there was no significant diference between those athletes who left sport prematurely in college and those who expended eligibility. Our statistical test was a chi-square analysis of association at the .05 level.)

One important factor that may be related to postcareer involvement concerns motivation or reasons for participation. In response to an open-ended question asking them to rank their reasons for intercollegiate participation, approximately 45% indicated "love of sport" as a primary reason, 27% listed "social experience" as a second reason, and 21% listed sport for self-improvement/conditioning as a third reason. The nature of the reasons listed seems to suggest that these athletes were more intrinsically (rather than extrinsically) motivated to participate in intercollegiate sport. Logically, it would seem that the more intrinsicially motivated the activity, the less dependent the athletes would be on the specific sport system or the rewards of the system. Consequently, expending eligibilty or voluntarily leaving a specific organizational setting may not be related to interest in and participation in the activity itself. From this perspective, then, postcareer participation would be expected.

Although some researchers have recently expressed concern about viewing sport retirement as a terminal experience (Coakley, 1983; Greendorfer, 1983), the appropriateness of this framework has remained unchallenged. Our data seem to suggest a continuation in sport on the part of the "retired" athlete. Rather than termination, the process seems to represent a transition from one competitive level to another. Although the athlete relinquishes the formal role of sport competitor in a specific institutionalized setting (i.e., the school), this severance does not represent total activity withdrawal. Thus, retirement may be an inappropriate framework from which to conceptualize the process of leaving competitive sport.

How Traumatic Is Retirement from Sport?

A primary focus of existing sport retirement research has been on psychosocial adjustment. Several empirical investigations have focused on difficulties experienced by athletes who disengage from sport roles—perception of failure, loss of status, and downward mobility, to mention a few. Despite the number of studies suggesting the need for psychosocial adjustment, however, investigators have not clearly indicated whether these difficulties are inherent in the sport retirement process or whether specific circumstances and antecedent factors contribute to these adjustment problems. Obviously, research attention devoted to this question would be a worthy endeavor.

Although empirical data (as well as anecdotal case studies) do indicate that former athletes experience sadness, disappointment, or unhappiness with their "retirement," the relationship between such feelings and psychosocial adjustment has never been conceptually explained. Although it is commonly assumed that athletes experience intense feelings immediately upon leaving sport, it is theoretically possible for some attenuation to occur. Were this the case, an adjustment perspective might be questioned. There are some empirical data that suggest that attenuation does occur. For example, Greendorfer and Kleiber (1982) found it was not uncommon for athletes to indicate that they felt "very sad at first, but feel much better now."

Similarly, there is very little in our data to suggest that sport retirement was in any way traumatic for these women. For example, 89% of our sample indicated that they looked forward to life after retirement. When asked how satisfied they felt with themselves when their sport career ended, 54% indicated they were either "quite" or "extremely" satisfied. Another 28% indicated they were "moderately" satisfied, while approximately 17% indicated they were "extremely" or "somewhat" unsatisfied. Such findings suggest that the majority of athletes in this study did not view sport retirement from extreme perspectives.

One explanation for this finding can be found in the data suggesting that a shift of interests and orientations occurred during the college years (see Tables 1 and 2). Such a shift may suggest that some preparation for leaving sport could have occurred prior to actually leaving the role of intercollegiate athlete. More specifically, the data in Table 1 indicate a gradual increase from childhood through high school in importance of sport, devotion to sport, and perception of ability in sport. In contrast, the importance of sport and perception of ability declined substantially during the college years. The data in Table 2 demonstrate that, concurrent with this decline, there was an increase in importance of schoolwork and social life during the freshman and senior years of college. Thus, it appears that some shift in priorities took place. Perhaps this change in attitude is an indication that these intercollegiate athletes consciously or subconsciously made some preliminary preparation for leaving the sport role.

This pattern of shifting priorities characterized the entire sample; however, our data suggest that there may be some differences between those athletes who prematurely left sport and those who expended eligibility. Specifically, the data suggest that this reshuffling of priorities between sport, school, and social life might occur at different points in time for each group; however, this shift does take place for both during the college years. For the athletes who had eligibility remaining, a decrease in importance of sport,

TABLE 1
Importance of Sport over Life Cycle Stages

	Importance of Sport		Devotion to Sport		Ability in Sport	
	N	*%*	*N*	*%*	*N*	*%*
Childhood	319	46	334	48	526	75
Junior high	432	62	462	66	570	82
High school	624	90	636	91	631	91
Freshman year college	547	79	622	89[a]	502	72
Senior year college	368	56				
At retirement	364	53	—	—	—	—
Now	384	56	416	60	524	75

Note. Figures (*N*s) represent sum of responses to "extremely" and "very" important, "extremely" and "very" devoted, or "well above" and "above" average.
[a]Question did not specify year in college—response is to "college years"

TABLE 2
Importance of Schoolwork/Social Life

	School		Social	
	N	*%*	*N*	*%*
Freshman year	503	72	426	61
Senior year	554	84	432	66
After retirement	492	73	493	71

Note. *N*s represent sum of responses to "extremely" and "very" important.

devotion to sport, and perception of ability seemed to occur at an earlier point during the college years. In contrast, this shift in orientation seemed to occur closer to the senior year for those athletes who expended their eligibility. It is not known whether this reshuffling of priorities during the college years may have contributed to the formation of these two distinct groups. Regardless, the data clearly indicate that these two groups did not differ in sport-related dimensions prior to their freshman year in college. Moreover, the differences that emerged during the college years disappeared after college.

This reshuffling of priorities suggests that some anticipatory socialization may have occurred. Perhaps as an athlete anticipates the need to move into alternative roles, other skills or activities become more important. Thus, the extent to which an athlete reshuffles or shifts priorities of various social roles may be reflected in the importance and commitment attached to a sport role. Also, the degree to which an athlete considers alternative role possibilities *during* her career could be a strong indicator of the likelihood of successful transition. As other realms increase in importance to the athlete—during her career—the *personal investment* in the singular role of athlete may decline. Obviously, a somewhat different assumption underlies this discussion; namely, the consideration that role occupancy, enactment, and "withdrawal" are complex and multidimensional in nature. Perhaps it is time to discard unidimensional notions such as "endings" and begin to consider sport retirement from another perspective.

SUMMARY AND CONCLUSIONS

The patterns obtained from our data suggest that retirement is not a termination of a sport role, is not traumatic, and may not require tremendous adjustment. Obviously, these patterns are contrary to existing conceptual notions. Although several factors could have contributed to our findings—the sex of the subjects in addition to the competitive level of the sample, or the type of sport retiree (voluntary and involuntary)—these findings are supportive of Coakley's (1983) notion of sport retirement as transition.

By selecting the specific sample frame and attempting to generalize beyond the male professional athlete, our data do more than challenge existing conceptual notions. They introduce a host of additional factors that should be considered in any analysis of sport retirement. Recognizing that it would be more convenient to disregard data which do not conform to theory than it would be to reconceptualize theoretical structures, we feel that some attempt should be made to reconcile empirical data with theoretical perspectives. We sense that, in their present form, current notions are not generalizable because the male professional athlete has been considered the "standard" rather than a select sample. Consequently, popular conceptual notions may not be capturing the general process of sport retirement. In conclusion, then, we suggest that underlying assumptions behind sport retirement research be seriously reexamined and that every effort be made to broaden perspectives in order to achieve a theoretical-empirical balance.

REFERENCES

Atchley, R. C. (1976). *The sociology of retirement.* New York: Wiley.

Ball, D. W. (1976). Failure in sport. *American Sociological Review, 41,* 726–739.

Coakley, J. J. (1983). Leaving competitive sport: Retirement or rebirth? *Quest, 35,* 1–11.

Eitzen, D. S., & Sage, G. H. (Eds.). (1982). *Sociology of American sport* (2nd ed.). Dubuque, IA: Brown.

Greendorfer, S. L. (1983, October). *Letting the data speak: The reality of sport retirement.* Paper presented at the annual meeting of the North American Society for the Sociology of Sport, St. Louis.

Greendorfer, S. L., & Kleiber, D. A. (1982, November). *Sport retirement as social death: The college athlete.* Paper presented at the annual meeting of the North American Society for the Sociology of Sport, Toronto.

Haerle, R. (1975). Career patterns and career contingencies of professional baseball players. In D. Ball & J. Loy (Eds.), *Sport and social order* (pp. 461–519). Reading, MA: Addison-Wesley.

Hare, N. (1971). A study of the black fighter. *Black Scholar, 3,* 2–9.

Hill, P., & Lowe, B. (1974). The inevitable metathesis of the retiring athlete. *International Review of Sport Sociology, 4,* 5–29.

Lerch, S. H. (1981). The adjustment to retirement of professional baseball players. In S. L. Greendorfer & A. Yiannakis (Eds.), *Sociology of sport: Diverse perspectives* (pp. 138–148). West Point, NY: Leisure Press.

McPherson, B. D. (1977, May). *The occupational and psychological adjustment of former professional athletes.* Paper presented at the Symposium on Former Athletes in Later Life, American College of Sports Medicine Annual Meeting, Chicago.

McPherson, B. D. (1980). Retirement from professional sport: The process and problems of occupational adjustment. *Sociological Symposium, 30,* 126–143.

Mihovilovic, M. A. (1968). The status of former sportsmen. *International Review of Sport Sociology, 3,* 73–96.

Reynolds, M. J. (1981). The effects of sport retirement on the job satisfaction of the former football player. In S. L. Grendorfer & A. Yiannakis (Eds.), *Sociology of sport: Diverse perspectives* (pp. 127–137). West Point, NY: Leisure Press.

Rosenberg, E. (1980). Social disorganizational aspects of professional sports careers. *Journal of Sport and Social Issues, 4,* 14–25.

Rosenberg, E. (1981). Gerontological theory and athletic retirement. In S. L. Greendorfer & A. Yiannakis (Eds.), *Sociology of sport: Diverse perspectives* (pp. 118–126). West Point, NY: Leisure Press.

Rosenberg, E. (1982, November). *Athletic retirement as social death: Concepts and perspectives.* Paper presented at the annual meeting of the North American Society for the Sociology of Sport, Toronto.

Snyder, E. E. (1981). A reflection on commitment and patterns of disengagement from recreational physical activity. In S. L. Greendorfer & A. Yiannakis (Eds.), *Sociology of sport: Diverse perspectives* (pp. 108–117). West Point, NY: Leisure Press.

Weinberg, S. K., & Arond, H. (1952). The occupational culture of the boxer. *American Journal of Sociology, 57,* 460–469.

12

RACIAL MAKEUP OF CENTRAL, STACKING, AND OTHER PLAYING POSITIONS IN SOUTHEASTERN CONFERENCE FOOTBALL TEAMS, 1967–1983

Richard V. McGehee

M. Joan Paul

Studies of the racial composition of team positions in professional and collegiate football have shown blacks to be underrepresented in certain spatially central positions and to be overrepresented in the more peripheral positions. The Southeastern Conference, for the period from the first year of integration through the 1983 season, showed significant underrepresentation of black players in the central positions of quarterback, center, and offensive guard; blacks are also underrepresented at offensive tackle, as kickers, and in the total offensive line. During the same period blacks were significantly overrepresented in the stacking positions of running back, wide receiver, and defensive back. Blacks were also overrepresented at defensive guard and in the offensive and defensive backfields. Since the integration of all football teams in the Conference in 1973, the percentage of black football players has increased from 8% to over 41%. The percentages of blacks in all position categories and in each position except quarterback, center, and kicker have shown moderate to large increases. The data for 1983 show that black players make up a larger proportion of first-team players than would be expected from their numbers on the team rosters.

In the early 1960s sport was widely thought to be an ideal integrating force in the United States, providing fair and equal opportunity and treatment for all its participants (Tobin, 1967). However, in 1968 Jack Olsen presented a powerful exposé of the discriminatory social practices in American sport in a five-part series in *Sports Illustrated*. The articles by Olsen, followed by the Olympic protest organized by Harry Edwards and the dramatic black glove salute by Tommy Smith and John Carlos at the 1968 Olympic Games in Mexico City, brought into prominence the need for studies seeking the truth regarding the accusations of racial discrimination in sport. The investigations of race in sport which followed also played an important role in the development of the fledging discipline of sport sociology.

In 1970 Loy and McElvogue published their classic analytic study of the racial composition of player positions in professional sport. Using the work of Blalock (1962) and Grusky (1963) as a framework, they examined the occupational discrimination in sport by comparing the racial makeup of the central and noncentral positions on professional baseball and football teams. The concept of "centrality" is that those positions located closest to the physical center of the team's network permit greater social interaction, demand more leadership ability, and provide more prestige for those occupying them. In short, they are more important for team success. Loy and McElvogue defined the central positions in football as the quarterback, the center, and the two guards on the offensive team and the linebacker positions on the defensive team. They found the central positions to be occupied primarily by white players. The noncentral positions are physically peripheral and were overrepresented (stacked) by black players. The most stacked positions are running back and wide receiver on the offensive team and cornerback and safety on the defensive team. Loy and McElvogue noted that black players seemed to be concentrated in the same noncentral positions where they had to compete with one another and were not allowed to compete against whites for the central positions.

Following Loy and McElvogue's study, sport sociologists continued to test the centrality and stacking phenomena and provided several explanations for the racial patterns by position on football and baseball teams. For example, Eitzen and Sanford (1975) and Spivey and Jones (1975) used "position politics" to account for this pattern of discrimination: white coaches place white players in power positions in order to appease team owners and fans. At the same time black athletes, aware of their limitied opportunities, select peripheral positions because they perceive a greater chance to earn college scholarships or to be selected by professional football teams if they play noncentral positions. McPherson (1974) and Eitzen and Sanford (1975) suggested that modeling, the emulation of black stars by young black athletes, is the reason blacks select noncentral positions. Other explanations include integration avoidance (Eitzen & Sanford, 1975; McPherson, 1974) and reactive versus self-paced performance requirements of the different positions (Worthy & Markle, 1970). However, most of the studies reporting evidence of discrimination by race in playing positions conclude that stereotyping probably accounts for the dominance of whites in central positions and the stacking of blacks in noncentral or peripheral positions (Williams & Youssef, 1972, 1975). In short, coaches assign players to positions according to their beliefs about the capabilities of whites and blacks.

In 1978 Curtis and Loy reviewed all previous research on the stacking phenomenon. Of the 17 articles they summarized, 8 presented information on professional football and 2 focused on collegiate football (Eitzen & Sanford, 1975: Williams & Youssef, 1975). Eitzen and Sanford studied 553 players from 38 colleges (including some all-black schools) drafted by professional football teams between 1962 and 1971). They compared the percentages of blacks who played in central with those who played in noncentral positions. Blacks were overrepresented in one central position, offensive guard, and underrepresented in all other central positions. Conversely, they were overrepresented in the three noncentral positions, wide receiver, running back, and defensive back. Williams and Youssef studied 785 players from 15 collegiate teams in the Midwest and West during the 1974 football season and reported that black players were underrepresented in all central positions and overrepresented in the three stacking positions.

More recently, Schneider and Eitzen (1979) analyzed the racial composition of several 1978 collegiate football teams in the Midwest and West (13 teams and 730 players) and found blacks to be underrepresented in central positions and overrepresented in the stacking positions plus among the defensive line (front four). Marsh and Heitman (1981) reported fewer blacks than expected (according to their proportion of the team) in all central positions except linebacker and more than expected in the stacking positions on the Senior Bowl teams between 1975 and 1981. Bowen and Fludd (1982) found a similar pattern among the starting and second teams on football squads in the Southeastern Conference (SEC) in 1979.

SEC football is an interesting area in which to study centrality because it is composed of southern schools with a history of segregation. Established in 1932, the SEC was the last major intercollegiate conference in the United States to integrate its sports teams. The University of Kentucky awarded the first two football scholarships to blacks in 1966, but because of the freshman eligibility rule, the first year of integrated varsity football in the Conference was 1967. The last school to have black football players was the University of Mississippi, which integrated its team in 1973.

The purpose of the present study was to investigate (a) whether the phenomena of centrality and stacking occur in SEC football, (b) whether player occupancy of individual positions in collegiate football is related to race, (c) whether the racial composition patterns of central and noncentral positions have changed since the beginning of integration in the Conference (1967) through the 1983 season, and (d) whether there are differences in the skill levels of black and white players on collegiate football teams.

METHOD

The present investigation is an outgrowth of our study of the history of integration of sports teams among the 10 members of the Southeastern Conference (Paul, Fant, & McGehee, 1983). Team rosters for each intercollegiate sport for all years from the mid-1960s through the 1979−1980 season were mailed to the sports information directors at all Conference schools, who were asked to identify which athletes were black. In the one case in which cooperation was refused, the information was obtained from SEC media guides in the Conference Office. Similar data for 1980−1983 were obtained directly from the photo rosters in the football media guides; the starting players on the 1983 teams were identified from game programs. Information was collected on every player for each year of the study, a total of 10,230 athletes. Chi-square tests of independence were applied to the data for each position and groups of positions. The .05 level of significance was used for all analyses.

RESULTS

The number of blacks and whites who played in the SEC football teams between 1967, the first year of integrated football teams, and 1983 are shown in Table 1. The chi-square analyses reveal that black players were under-represented in all central positions except linebacker. Blacks were over-represented in all stacking positions, wide receiver, running back, and defensive back, and were also overrepresented at defensive guard (nose guard). Blacks were underrepresented at offensive tackle, kicker, in the overall offensive line, and in the combined offensive and defensive lines.

A breakdown of the black−white differences by position for the 10 SEC schools is shown in Table 2. For example, blacks were underrepresented at the offensive guard position at all 10 schools, but were underrepresented at linebacker at only 2 schools and were even overrepresented at linebacker at 1 school.

With the exception of kickers, few members of the special teams, for example, punting team, extra point team, and kickoff receiving team, could be identified and were not included in the analyses. A few long snappers— centers who are responsible for getting the ball to the punters or the field goal kickers—were known and they were all white. Casual observation suggests that most kickoff and punt return specialists are black.

Figures 1 through 4 show the changes in black occupancy of individual positions and position categories from 1973, the first year that all 10 schools had at least one black player, through 1983. Data from all schools were combined for each year with the yearly Ns ranging from 684 players in 1981 to 794 players in 1975.

The overall percentage of blacks on the football rosters has increased from 8% in 1973 to over 41% in 1983 (see Figure 1). The rate of increase has

TABLE 1
Occupancy of Positions by Race

Position	Black Players	White Players	Percentage Black	Chi-Square	Pearson's Coef.
Central	396.5	2727.5	12.7	223.19^{a}*	.14
Quarterback	54.5	504.5	9.7	51.08^{a}*	.07
Center	26.5	450.5	5.6	78.19^{a}*	.09
Offen. guard	56.0	763.5	6.8	118.31^{a}*	.11
Linebacker	259.5	1009.0	20.5	1.78	
Stacking	1204.5	2150.5	35.9	571.59^{b}*	.23
Running back	533.0	652.0	45.0	417.06^{b}*	.20
Wide receiver	235.0	494.0	32.2	48.96^{b}*	.07
Defen. back	383.0	954.5	28.6	40.73^{b}*	.06
Other positions and categories					
Defen. guard	89.8	185.5	32.6	19.01^{b}*	.04
Defen. tackle	198.3	672.0	22.8	0.43	
Defen. end	166.8	660.0	20.2	1.57	
Offen. tackle	65.5	793.0	7.6	111.65^{a}*	.10
Offen. end	114.0	451.5	20.2	1.07	
Kicker	5.5	349.0	1.6	88.94^{a}*	.09
Offen. line	262.0	2458.5	9.6	326.45^{a}*	.18
Offen. bkfld.	822.5	1650.5	33.3	245.72^{b}*	.15
Total offen.	1084.5	4009.0	21.3	2.24	
Defen. line	455.0	1517.5	23.1	1.93	
Defen. bkfld.	696.0	2013.5	25.7	30.80^{b}*	.06
Total defen.	1155.0	3519.0	24.7	39.58^{b}*	.06
Total line	717.0	3976.0	15.3	222.66^{a}*	.15
Total bkfld.	1518.5	3664.0	29.3	335.71^{b}*	.18

Note. Based on all players for the 10 SEC schools in all years from the first year of integration through 1983. Total players = 10,230. Total black players = 2,241. Overall percentage blacks = 21.9. Players listed in multiple positions were counted fractionally in each.

^{a}Black underrepresentation.

^{b}Black overrepresentation.

*p<.0001, df=1.

been regular, about 4% per year with breaks in the pattern in 1979, 1982, and 1983. The rate seems to be leveling off since 1981, but it is too recent to draw any conclusions. Black occupancy of both central and stacking positions has also increased regularly, but the rate of increase for blacks in stacking positions has been greater than the overall growth for blacks on the team. Increases in the number of blacks in central positions have been slower.

TABLE 2
Individual Team Differences in Racial Composition of Positions

Position	Number of Teams		
	Signif. Black Overrepresent.	Signif. Black Underrepresent.	Nonsignif. Difference
Central		9	1
Quarterback		6	4
Center		9	1
Offen. guard		10	
Linebacker	1	2	7
Stacking	10		
Running back	10		
Wide receiver	4		6
Defen. back	6		4
Other positions and categories			
Defen. guard	2		4
Defen. tackle	1	1	8
Defen. end		2	8
Offen. tackle		9	1
Offen. end	1		9
Kicker		8	
Offen. line		9	1
Offen. bkfld.	10		
Total offen.		2	8
Defen. line	3		7
Defen. bkfld.	3		7
Total defen.	6		4
Total line		9	1
Total bkfld.	10		

$p < .05$ (level of significance used for all comparisons made to determine whether the team was in the overrepresented, underrepresented, or nonsignificant category).

Figure 2 shows the patterns of change in the specific central and stacking positions. The percentage of blacks who played linebacker are very similar to the overall black membership on football teams in the Conference. The other central positions (quarterback, center, and offensive guard) have much lower percentages of blacks, although the number of blacks playing offensive guard has been increasing gradually, from none in 1973 to 18% in 1983. Black occupancy of all three stacking positions (wide receiver, running back, and defensive back) has increased rapidly. The greatest increase is for running back, with the position 21% black in 1973 and 80% in 1980 and 1981. However, the percentage dropped slightly to 73% in 1983.

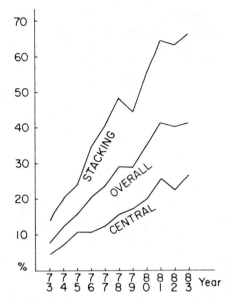

FIGURE 1. Percentage of blacks in central and stacking position categories by year, 1973–1983.

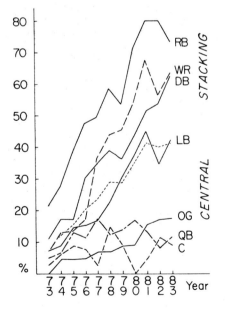

FIGURE 2. Percentage of blacks in the component positions of the central and stacking categories by year, 1973–1983. (RB = running back; WR = wide receiver; DB = defensive back; LB = linebacker; OG = offensive guard; QB = quarterback; C = center; dotted line is overall black percentage)

The percentage of blacks playing positions other than the central and noncentral (stacking) positions are similar to the proportion of blacks on the team with two exceptions, offensive tackle and kicker (see Figure 3). When individual playing positions were combined into larger units such as offensive backfield, defensive line, or the entire defensive team, black representation in all position groupings shows consistent increases over time (see Figure 4).

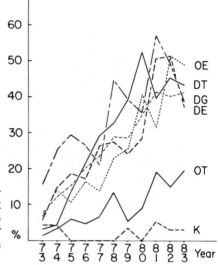

FIGURE 3. Percentage of blacks in other individual positions by year, 1973–1983. (OE = offensive end; DT = defensive tackle; DG = defensive guard; DE = defensive end; OT = offensive tackle; K = kicker; dotted line is overall black percentage)

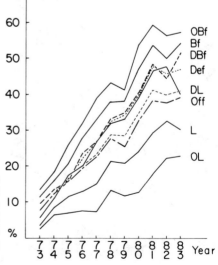

FIGURE 4. Percentage of blacks in various position groupings by year, 1973–1983. (OBf = offensive backfield; Bf = total backfield; DBf = defensive backfield; Def = total defense; DL = defensive line; Off = total offense; L = total line; OL = offensive line; dotted line is overall black percentage)

Since 1973 the percentage of black players in central positions has been between 15% and 20% (see Figure 5). Moreover, the number of blacks in the stacking positions has also been consistent, between 50% and 60%. However, the percentage of blacks in the stacking positons has declined slightly since 1977.

The bar graphs in Figures 6 through 8 compare the proportion of blacks on 1983 team rosters and starting line-ups. For example, in 1983 blacks comprised 43% of all football players, but made up 55% of the starting

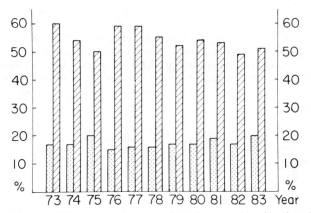

FIGURE 5. Partition of black players into central (dots) and stacking (lines) position categories by year, 1973–1983.

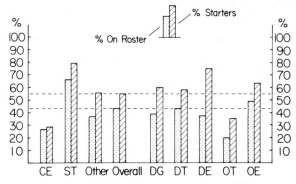

FIGURE 6. Comparison of proportions of black players on 1983 team rosters (dots) and starting line-ups (lines) for the central and stacking categories and other individual positions. (CE = central; ST = stacking; DG = defensive guard; DT = defensive tackle; DE = defensive end; OT = offensive tackle; OE = offensive end; lower horizontal dashed line is overall percentage of blacks on team, upper horizontal dashed line is overall percentage of black starters)

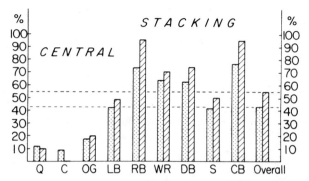

FIGURE 7. Comparison of proportions of black players on 1983 team rosters (dots) and starting line-ups (lines) for the component positions of the central and stacking categories. (Q = quarterback; C = center; OG = offensive guard; LB = linebacker; RB = running back; WR = wide receiver; DB = defensive back; S = safety; CB = cornerback; lower horizontal dashed line is overall percentage of blacks on team, upper horizontal dashed line is overall percentage of black starters)

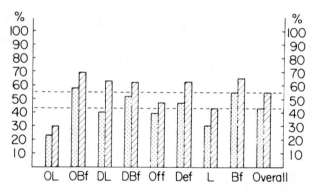

FIGURE 8. Comparison of proportions of black players on 1983 team rosters (dots) and starting line-ups (lines) for various position groupings. (OL = offensive line; OBf = offensive backfield; DL = defensive line; DBf = defensive backfield; Off = total offense; Def = total defense; L = total line; Bf = total backfield; lower horizontal dashed line is overall percentage of blacks on team, upper horizontal dashed line is overall percentage of black starters)

teams. For all positions except quarterback and center, the percentage of black starters is higher than the percentage of blacks listed at the position on the team rosters.

In order to put black participation in the Southeastern Conference into a more meaningful perspective, one should compare the percentages of blacks on football teams with the racial composition of the undergraduate student population and the overall black population in the states in which the schools are located (see Figure 9). Georgia and Tennessee have the

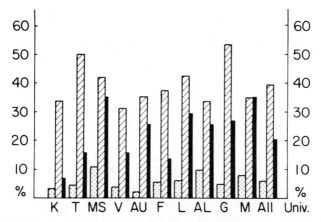

FIGURE 9. Percentages of blacks in undergraduate student bodies (dots), football rosters (lines), and state populations (solid) for SEC universities. Student body and player racial percentages are from 1981–1982; state racial percentages are based on the 1980 census. (K = Kentucky; T = Tennessee; MS = Mississippi State; V = Vanderbilt; AU = Auburn; F = Florida; L = Louisiana State; AL = Alabama; G = Georgia; M = Mississippi)

highest percentage of blacks on their football rosters (50% or more); Kentucky, Vanderbilt, Auburn, Florida, Mississippi, and Alabama have approximately one third of their varsity teams comprised of blacks. The ratio of blacks in football to blacks in the student body ranges from the lowest at Alabama (approximately 3 to 1) to the highest at Auburn (over 14 to 1). A comparison of the percentage of blacks on football teams with the percentage of blacks in the state population shows that the percentages of blacks on football teams at schools in Alabama—Alabama and Auburn— and those in Mississippi— Mississippi and Mississippi State—are most similar to the black population in the state. Conversely, the universities of Kentucky, Tennessee, Florida, and Vanderbilt (Tennessee) have the largest discrepancies between the percentage of blacks on the football team and those living in the state.

CONCLUSIONS

Although the number of blacks on SEC football teams has been steadily increasing since 1967, there has been little change in the positions occupied by black players. Over the period 1973–1983 the percentage of black players increased in every position grouping and in all positions except quarterback, center, and kicker. The data reveal a significant relationship between race and position played, a pattern which supports the centrality theory in football initially demonstrated by Loy and McElvogue (1970). Although SEC schools heavily recruit black football players, a fact supported by the black representation on football squads compared with the black undergraduate enrollments and the number of blacks living in the respective states, the Conference schools have continually discriminated against blacks in terms of the positions they are allowed to occupy. Thus, the data are consistent with the earlier findings of discrimination in professional football (Ball, 1973; Brower, 1972: Dougherty, 1976; Eitzen & Sanford, 1975; Eitzen & Yetman, 1977; Loy and McElvogue, 1970) and in college football (Bowen & Fludd, 1982; Eitzen & Sanford, 1975; Marsh & Heitman, 1981; Schneider & Eitzen, 1979; Williams & Youssef, 1975). Whether this pattern is a result of modeling, player preferences, coaches' stereotypes, or other causes, a self-perpetuating myth has developed that reinforces the belief of coaches, players, and even the general public, that racially linked traits account for the overrepresentation of blacks in some positions and their underrepresentation in others.

These data from the SEC also support earlier findings that blacks must be better athletes in order to make the football teams. The percentage of blacks on the starting teams (1983) is higher than their presence on the overall team roster. On the average the performance of blacks is superior to that of whites, a conclusion based not only on the higher number of blacks on starting teams, but also by the number of blacks who earn letters and set school and conference athletic records. In short, blacks are not recruited to sit on the bench.

ACKNOWLEDGMENT

We gratefully acknowledge the assistance of Helen Fant, Louisiana State University, for her assistance in the data collection. This article was presented in part at the Clemson Conference on Sport and Society, Clemson, South Carolina, March 30, 1984.

REFERENCES

Ball, D. W. (1973). Ascription and position: A comparative analysis of "stacking" in professional football. *Canadian Review of Sociology and Anthropology, 10,* 97–113.
Blalock, H. M., Jr. (1962). Occupational discrimination: Some theoretical propositions. *Social Problems, 9,* 240–247.
Bowen, R. T., & Fludd, C. (1982). Race, home town and experience as factors in Deep South major college football. *International Review of Sport Sociology, 17,* 41–51.
Brower, J. (1972, April). *The racial basis of the division of labor among players in the National Football League as a function of racial stereotypes.* Paper presented at the meeting of the Pacific Sociological Association, Portland, OR.

Curtis, J. E., & Loy, J. W. (1978). Race/ethnicity and relative centrality of playing positions in team sports. In R. S. Hutton (Ed.), *Exercise and Sport Sciences Reviews* (Vol. 6, pp. 285–313). Philadelphia: Franklin Institute Press.

Dougherty, J. (1976). Race and sport: A follow-up study. *Sport Sociology Bulletin, 5,* 1–12.

Eitzen, D. S., & Sanford, D. C. (1975). The segregation of blacks by playing position in football: Accident or design? *Social Science Quarterly, 55,* 948–959.

Eitzen, D. S., & Yetman, N. R. (1977). Immune from racism? *Civil Rights Digest, 9,* 3–13.

Grusky, O. (1963). The effects of formal structure on managerial recruitment: A study of baseball organization. *Sociometry, 26,* 345–353.

Loy, J. W., & McElvogue, J. F. (1970). Racial segregation in American sport. *International Review of Sport Sociology, 5,* 5–24.

Marsh, R. L., & Heitman, R. J. (1981). The centrality phenomenon in football: Senior Bowl, 1975–1981. *Journal of Sport Behavior, 4,* 111–118.

McPherson, B. D. (1974). Minority group involvement in sport. In J. Wilmore (Ed.), *Exercise and Sport Sciences Reviews,* (Vol. 2, pp. 71–101). New York: Academic Press.

Olsen, J. (1968, July 1). The black athlete—a shameful story: The cruel deception. *Sports Illustrated,* 12–27.

Olsen, J. (1968, July 8). The black athlete: Pride and prejudice. *Sports Illustrated,* 18–31.

Olsen, J. (1968, July 15). The black athlete: In an alien world. *Sports Illustrated,* 29–43.

Olsen, J. (1968, July 22). The black athlete: In the back of the bus. *Sports Illustrated,* 28–41.

Olsen, J. (1968, July 29). The black athlete: The anguish of the team divided. *Sports Illustrated,* 20–35.

Paul, J., Fant, H., & McGehee, R. (1983). The arrival and ascendence of the black athlete in the Southeastern Conference: 1966–1980 [Abstract]. *Proceedings of the 11th Annual Meeting of the North American Society for Sport History* (Vol. 19, pp. 16–29).

Schneider, J., & Eitzen, D. S. (1979). Racial discrimination in American sport: Continuity or change? *Journal of Sports Behavior, 2,* 136–142.

Spivey, D., & Jones, T. A. (1975). Intercollegiate athletic servitude: A case study of the black Illinois student athletes, 1931–1967. *Social Science Quarterly, 55,* 939–947.

Tobin, R. L. (1967, January 21). Sports as an integrator. *Saturday Review,* p. 32.

Williams, R. L., & Youssef, Z. I. (1972). Consistency of football coaches in stereotyping the personality of each position's player. *International Journal of Sport Psychology, 3,* 3–11.

Williams, R. L., & Youssef, Z. I. (1975). Division of labor in college football along racial lines. *International Journal of Sport Psychology, 6,* 3–13.

Worthy, M., & Markle, A. (1970). Black Americans in reactive versus self-paced sports activities. *Journal of Personality and Social Psychology, 16,* 439–443.

13

MORAL DEVELOPMENT LEVELS OF ATHLETES IN SPORT-SPECIFIC AND GENERAL SOCIAL SITUATIONS

Elizabeth R. Hall

The purpose of this study was to determine whether athletes use a different level of moral reasoning to resolve sport-specific dilemmas than to resolve dilemmas that are of a general social nature. Forty-three female and 21 male basketball players from NCAA Division I schools completed Kohlberg's Moral Judgment Questionnaire and an especially prepared questionnaire requiring responses to sport-specific dilemmas. Female athletes displayed a higher level of moral reasoning than male athletes (p <.003) in both the general and the sport situations. Male and female athletes in the 20−23 age group did not reach the normative level of moral reasoning reported by Kohlberg. Male and female athletes displayed a higher level of moral reasoning on the sport-specific dilemmas than on the general social situations.

Historically, sport institutions have been regarded as vehicles for social learning, providing solid support for traditional values. However, recently the negative behavior of athletes, coaches, administrators, and fans has focused public attention on the kinds of lessons sport teaches. Although those critical of organized sport often blame the system, the organization and administration of institutionalized sport, sport participants must also be scrutinized because they make the actual decisions to commit, avoid, condone, or denounce unethical behavior.

Edwards (1973) presented a review of the basic themes that have been analyzed by researchers interested in the effect of sport participation on the social development of athletes and some decisions regarding what research illuminates about each: (a) sport participation builds character—INCONCLUSIVE; (b) sport participation develops a value orientation towards loyalty—NO EVIDENCE; (c) sport participation generates altruism—INCONCLUSIVE; (d) sport participation generates a value orientation toward social and/or self-control—INCONCLUSIVE; and (e) sport provides opportunities for individual advancement—INCONCLUSIVE.

It appears that this fragmented approach to determining the effect of athletics on the individual has yielded little concrete knowledge. Porter and Taylor (1972) summarized the plight of sport sociologists and psychologists interested in the effect of sport on the individual:

> The study of moral attitudes and development took the form of assessing character strength—honesty, friendliness, self-control, and so on. This bag

of virtues approach provided little understanding of the nature of moral development and moral thinking. (p. 1)

In order to expand the knowledge concerning athletic competition and moral development, we must reject this "bag of virtues" approach in favor of the establishment of a base of knowledge which is developmental and general and may explain behavior in terms of the cognitive development of the individual. Hoffman (1970) stated: "The guiding concept in most moral development research is internalization of socially-sanctioned prohibitions and mandates" (p. 262). This process of internalization may be said to have a direct effect on certain traits, summarized by Edwards (1973) as altruism, social and self-control, fortitude, individual advancement, and preparation for life. The social scientist interested in sport, then, has a responsibility to determine what influences the internalization of values—acted out within the sport environment—might have on the moral development of individual athletes.

THEORETICAL BASES

Kohlberg (1969) provided a theoretical framework which can guide investigation into the nature of moral development. He described three levels of moral development which comprise six stages of moral development. Level I identifies the basis of moral judgment as external, quasi-physical acts or needs rather than acts based on awareness of norms or individuals. Level I has been labeled "preconventional" and includes Stages 1 and 2 of the developmental process. Individuals functioning at Stage 1 defer to prestige or power in order to avoid punishment. Those at Stage 2 are considered "naively egoistic" and direct their actions strictly to satisfy their own needs.

Level II is labeled "conventional" and contains Stages 3 and 4 of the developmental sequence. A Level II orientation reflects the desire to perform proper and socially acceptable behaviors to gain the approval of others. An individual functioning from a Stage 3 orientation conforms to stereotypical models and indulges in very little behavior that is not pleasing to others. Those at Stage 4 are now aware of laws for their own sake, and doing one's duty is important.

Level III is called "post conventional" and includes Stages 5 and 6. Individuals who have reached this level are considered autonomous; conformity is dictated by the self and based on internalized standards. Individuals who have reached the fifth stage of development display great concern for the rights of others and the will of the majority. Often referred to as the

"Universal Ethical Principle Orientation," Stage 6 emphasizes the importance of conscience and principle. The conscience directs behavior with an emphasis on mutual respect and trust.

Studies undertaken since the original proposal have led Kohlberg to identify a transitional stage between Stage 4 (the last conventional level) and Stage 5 (the first postconventional level). This stage occurs for most people about the time they complete high school. Labeled "Stage 4½," it is defined as the Outside Society Perspective. It is a transition stage necessary for one to achieve autonomy and is characterized by skepticism, egoism, and relativism. These characteristics develop from the realization that laws and rules are merely man-made dictates of behavior and do not represent a universal mode of conduct. It is this realization that prompts the individual to begin to look to the self to determine right and wrong and is the impetus for moving into Stage 5. The following chart summarizes Kohlberg's levels and stages of moral development:

Level I *Preconventional*
   Stage 1   Reward and Punishment (right is that which avoids punishment
   Stage 2   Personal Interest (right is what pleases me)
Level II *Conventional*
   Stage 3   Peer Group Interest (right is what makes me acceptable to others)
   Stage 4   Authority and Law (right coincides with written agreed-upon law [rules])
   Stage 4½ Outside Society Perspective
Level III *Post Conventional*
   Stage 5   Respect for Personal Freedom of the Other (right promotes freedom of individual and community)
   Stage 6   Awareness of Universal Responsibility (right is to publicly promote and protect freedom in society)

Kohlberg's emphasis on reasons for behavior rather than the behaviors themselves allows the examination of differences in overall moral outlook. Duska and Whelan (1975) explained: "Whereas one person might indicate that cheating is wrong because one can get caught doing it, another person might indicate that cheating undermines the trust necessary to preserve society. Here a significant difference in the maturity of the reasoning process and in the reasons given is obvious." (p. 43)

Kohlberg's six stages of moral development are considered hierarchical. Kohlberg (1969) stated: "An individual's response profile, then, typically represents a pattern composed of the dominant stage he is in, a stage he is leaving, but still uses somewhat and a stage he is moving into but has not yet crystallized . . . all other stages are available or at least comprehensible to the S[ubject]." (p. 387)

To summarize, Kohlberg's stages represent a developmental sequence which does not vary. All development is forward in sequence. An individual may reach a particular stage and never progress any further, but any movement is in accord with the developmental steps. For example, conventional reasoning never occurs before preconventional, and postconventional reasoning never precedes conventional (Kohlberg, 1958).

Kohlberg (1969) explained that the most important assumption of cognitive development theory is that "basic mental structure is the result of an interaction between certain organismic structuring tendencies and the structure of the outside world, rather than either one directly" (p. 352). For example, one unique outside world situation is sport, and for a long time many have suggested that the experiences gained in sport situations may contribute to the development of values.

The sport environment can be characterized by a number of factors which could affect the cognitive moral development of participants. Three of the most obvious components are authoritarian leadership (Lilly, 1980), competitiveness, and a "winning is everything" ethic. These three are major characteristics of the outside world of sport with which the athlete interacts.

Authoritarian Leadership

Ogilvie and Tutko (1970) described male coaches as

high in achievement need, deference, order, dominance, endurance, abasement, and aggression. They are low in needs intraception, exhibition, nurturance, and change. This study supports the generalization that for those traits which determine getting ahead and succeeding that do not necessitate personal involvement, coaches score high. In those traits of personality which contribute most to being sensitive and also support close interpersonal relationships they score low. (p. 76)

Competitiveness

Competitiveness enters into the athletic world in many different ways and often leads to violations in the spirit of the rules as well as the letter. The most obvious example, competition between teams or individuals on opposing sides, will be discussed under the winning is everything ethic discussion. Competition within teams, defined by Cartwright and Zander (1968, p. 412) as "competitive interdependence," often leads to less positive relationships among team members. For example, in team sports like basketball, teams composed of 10 to 12 players are allowed to have only 5 team members playing at any one time. The competition among the players for playing time can create an environment in which individuals learn to disregard their teammates as people and see them as obstacles which must be overcome in order to play the game.

Winning Is Everything Ethic

Perhaps the most important and far-reaching of the three components is the winning is everything ethic, which seems to dominate competitive athletics. Sage (1972) provided some insight into the scope of this emphasis: "In recent years America's high school and college athletic coaches have been vigorously attacked by individuals from within and outside the field of education. These attacks have centered on the alleged ruthless methods that athletic coaches use in carrying out the tasks of coaching their teams." (p. 45) These "ruthless acts" are justified by the payoff—winning. This ultimate goal and the fact that it is clearly defined in every sport endeavor by intricate and explicit rules, may be the most significant factor which sets the sport environment apart from other competitive environments.

PURPOSE AND HYPOTHESES

The present study was designed to determine the functional stage of moral development of athletes in situations which are related to general social dilemmas (Kohlberg, 1958) and situations which are sport specific. In addition, the moral maturity levels of athletes were compared with the general norms developed by Kohlberg to identify the various levels of moral development (L. Kohlberg, personal communication, October 1980).

It has been pointed out that the interaction with the environment affects the rate at which moral development occurs, and that athletics is one kind of environment that may have a strong influence on participants. The athletic subculture has been characterized by authoritarian leadership, competitiveness, and the importance of winning. Because of these factors, especially the emphasis on winning, the athletic environment may retard the moral development of those who spend considerable time in athletic situations.

Hypothesis I: Athletes display a stage of moral development lower than the norm for others in their age group.

Although an individual may have progressed to a particular stage of development, he or she is still able to reason at lower levels. It is also possible that individuals may interact at different stages in varying situations. Thus, the effect of the athletic environment may influence athletes to solve conflicts in sport at lower levels than they solve dilemmas of a more general social nature.

Hypothesis II: Athletes display a lower stage of moral development in sport situations than in nonsport situations.

It is also possible that a particular situation or environment may affect people differently. For example, women have not been exposed to the same pressures to win in athletics as have men. The win-loss records of female coaches have not been significant factors in either their employment or their job security as they have been for male coaches. Moreover, women's teams seldom function as identity symbols for the students, faculty, or alumni. In short, women may not have experienced the same athletic environment that men have.

Hyposthesis III: Female athletes demonstrate higher moral development than male athletes in nonsport situations.

Hypothesis IV: Female athletes show higher moral development than male athletes in sport situations.

METHOD

Subjects

Subjects in this study were 64 college athletes, 21 men and 43 women, who participated on NCAA Division I basketball teams during the 1980–1981 basketball season. All subjects competed for schools in the Dallas–Fort Worth Metroplex. Sixty-seven subjects completed questionnaires which contained four social dilemmas developed by Kohlberg (1958) and four sport-specific dilemmas developed especially for this project. Following each dilemma were a series of questions concerning the behavioral alternatives to solving the problem. Each subject responded in writing to the questions. Three athletes whose questionnaires were incomplete were eliminated from the study.

Instruments

Kohlberg's Moral Judgment Questionnaire.

The Moral Judgment instrument is composed of nine scenarios and is self-administered. The following example is one of the four nonsport scenarios used in the project:

In Europe, a woman was near death from a special kind of cancer. There was one drug that the doctors thought might save her. It was a form of radium that a druggist in the same town had recently discovered. The drug was expensive to make, but the druggist was charging ten times what the drug cost him to make. He paid $200.00 for the radium and charged $2,000.00 for a small dose of the drug. The sick woman's husband, Heinz, went to everyone he knew to borrow the money, but he could only get together about $1,000.00, which is half of what it cost. He told the druggist that his wife was dying and asked him to sell it cheaper or let him pay later. But the druggist said, "No. I discovered the drug and I'm going to make money from it." So Heinz got desperate and broke into the man's store to steal the drug for his wife.

1. Should Heinz have done that? Was it actually wrong or right? Why?
2. Is it a husband's duty to steal the drug for his wife if he can get it no other way? Would a good husband do it?
3. Did the druggist have the right to charge that much when there was no law actually setting a limit to the price? Why?

Answer 4a and 4b only if you think Heinz should steal the drug.

4a. If the husband does not feel very close or affectionate to his wife, should he steal the drug?
4b. Suppose it wasn't Heinz's wife who was dying of cancer, but it was Heinz's best friend. His friend didn't have any money and there was no one in his family willing to steal the drug. Should Heinz steal the drug for his friend in that case? Why?

Answer questions 5a and 5b only if you think Heinz should not steal the drug.

5a. Would you steal the drug to save your wife's life?
5b. If you were dying of cancer, but were strong enough, would you steal the drug to save your own life?
6. Heinz broke into the store and stole the drug and gave it to his wife. He was caught and brought before the judge. Should the judge send Heinz to jail for stealing or let him go free? Why?

Sport-Specific Questionnaire

Sport-specific dilemmas were developed by the investigator using the guidelines suggested by Mattox (1975). Completed scenarios were reviewed by an expert sport sociologist and an intercollegiate basketball coach to ensure that each dilemma presented a problem in a realistic setting, created cognitive conflict, addressed a focal question, and was a serious concern. Suggestions made by these experts were incorporated into the final draft of scenarios.

The investigator then instructed 20 college-aged men and women in the characteristics of Kohlberg's moral stages. Each of the men ($n=10$) and women ($n=10$) completed each of the sport scenarios six times. Each time they completed the questionnaire they were to respond according to one of Kohlberg's six stages of moral reasoning. Similar responses were obtained from graduate students in group dynamics at Texas Woman's University.

Next, three judges, familiar with Kohlberg's work from both a theoretical and a practical perspective, reviewed all sample answers and prepared a scoring frame of reference for each question for each dilemma. Examples of the kind of thinking (i.e., typical responses) for each stage of moral reasoning were incorporated into a training manual which was given to each scorer.

The following example is one of the four sport-specific scenarios used in the study:

> Coach Miller needs a winning season to convince the school administration to keep basketball in the athletic program. Tonight the team will play the final game of the season and their win-loss record is even. At the end of the first half Coach Miller's team is behind so the coach instructs the team's official timekeeper to delay starting the clock on throw-ins and jump balls in order to give the home team a time advantage that could allow them to win the game. Further, the coach made it clear to the timer that failure to follow these instructions will result in the timekeeper not being rehired next season. The timekeeper is supported by the money earned working for the team and was counting on income from this job next season.
>
> 1. Should the timekeeper follow the coach's instructions: Why?
> 2. Is the coach to do everything possible to save the basketball program? Why?
>
> Answer 3 and 4 only if you think the timer should follow the coach's instructions.
>
> 3. If the timekeeper does not feel any loyalty to the team, but keeps time only as a means of making money, should the timekeeper follow the coach's instructions? Why?
> 4. The timekeeper followed the coach's instructions and was caught by the officials. The result was being brought before the conference disciplinary review board. Should the timekeeper receive individual punishment for adjusting the time? Why?
>
> Answer questions 5 and 6 only if you think the timer should not follow the coach's orders.
>
> 5. Would you adjust the time to save your own job? Why?
> 6. Suppose the timer's best friend is on the team and will lose the only possible chance at an education if the basketball team is dropped from the athletic program because all scholarships would be cancelled. Should the timer adjust the time? Why?

Scoring

Six adults served as scorers. Each held at least a master's degree and had experience in social research and/or previous exposure to Kohlberg's work. All scorers attended a 1-day workshop devoted to a discussion of Kohlberg's approach to moral development, an explanation of the scoring procedures, the scoring of practice scenarios, and an analysis of and the scoring of the specific scenarios used in the study.

The six scorers scored each questionnaire using the procedures outlined by Porter and Taylor (1972), who developed the scoring frame of reference for Kohlberg's dilemmas. The sport-specific dilemmas were evaluated using the frame of reference developed by the three judges.

Each subject received a stage score for each sport and nonsport scenario from each of the six scorers; the scores were then converted into a single moral reasoning score for each of the two situations, sport and nonsport. Specifically, a measure of interrater reliability was determined by using Kendall's Coefficient of Concordance to compare the scores given to each subject by various combinations of three scorers. The set of scores with the highest interrater reliability was used; the high and low scores within the set were discarded and the median score was used as the subject's moral reasoning score. The interrater reliability for Kohlberg's dilemmas was $W=.70$; the reliability for the sport-specific situations was $W=.72$.

Individual scores were then combined for the men and women within each age grouping, 16–19 and 20–23, used by Kohlberg to establish his norms for moral reasoning. Thus, eight group scores, one for each sex, age, and situation—sport or nonsport—combination, were available for the analyses. The means for moral reasoning were also compared with the norms established by Kohlberg.

The three-digit (e.g., 312, 296) scores used in the analyses are a combination of the stage (first digit) and the degree of proximity to that stage (last two digits).

RESULTS

Table 1 presents the results for all subjects by age.

TABLE 1
Results of Data Collection on All Subjects by Age

		Kohlberg		Sport-Specific	
		Males $(N=21)$	**Females** $(N=43)$	**Males** $(N=21)$	**Females** $(N=43)$
Age:	16–19	$(N=9)$	$(N=18)$	$(N=9)$	$(N=18)$
	Median	233	300	275	316.5
	Mode	255/233	300	242/325	325
Age:	20–23	$(N=12)$	$(N=25)$	$(N=12)$	$(N=25)$
	Median	271	283	279	317
	Mode	225	308	250/292/308	325
Total/sex					
	Median	233	275	279	321
	Mode	225	300/308	242	325
Total					
	Median	279		304	
	Mode	300		325	

The mean moral reasoning scores for athletes in the 16−19 and the 20−23 age groupings were lower than the norms reported by Kohlberg *(Table 2)*. Although no statistical tests were carried out, athletes in both age groups scored below the mean; athletes in the 20−23 group were considerably below the norm.

TABLE 2
Comparison of Mean Moral Reasoning Scores Reported by Kohlberg[a] and Those of Athletes on Kohlberg's Moral Judgment Questionnaire

	Kohlberg		Hall	
Age	N	Norm	N	Athletes
16−19	43	287.68	27	279.30
			9	247.11 (Male)
			18	295.39 (Female)
20−23	30	324.72	37	274.24
			12	252.00 (Male)
			25	284.92 (Female)

[a]Mean scores only available.

The Wilcoxon Matched-Pairs Signed-Ranks procedures were used to test the difference between the athletes' levels of reasoning on the general moral judgment situations and their levels in the sport-specific dilemmas (Table 3). Only 16 subjects scored higher on the general moral reasoning situations than on the sport dilemmas, a finding opposite that predicted in Hypothesis II. Thus, athletes demonstrated a higher level of moral reasoning in sport situations.

The Mann-Whitney U Test was used to compare the levels of reasoning of male and female athletes in both the general moral reasoning situations and the sport-specific dilemmas (Table 4). Women scored higher in both the sport and nonsport situations.

The results may be summarized as follows:
Hypothesis I: Athletes display a stage of moral development lower than the norm for others in their age group. SUPPORTED (Table 2)
Hypothesis II: Athletes display a lower stage of moral development in sport situations than in nonsport situations. NOT SUPPORTED (Table 3)
Hypothesis III: Female athletes demonstrate higher moral development than male athletes in nonsport situations. SUPPORTED (Table 4)
Hypothesis IV: Female athletes show higher moral development than male athletes in sport-specific situations. SUPPORTED (Table 4)

TABLE 3
Degree of Difference between Athletes' Moral Reasoning
Scores on Kohlberg's Moral Judgment Questionnaire
and the Sport-Specific Dilemmas

Number of Pairs	Number Scoring Higher on Kohlberg's Moral Reasoning Questionnaire	Wilcoxon T	z
59[a]	16	348	4.06*

[a]Six pairs of Moral Reasoning Scores were equal and therefore not considered.
*$p<.003$, one-tailed.

TABLE 4
Summary Results of the Mann-Whitney *U* Test Applied to
Moral Reasoning Scores for Male and Female Athletes

	Moral Reasoning Scores			
	Kohlberg's Questionnaire		Sport-Specific Dilemmas	
Statistic	Male (N=21)	Female (N=43)	Male (N=21)	Female (N=43)
R[a]	492	1643	478	1667
U	239		225	
z	2.76*		3.45**	

[a]R is the sum of ranks for each of the male and female subgroups.
*$p<.0029$, one-tailed.
**$p<.0003$, one-tailed.

DISCUSSION

From a cognitive development perspective there should be no difference between men and women in their levels of moral reasoning. Boyce and Jensen (1978) stated that "the authors know of no theories of moral reasoning that posit a significant sex difference in the development of moral reasoning" (p. 130). Earlier, Hoffman (1975) had concluded:

Despite the theory that males are more internalized, the research gives the edge to neither sex . . . moral judgment research is also inconclusive. The measures tap dimensions advanced by Piaget (1932) and Kohlberg (1958) as reflecting moral reasoning, but they do not pertain to moral internalization and the findings are ambiguous. Though girls obtained higher moral scores in two studies (Porteus & Johnson, 1965; Nelson, Grinder, & Challas, 1967) and boys in one (LeFurgy & Woloshin, 1969), no sex differences have been the rule (Boehm & Nass, 1962; Durkin, 1960; Grinder, 1964; Hebble, 1971; Keasey, 1972; Sullivan, McCullogh, & Stager, 1970; White & Kosier, 1964). (p. 720)

Kohlberg (1968), however, noted that cultural differences can affect the rate of moral development. The hypotheses that athletes reason at lower levels than others in their age groups and that female athletes reason at a higher level than male athletes were based on this assumption. For example, it was assumed not only that sport provided a significant outside influence that would retard the moral development of athletes, but also that the athletic environments for men and women are sufficiently different that they can be considered as two different cultures. By exerting less pressure to win on the women, the athletic environment may provide a positive influence on the moral development of women. Conversely, the need to win may contribute to negative pressures on men. Moreover, the data support such an interpretation; female athletes exhibit a higher level of moral reasoning than the male athletes in both the sport and nonsport settings. Thus, if these findings can be replicated, they could support a move to restructure the athletic environment.

Although it was hypothesized that the moral reasoning in sport would be at a lower level than in nonsport situations, the findings show that athletes used a higher level of reasoning in sport situations. It may be that it is easier to make a high-level moral judgment in sport. The rules in sport may be clearer to athletes and spectators; moreover, the rules in sport are enforced by officials. Unfortunately, this ability to make higher-level moral decisions does not appear to carry over into nonsport settings.

Bales (1960) stated that the transfer of learning will occur "if and when—and only if and when—(1) opportunity offers, (2) a trained individual sees or senses it as an opportunity, and (3) he is disposed to take advantage of the opportunity" (p. 58). However, the fact that athletes were able to display a higher level of reasoning demonstrates that at least they have the capability to reason at the higher level.

Finally, it should be mentioned that the project was, in part, a validation of the sport-specific dilemmas especially prepared for this investigation. Whereas the failure to support the hypothesis that athletes make decisions at a lower level of moral development in sport situations than in nonsport settings can be discussed conceptually, it is also possible that the sport and nonsport situations were not comparable. For example, despite the procedures used the sport situations may have lacked the realism and/or seriousness of the nonsport dilemmas. The seriousness of the timekeeper situation may be less than the life-and-death drama of the cancer patient scenario. After all, sport is only play. On the other hand, the hypothesis that women make decisions at a higher level of moral development than men do was supported in both the sport and nonsport settings. Such a finding provides support for the utility of the sport-specific scenarios.

CONCLUSIONS AND RECOMMENDATIONS

The following conclusions are based on the results of this investigation:

1. The older intercollegiate athletes are less well developed in their levels of general moral reasoning. Specifically, 20–23-year-old athletes appear to be less mature in their levels of reasoning than their nonathletic peers.
2. Intercollegiate athletes are significantly more mature in their reasoning in sport-specific situations than in nonsport dilemmas.
3. Female intercollegiate athletes are more mature in moral reasoning than their male counterparts in both the general and the sport-specific situations.

Further investigations should initially focus on the quality of the sport-specific scenarios. Attention should also be given to a replication and/or explanation for the sex differences in moral reasoning among athletes. Such replications should also attempt to identify those factors in the athletic environment which could contribute to differences between male and female athletes.

REFERENCES

Bales, E. E. (1960). *Democratic educational theory.* New York: Harper & Row.
Boyce, W. D., & Jensen, L. C. (1978). *Moral reasoning: A psychological-philosophical approach.* Lincoln: University of Nebraska Press.
Cartwright, D., & Zander, A. (1968). Motivational processes in groups. Introduction to *Group Dynamics: Research and theory.* New York: Harper & Row.
Duska, R., & Whelan, M. (1975). *Moral development: A guide to Piaget and Kohlberg.* New York: Paulist Press.
Edwards,. H. (1973). *Sociology of sport.* Homewood, IL: Dorsey Press.
Hoffman, L. (1970). Moral development. In P. H. Musser (Ed.), *Carmichael's manual of child psychology* (Vol. 2, 3rd ed., pp. 261–359). New York: Wiley Press.
Hoffman, M. L. (1975). Sex differences in moral internalization and values. *Journal of Personality and Social Psychology, 32,* 720–729.

Kohlberg, L. (1958). *The development of modes of moral thinking in the years ten to sixteen.* Unpublished doctoral dissertation, University of Chicago.

Kohlberg, L. (1968). *The child as a moral philosopher. Psychology Today, 2,* 24–31.

Kohlberg, L. (1969). Stage and sequence: The cognitive developmental approach to socialization. In D. A. Goslin (Ed.), *Handbook of socialization theory* (pp. 347–480). Chicago: Rand McNally.

Lake, D. G., Miles, M. B., & Earle, R. B. (Eds.). (1973). *Measuring behavior: Tools for the assessment of social functioning.* New York: Teachers College Press.

Lilly, A. (1980). *A study of autocratic and democratic leadership styles of selected successful and unsuccessful coaches.* Unpublished manuscript, Texas Woman's University.

Mattox, B. A. (1975). *Getting it together: Dilemmas for the classroom.* San Diego: Pennant Press.

Ogilvie, B. C., & Tutko, T. (1970). Self perception as compared with measured personality of selected male physical educators. In G. S. Kenyon (Ed.), *Contemporary psychology of sport* (pp. 73–77). Washington, DC: International Society of Sport Psychology.

Porter, N., & Taylor, N. (1972). *How to assess the moral reasoning of students.* Toronto: Ontario Institute for Studies in Education.

Sage, G. (1972). *Machiavellianism among college and high school coaches.* Paper presented at the 75th National Physical Education Association for Men.

14

HEROES AND BAD WINNERS:
CULTURAL DIFFERENCES

Lee Vander Velden

Undergraduate men and women, both blacks and whites, identified their favorite (heroes) and least favorite (bad winners) athletes and then described their choices according to the traits they most admired or least admired about them. Both men and women chose male heroes; whites chose white heroes and blacks selected black heroes. Muhammad Ali received the most mentions as a hero, but he was more often mentioned as a bad winner. Overall, heroes are admired for their ability and competitiveness—hard work and hustle— while bad winners are criticized for arrogance. Blacks mention ability more often than whites, who admire competitiveness almost as much. The finding that blacks and whites evaluate sports heroes differently was related to other clashes of culture such as the contrast between styles of play in basketball and the increased taunting and flaunting behavior in organized sports.

A popular theme in sport sociology is that sport is a mirror of society: the characteristics dominant in the larger society are also most evident in sport situations. Not only are personal attributes like achievement motivation emphasized in both settings, but social problems such as sexism and racism are also found in both (Hoch, 1972). Social scientists studying the role of sport in the socialization process have also supported the sport as a mirror concept with their findings that warlike societies have more aggressive games than the relatively peaceful societies (Roberts & Sutton-Smith, 1962; Sipes, 1973). Others have reported that increased participation in organized sport is associated with a more professionalized (achievement-oriented) attitude toward play (e.g., Mantel & Vander Velden, 1974; Webb, 1969). Thus, sports and games are considered to be educational, teaching participants the lessons necessary for their enculturation, enabling them to take their places in society. Finally, social reformers, although critical of sport, seem to acknowledge the sport as a mirror phenomenon by advocating that changes in sport can lead to an improved society (Hoch, 1972; Lapchick, 1975).[1]

[1]Richard Lapchick has been an outspoken leader of the sports boycott of South Africa. His goal has been to ultimately effect changes in South African racial policies by forcing the authorities to first make changes in sport. His optimism for success of the boycott has been based on the significant role that international sport has in the national and international policies of the South African government.

The notion of sport as a mirror of society has also been extended within the socialization process to include the use of athletes as significant others (socializing agents) whose influence helps to shape the attitudes and behavior of those being socialized. Those athletes revered as heroes are considered as role models who embody the best attributes of the larger group or society. A hero is one who repesents or serves as a mirror of a society or culture; specifically, heroes are "mythical or real, alive or dead [individuals] who symbolize by [their] past or present social roles or deeds some important aspect of the values of a culture or subculture" (Theodorson & Theodorson, 1969, p.185). Heroes in America, therefore, could reflect either those traits and characteristics of Americans—some part of our national character—or those attributes salient in one of the several racial and ethnic subcultures in America. In the past, superstars like Babe Ruth, Ty Cobb, Jim Thorpe, Joe Louis, Jack Dempsey, and Jesse Owens in real life and Frank Merriwell in fiction are thought to have symbolized the American character.

The concept of national character suggests a consistency in the values, attitudes, and behaviors which permits distinctions to be made between cultures. Accordingly, Americans could be considered as distinct from the British, the Germans, or the Russians. It also holds that whether or not some innovation is embraced within a society depends on its compatibility with the traditional culture. For example, the Americanization of soccer not only reflects the sport as a mirror argument, but also illustrates the reaction of a society faced with change. The kind of people we are seems to conflict with the rules and traditions of soccer. For many Americans the game is boring with too little scoring; therefore, we changed the offside and substitution rules and added a tie-breaking shootout to satisfy those achievement-oriented Americans who need to know who won, who is best. To soccer fans throughout the world, these changes were heresy; the game was exciting as it was. However, despite the changes, soccer is still not as popular in the United States as it is around the world. The final straw for Americans was that it did not fit the television format.

Kirchner and Kirchner (1973) discussed the Americanization of chess, pointing out that the chess rating system—who is number one, number two, and number three—and the social hoopla now a part of major chess tournaments in this country are American innovations. However, the Kirchners concluded that despite a growing number of chess players in the United States, chess will never become our national game because it clashes with our anti-intellectualism, gregariousness, and pragmatism. Poker, they argued, is more compatible with our character because it prepares us for life—attaining success any way we can, bluffing, lying, and even cheating. It is not the cards you have, but the appearance you give, your style, that counts.

On the other hand, a society with many racial, ethnic, and religious cleavages has identifiable subcultures which may preclude the development of a national character. Gilbert (1972) elaborated on this theme by citing class differences as the reason for the absence of national heroes today. He pointed out that the "idealized image of a sports hero comes from an era when notable . . . sporting feats wre accomplished by members of a small affluent class" (p. 44). Unfortunately, he continued, those sportsmen who held these attitudes are gone; the most popular athletes recently have been the bad boys of sport such as Pete Rose, Reggie Jackson, Jimmy Connors, John McEnroe, Dwight Stones, and former chess champion Bobby Fischer. Yet, those currently in charge of sport still hold to the old view of winners: They are "white, clean, middle-class [athletes, who are] gregarious, charming, and casual" (p.43). They are better athletes. "They never complain about decisions, never bicker about rules; they accept high salaries only as a tribute to their talent" (p. 43).

Michener (1976) commented on the racial differences between the styles of those in charge of sport and those now playing the game.

> Spiking (slamming the ball exuberantly to the ground . . .), like dancing into the payoff zone, is a playground tradition of black players, and Bownes [black assistant coach at Hunter College] is probably correct in believing that it irritates the white establishment, which has outlawed spiking and may soon outlaw the victory dance. The black is free to participate in white sports, but he damned well better conduct himself like a white man. (p. 214)

Novak (1978) has also attributed the increased taunting and flaunting in sport to cultural differences. He added that the increasing numbers of blacks in sport has brought a new style into sport. This disparity, whether it is a consequence of age, race, or class, was highlighted in 1984 when the white custodians of the National Football League reacted to the infusion of this new style, a new culture, into sport by banning individual and group celebrations by players during games.

Arthur Ashe, a black in a white sport, provides further evidence of the changing scene in sport. An outsider because of his color, Ashe was sponsored by Dr. Walter Johnson from Richmond, Virginia, who not only coached his tennis, but also prepared him socially to compete in the white world of tennis (Ashe, 1975). He was taught the traditional standards of sportsmanship: to be forever courteous, never to dispute a call, and never to show emotion. His deportment was more like the traditional tennis behavior than that of many whites such as Connors, McEnroe, and Nastase now playing tennis. Ashe related that it used to upset him when some tennis patrons would tell him how good his manners were and how well he spoke (Michener, 1980). He added that now tennis has become more public; it is no longer a sport solely for the upper classes, and he predicted that before long many more blacks will be playing on the tennis circuit. He warned that these blacks will not look like him, talk like him, or act like him, and they will upset many, many people. Tennis would experience the clash of two cultures.

Whereas the variety of subcultures is one explanation for the dearth of sports heroes today, the media have also received a share of the blame. For example, the rise of television and the muckraking tradition of the press in the 1960s and 1970s exposed the athlete—warts, bad breath, and all—for public inspection. They have created popular athletes and publicized them because they are colorful or make good copy. Hook (1955) commented: "Today, more than ever before, *belief* in 'the hero' is a synthetic product. Whoever controls the microphones and printing presses can make or unmake belief overnight" (p. 10). Rosen (1980) added: "The great lesson about notoriety gleaned from the past decade is that it doesn't matter if you're right or wrong as long as the media knows where to get hold of you" (p. 13). Smith (1976) called these creations "anti-heroes," those who reject the traditional heroic qualities, yet are heroic or at least popular. While they share the spotlight, they are not likely to be imitated or modeled. To Gilbert (1972), they are bad winners.

Do we still have heroes? Is the popularity of arrogant, spoiled-brat athletes a sign that the number of athletes as well as other Americans with heroic qualities has diminished, as symbolized by the lyrics of the once popular song: "Where have you gone, Joe DiMaggio?" (Simon & Garfunkel, 1968). Has the infusion of racial and ethnic minorities precluded the possibility of any national heroes, permitting only local or special interest ones? Do the taunting and humiliation of opponents and the flaunting of success with "We're number one!" chants, gestures, and slogans signify a change in our character or are they merely reflections of the various subcultures now playing prominent roles in organized sport?

Prompted by such considerations I designed this project to: (a) determine whether American men and women have sports heroes; (b) identify those athletes held in highest regard, describing them by those characteristics most admired; (c) identify those athletes not held in high regard, describing them by those traits least admired; (d) ascertain any racial differences in the preferences for any kind of hero; and (e) identify any differences between blacks and whites in the characteristics attributed to those athletes most admired and those least admired.

METHOD

Sample

A specially prepared questionnaire was given to 158 undergraduate men and women, blacks and whites, at the University of Maryland and Bowie State College. Subjects were asked to identify their favorite sports performers, listing those qualities they most admired, and to identify one or more sports performers not liked, listing the qualities of each athlete which put him or her in the not-preferred category. Those athletes admired were subsequently labeled "heroes," even though no attempt was made to ascertain whether they were truly heroic. Conversely, athletes not liked were later labeled "bad winners," the term Gilbert (1972) used to refer to those highly successful athletes whose attitudes and/or behavior, such as arrogance, poor sportsmanship, and mercenary interests, were inconsistent with the traditional view of winners.[2] Each respondent could list two heroes, a current hero and a former hero, and from one to three bad winners. The sex, age, race, and hometown of each respondent was also recorded.

Treatment of Data

Because open-ended questions were used to ascertain the qualities attributed to heroes and bad winners, a wide range of responses had to be reduced to a smaller number of workable categories. Twelve categories were identified: ability, appearance, competitiveness, sportsmanship, individualism, self-confidence, public image, personality, intelligence, tells-it-like-it-is, prejudice, and miscellaneous. For example, an athlete idolized for his hustle and another disliked for his laziness represent opposite sides of the competitiveness coin; a sore loser opposes a noncomplainer on sportsmanship; and arrogance contrasts confidence on the self-confidence dimension. Table 1 shows the characteristics assigned to each of the twelve categories.

RESULTS

Seventy-two percent of the respondents were white, but only 59% of the heroes were white. At the same time, 52% of the bad winners were white. Whites chose white heroes and blacks chose black heroes; both men (97%) and women (87%) chose male heroes. (The latter finding is consistent with

---

[2]Although some might equate bad winners with anti-heroes, the failure to adhere to a strict definition of a hero prevented any contrast between heroes and anti-heroes.

TABLE 1
Characteristics of Heroes and Bad Winners

Trait	Comments	
	Positive	**Negative**
Ability	Skill	Lacks skill
	Great ability	
Appearance	Handsome	Ugly
	Good physique	Fat
Competitiveness	Disciplined	Lazy
	Hard worker	Quitter
	Hustles	Not putting out
Sportsmanship	Does not complain	Sore loser
	Even tempered	Complainer
	Quiet	Blames others
		Dirty player
Individualism	Unselfish	Selfish
	Team oriented	Concern for self, not for the team
Self-confidence	Confidence	Arrogant
	Supreme confidence	Too large an ego
	Enthusiasm	Conceit
Public image	All-American image	Overpaid
	Appeal	Bad for the sport
	Class	Overrated
Personality	Good personality	Bad attitude
	Nice person	Not realistic
	Honesty	Rude
Intelligence	Intelligent player	Lacks intelligence
		Stupid
Tells-it-like-it-is	Outspoken	
	Black and acts like it	
Prejudice	He's white	Symbol of Great White Hope
	He's black	
Miscellaneous	On favorite team	Not on favorite team
	Has other interests outside sport	Not good for the sport
		Too nice

Note. Comments from respondents were combined into 12 categories. Examples of both positive and negative comments given by respondents are listed for each of the categories.

the *Miller Lite Report on American Attitudes Toward Sports,* 1983, in which 98% of the men and 78% of the women chose male heroes.) Among those who crossed over (i.e., whites who named black heroes and blacks who named white heroes; see Table 2), white males were more likely to choose a black hero (30%) while black males were least likely to choose a white hero (13%).

Muhammad Ali generated the most activity, receiving 19 votes as a hero, but 32 votes as a bad winner. Tables 3 and 4 list the other heroes and bad winners. These lists reflect the year (1978) as well as the area (Baltimore–Washington D.C.) in which the survey was made. However, data gathered on heroes and bad winners since then reveal many of the same

TABLE 2
Race of Heroes by Race and Sex of Respondents

Race	Sex	N	White	Black
	Respondents		**Heroes**	
White	Male	71	70%	30%
	Female	36	83%	17%
Black	Male	23	13%	87%
	Female	17	24%	76%

TABLE 3
Athletes Selected as Sports Heroes

Hero	Current Hero	Former Hero	Not Liked	Sport	Sex	Race
	Mentions					
Muhammad Ali	19	4	32	Boxing	M	B
Brooks Robinson	10	6	0	Baseball	M	W
Julius Erving	9	2	2	Basketball	M	B
Bert Jones	6	2	3	Football	M	W
O.J. Simpson	6	3	0	Football	M	B
Bjorn Borg	5	2	0	Tennis	M	W
Jimmy Connors	5	1	16	Tennis	M	W
Arthur Ashe	5	1	0	Tennis	M	B
Joe Namath	3	5	4	Football	M	W
John Unitas	3	4	0	Football	M	W
Willie Mays	0	6	0	Baseball	M	B
John Havlicek	4	1	0	Basketball	M	W
Billie Jean King	4	1	3	Tennis	F	W
Pete Maravich	4	0	0	Basketball	M	W
Chris Evert	3	1	2	Tennis	F	W

Note. Only those mentioned at least four times, either past or present, were included.

TABLE 4
Athletes Selected as Bad Winners

	Mentions					
Bad Winner	Current Hero	Former Hero	Not Liked	Sport	Sex	Race
Muhammad Ali	19	4	32	Boxing	M	B
Reggie Jackson	1	1	26	Baseball	M	B
Jimmy Connors	5	1	16	Tennis	M	W
Ilie Nastase	1	0	12	Tennis	M	W
Rick Barry	1	1	6	Basketball	M	W
George Atkinson	0	0	6	Football	M	B
Conrad Dobler	0	0	6	Football	M	W
Billy Kilmer	2	1	5	Football	M	W
Pete Rose	0	0	5	Baseball	M	W
Roger Staubach	2	2	5	Football	M	W

Note. Only those mentioned at least five times as a bad winner were included.

athletes, such as Julius Erving, Muhammad Ali, Chris Evert Lloyd, Jimmy Connors, Reggie Jackson, and Pete Rose (Vander Velden, 1984). The greatest value of the data is the identification of the qualities admired in those athletes chosen as heroes and the attributes not admired in those named as bad winners. Although the names of particular athletes chosen as heroes or bad winners will change over time, it was assumed that the qualities admired or criticized are more stable. Moreover, the nature of the praise or criticism has been consistent for those athletes also mentioned in later polls or surveys. Julius Erving is still admired for his athletic prowess, and Muhammad Ali and Reggie Jackson continue to be criticized for their arrogance (Vander Velden, 1984).

Heroes are admired for their ability (28%), their competitiveness (17%), personality (11%), public image (11%), self-confidence (8%), and intelligence (8%). As shown in Table 5, black heroes are admired more for their ability (33%) than are whites (25%). Moreover, the intelligence (11%) and appearance (7%) of blacks are admired more than that of whites (6% and 2%, respectively). conversely, the competitiveness of white heroes is admired (24%), but not that of blacks (7%).

Contrasting the traits attributed to heroes by blacks and whites supports the racial differences in the importance of ability already reported. As shown in Table 6, blacks admire ability (35%) more than whites (26%) do, whereas whites appreciate competitiveness (20%)—hard work and hustle— more than do blacks (9%). Whites value intelligence (9%) and unselfishness (6%) more than do blacks (5% and 1%). Those whites who chose black

TABLE 5
Positive Attributes of White and Black Heroes

	Heroes	
Trait	White (N=208)[a]	Black (N=138)[b]
Ability	25%	33%
Competitiveness	24%	7%
Public image	10%	13%
Personality	11%	12%
Self-confidence	8%	9%
Intelligence	6%	11%
Appearance	2%	7%

[a]Responses given to white heroes, 198 by whites and 10 by blacks.
[b]Responses given to black heroes, 68 by whites and 70 by blacks.

TABLE 6
Positive Attributes of Heroes Identified by Whites and Blacks

	Respondents	
Trait	White (N=266)[a]	Black (N=80)[b]
Ability	26%	35%
Competitiveness	20%	9%
Public image	10%	14%
Personality	12%	10%
Intelligence	9%	5%
Appearance	1%	12%
Individualism	6%	1%

[a]Responses given to white and black heroes by whites.
[b]Responses given to white and black heroes by blacks.

heroes may respect them for their intelligence; specifically, white males were most likely to have black heroes and were also apt to respect intelligence. The appearance of an athlete was more important to blacks (12%).

Bad winners are criticized for their arrogance (33%), poor sportsmanship (19%), bad public image (12%), and selfishness (11%). As shown in Table 7, black bad winners are rejected for their large egos (40%) more than whites (27%); white bad winners are poor sports (24%)—complainers and sore losers—as opposed to blacks (15%). In two other categories black and white bad winners were similar, selfish and with a bad public image. In the miscellaneous category, whites (10%) criticized athletes like Roger Staubach, formerly of the Dallas Cowboys, for being "too nice" or "on the wrong team," the Cowboys.

Both blacks and whites consider arrogance a negative for any athlete, but they differ on other traits. As shown in Table 8, white descriptions of bad winners mention arrogance, poor sportsmanship (23%), and selfishness (11%), as opposed to black descriptions of arrogance, bad public image (20%)—overpaid or overrated—and bad personality (18%).

TABLE 7
Negative Attributes of White and Black Bad Winners

	Bad Winners	
Trait	White (N=157)[a]	Black (N=140)[b]
Self-confidence	27%	40%
Sportsmanship	24%	15%
Public image	13%	12%
Individualism	9%	12%
Miscellaneous	10%	4%

[a]Responses given to white bad winners, 127 by whites and 30 by blacks.
[b]Responses given to black bad winners, 121 by whites and 19 by blacks.

TABLE 8
Negative Attributes of Bad Winners
Identified by Whites and Blacks

	Respondents	
Trait	White (N=248)[a]	Black (N=49)[b]
Self-confidence	33%	37%
Sportsmanship	23%	4%
Public image	11%	20%
Personality	3%	18%
Individualism	11%	6%
Miscellaneous	8%	2%

[a]Responses given to white and black bad winners by whites.
[b]Responses given to white and black bad winners by blacks.

DISCUSSION

The results are consistent with those reported by Smith (1976), who studied Canadian heroes in one (if not the only) other project seeking to link admired characteristics with specific individuals. Just as the Canadians chose Canadian heroes, Americans chose Americans; Muhammad Ali was the only athlete named in both studies. Although Ali is perhaps the only athlete named with the potential to be classified as truly heroic, he received more votes as a bad winner than as a hero. Both Canadian and American respondents rated athletic prowess as the primary attraction of heroes; personality was not a factor in either country.

Although Smith found that both men and women chose male heroes, two Canadian women, Nancy Greene (skier) and Karen Magnusson (skater), were listed third and fourth, respectively, in the list of popular athletes. Conversely, in my study the most popular American women were tennis players, Billie Jean King and Chris Evert Lloyd, who were ranked 13th and 15th. Only 13% of the American women identified a female hero. The tendency of men and women to choose male heroes has been confirmed by my subsequent work (Vander Velden, 1984) as well as by Balswick and Ignoldsby (1982) and the *Miller Lite Report* (1983). However, in my most recent survey, Chris Evert Lloyd and Martina Navratilova ranked 3 and 4, respectively, among those athletes most admired (Vander Velden, 1984).

A final similarity with Smith's findings was the reluctance of adults to admit to having a sports hero. Only 15% of the American sample considered their favorite athletes as heroes; most (58%) referred to them as favorite players. Whether this finding is evidence of the absence of sports heroes or only the reactions of young adults too embarrassed to admit having sports heroes is conjecture. The data, however, do support Gilbert's (1972) observation that many successful American athletes do not measure up to the heroic image of good American winners like Julius Erving or Brooks Robinson. Gilbert (1972) labeled Billie Jean King (tennis), Bobby Fischer (chess), Mark Spitz (swimming), Vince Mathews (track), and Dan Gable (wrestling) as bad winners. They were rude, spoiled, arrogant athletes who insulted officials, argued with teammates, alibied for their losses, and were disrespectful of the flag. Reggie Jackson, Jimmy Connors, Ilie Nastase, Pete Rose, and John McEnroe follow the same pattern. Successful and highly publicized, they are bad winners who are not liked (Vander Velden, 1984). Others, like Billie Jean King and Muhammad Ali, were both idolized and condemned. The negative reaction to Mary Decker's behavior following her unfortunate fall during the 1,500-meter race in the 1984 Olympic Games is another illustration of the disappointment Americans have in the behavior of their athletes.

The finding that blacks and whites do not value the same characteristics in their heroes is consistent with several other observations of blacks and whites in sport, including the different styles of play within basketball and the varying modes of behavior throughout all sports (Kochman, 1981). Such differences also contribute to the preclusion of having any national sports heroes. For example, during a recent Philadelphia 76ers – Washington Bullets basketball game, superstar Julius Erving (Dr. J) dribbled the ball under the basket, leaped high above the rim, and executed a spectacular slam dunk with the ball hitting the floor before the shooter did. The crowd erupted enthusiastically with most white fans applauding while many blacks, jumping to their feet, slapped hands in "high five" gestures of glee. Although everyone, black as well as white, acknowledges the athletic prowess of Dr. J., a well-liked, respected individual—number three on the list of heroes— the responses of white fans were muted in comparison to those of the blacks. Why the difference?

The data suggest why the black fans were so demonstrative while the whites merely clapped their appreciation for the slam dunk. Each was looking for something different: basketball was in the eyes of the beholders. The results suggest that both blacks and whites appreciate ability, but it means more to blacks; moreover, blacks appreciate a stylistic performance— making a difficult task look easy—more than whites, who have more respect for hard work, hustle, discipline, and teamwork. Such cultural differences are also revealed in comparisons between the city game and the rural game in basketball. The city game is the black game; the rural game, the white game. DuPree (1978) explained:

> The city game is a smooth, free flowing, coming together of slam dunks, soft jumpers, and spin moves. Style and flair is the most important thing. If it looks good and feels good and the fans like it, then do it . . . the emphasis is on the individual. The noncity game is a game of screens and picks, backdoor plays, and people taking the charging foul. It is a world of the good percentage shot; diving on the floor for loose balls, and the sure pass. "Don't be flashy, just be good" is the game's motto. It is often dull, usually efficient. (pp. E1, E6)

Whereas some deny that the contrast in games is a racial difference, citing blacks who play the rural game and whites who play the city game, many sports observers refer to the contrast as the black game versus the white game. Kochman (1981) pointed out that blacks do not like white performers getting credit for reproducing the styles that individual black performers have developed. For example, a black colleague commented that blacks have ambivalent feelings toward Larry Bird, a white baskeball star who plays like a black (J. Calloway, personal communication, June 4, 1984).

George Raveling, one of the few black basketball coaches at an NCAA Division I school (USC), attributed the contrasts in style to varying training regimes and opportunity (Attner, 1978). Most blacks, he pointed out, learn their skills on city playgrounds while whites learn from books, coaches, and summer clinics. Furthermore, basketball is more important to blacks who have few options to achieve success. They are hungrier than suburban whites. For the black to survive, he has to be better. Raveling added that the kids in the suburbs tend to practice alone and with their good coaching they become fundamentally sound players. Outsiders to the white game find it dull, boring. Conversely, those not familiar with the stylish city game criticize the individual showmanship, adding that playing as a team is the only way to play basketball.

Kochman (1981) pointed out that differences in style between the black and the white cultures are evident in *all* aspects of life: "Black style is more self-conscious, more expressive, more expansive, more colorful, more intense, more assertive, more aggressive, and more focused on the individual than is the style of the larger society of which blacks are part." (p. 130) He illustrated such differences in dress, language, the interaction between the sexes, the classroom, and sports. Concerning the black and white styles of play in sport, he commented that the differences in style are not easily resolved because they are based on cultural attitudes—"attitudes not only about expressiveness, but also about competition, winning and losing, and even (perhaps especially) about the nature and definition of individuality within the context of team play" (p. 14). He added that "whites view competitive sports in terms of winning and losing" (p. 148); blacks, on the other hand, see sports competition as dominating the field, being the best, and performing in a show. He concluded that the failure to recognize differences in style contributes to the negative feelings between blacks and whites. For example, whites view many of the moves blacks make as unnecessary and inefficient within the context of winning and losing. Individual style conflicts with the team concept; blacks are often criticized for not being team players. The differences in the characteristics attributed to white and black heroes and bad winners from blacks and whites seem to support the distinct styles outlined by Kochman.

The data also support Novak's (1978) contention that the flaunting and taunting in sport stem from such cultural differences: "Skin color doesn't make much difference in human affairs, but culture does. The rising number of ghetto athletes has brought into our sports a new culture, a new temperature, a new style. So pervasive has this style become among the young that nearly all athletes now participate in it." (p. E3) Novak says that his white culture tells him to ignore the flash and grandstanding play in sport, to work hard, to learn the basic skills, and to concentrate on teamwork. However, he concluded that modern professional sport is the clash of two cultures. One says to be skillful, but not to humiliate your opponent; the other requires winning, but with a personal style, strutting before the world, above the loser. He contended that television fuels such personal duels between players by concentrating on individual matchups, rather than on the game itself. Ultimately, when those who are humiliated try to get even, the result is violence. Recent examples of retaliation to the taunts and flaunts of opponents include a number of offensive linemen (football) who started fights with Mark Gastineau (New York Jets), who performs a special dance after "sacking" a quarterback. The linemen, upset over not being able to block Gastineau, perceived his dance as a taunt and tried to get even. Similarly, several Dallas Cowboys players, provoked by a victory dance performed by a few Washington players, ran into the circle of Redskins players in an attempt to disrupt the rite. Only quick action by the referees prevented a bench-clearing brawl. To whites, showboating and gloating over the demise of an opponent is poor sportsmanship (Kochman, 1981). Blacks do not agree; it is part of the show. Recall that next to arrogance, whites were more likely (23%) to criticize bad winners for sportsmanship than were blacks (4%) (see Table 8).

Acknowledging his amateur anthropological skills, Novak declined to speculate on the sources of these behaviors but others have suggested that the increasing number of blacks in professional sport has changed sport. This was the gist of Arthur Ashe's warning to the tennis world.

What is not different from past attitudes, however, is the importance of humility. Both blacks and whites disapprove of the cocky, arrogant athlete. Whites, especially, were critical of conceited black bad winners, a result, in part, of the negative reaction to Muhammad Ali, the most outspoken of all athletes. Reggie Jackson, another bad winner, was criticized for the same fault. The white norms of modesty and understatement are evident in the praise for Mike Peterson, "The Greatest Athlete in Yates Center, Kansas" (Johnson, 1971); Peterson was idolized not only for his athletic prowess, but also for his humility. "Mike is modest, very modest. In Yates Center the trait seems almost requisite to his prowess at sports; to hear people talk, the lacking of the BIG HEAD is perhaps only behind godliness and cleanliness in the book of virtues." (p. 26)

Kochman (1981) explained that while blacks admire a stylistic performance, the performer must be successful, otherwise the "audience will regard a performer as having laid claim to greater expertise than he can demonstrate" (p. 139). Dr. J. is acceptable as long as the ball goes in the basket. Perhaps Reggie Jackson—a bad winner—best illustrates this pattern. To whites he simply talks too much, but to blacks his talk is not supported; his lifetime batting average is less than .250 and he has a reputation as a poor outfielder. To both groups, he is arrogant. Overall, those most admired were the highly skilled athletes who, like Mike Peterson, kept their mouths shut; they include Dr. J., Brooks Robinson, O. J. Simpson, Bert Jones, and John Unitas.

CONCLUSIONS

Although American men and women have favorite sports performers, they are reluctant to refer to them as heroes or heroines. Whether this is evidence that we no longer have heroes or merely that young adults are not willing to admit to having heroes is conjecture. Moreover, media attention does not automatically lead to admiration; the characteristics of the individual were most important in the selection of most and least preferred athletes. On the other hand, the gatekeeping function of the media may regulate which image of an athlete the public gets to see (Cramer, Walker, & Rado, 1980). For example, media summaries of John McEnroe's tennis matches shown on the evening news or on sports programs highlight his disagreements with umpires, photgraphers, and fans at the expense of his tennis prowess. The athletes most favored are admired for their athletic prowess and their humility. Those not admired are most often criticized for arrogance.

The data also support the cultural differences between blacks and whites. For example, whites appreciate hard work, hustle, and teamwork in their heroes and criticize the showmanship of the stylistic performances of blacks as poor sportsmanship. Finally, cultural differences between blacks and whites were suggested as a possible cause for some of the changes in sport such as the increase in taunting and flaunting behaviors.

As the athletic ranks are increasingly filled by those from later generations and from different subcultures, sport will no longer be as it was when Novak, Gilbert, and I grew up. Whereas we experience surprise, discomfort, and even disgust over these deviations, our children accept them as the norms. They chant "We're number one!" slap hands and shout "in your face" after successful one-on-one encounters. Is it for the better? Perhaps we should heed Gilbert's (1972) blunt advice: "If we want to continue to admire athletic winners we had better learn to admire the virtues of people like Fischer, Spitz, King, and Gable. Sports having been opened to all classes . . . Winners will probably be increasingly temperamental and personally aggravating." (p. 44) We will also have to pay attention to Kochman's (1981) caveat that the failure to recognize the differences in style will contribute to negative feelings between blacks and whites.

ACKNOWLEDGMENT

This project was supported by the Computer Science Center, University of Maryland, College Park, Maryland.

REFERENCES

Ashe, A. (1975). *Portrait in motion.* Boston: Houghton Mifflin.

Attner, P. (1978, February 11). Layup vs slam-dunk: Two ways to the hoop. *The Washington Post,* pp. C1, C2.

Balswick, J., & Ignoldsby, B. (1982). Heroes and heroines among American adolescents. *Sex Roles, 8,* 243–249.

Cramer, J., Walker, J., & Rado, L. (1980). Athletic heroes and heroines: The role of the press in their creation. *Journal of Sport Behavior, 3–4,* 175–185.

DuPree, D. (1978, February 8). Country, city worlds apart in basketball. *The Washington Post,* pp. E1, E6.

Gilbert, B. (1972, December 25). Gleanings from a troubled time. *Sports Illustrated,* pp. 34–38, 43–46.

Hoch, P. (1972). *Rip off the big game.* Garden City, NY: Anchor Books.

Hook, P. (1955). *The hero in history.* Boston: Beacon Press.

Johnson, W.O. (1971, August 9). The greatest athlete in Yates Center, Kansas. *Sports Illustrated,* pp. 26–31.

Kirchner, E., & Kirchner, M. (1973, July). Why chess? *Intellectual Digest,* pp. 66–67.

Kochman, T. (1981. *Black and white styles in conflict.* Chicago: University of Chicago Press.

Lapchick, R. E. (1975). *The politics of race and international sport: The case of South Africa.* Westport, CT: Greenwood Press.

Mantel, R., & Vander Velden, L. (1974). The relationship between the professionalization of attitude toward play of preadolescent boys and participation in organized sport. In G. S. Sage (Ed.), *Sport and American society: Selected readings* (2nd ed., pp. 172–178). Reading, MA: Addison-Wesley.

Michener, J. (1976). *Sports in America.* Greenwich, CT: Fawcett Publications.

Michener, J. (Interviewer), & Greenspan, B. (Director). (1980). *The Black athlete* [Casette]. Santa Monica, CA: Cappy Productions.

Miller Lite report on American attitudes toward sports. (1983). Milwaukee: Miller Brewing Company.

Novak, M. (1978, January 29). Flaunts, taunts, and violence in sports. *The Washington Star,* p. E3.

Roberts, J.M., & Sutton-Smith, B. (1962). Child training and game involvement. *Ethnology, 1,* 166–185.

Rosen, R.D. (1980, November 15). Epping. *The New Republic,* pp. 13–14.

Simon, P., & Garfunkel, A. (1968). Mrs. Robinson. Song 3 on Side 2 of *Bookends* (KCS 9529). Columbia Records/CBS.

Sipes, R. (1973, February). War, sports and aggression: An empirical test of two rival theories. *American Anthropologist, 75,* 64–87.

Smith, G. (1976, December). An examination of the phenomenon of sports hero worship. *Canadian Journal of Applied Sport Sciences, 1,* 259–270.

Theodorson, G.A., & Theodorson, A. G. (1969). *Modern dictionary of sociology.* New York: Thomas Y. Crowell.

Vander Velden, L. (1984). [Heroes and bad winners in North America]. Unpublished raw data.

Webb, H. (1969). Professionalization of attitudes toward play among adolescents. In G.S. Kenyon (Ed.), *Aspects of contemporary sport sociology,* (pp. 163–187). Chicago: The Athletic Institute.

15

COMPARISONS OF LEADER STYLE, BEHAVIORS, AND EFFECTIVENESS OF MALE AND FEMALE COACHES

Judith C. Young

This investigation examined the leadership characteristics and effectiveness of male and female coaches of high school basketball teams. Eighty-nine varsity basketball coaches completed established instruments to determine leadership style and behaviors. At least five players from each team also completed a questionnaire concerning coaching behaviors. Career and season winning percentages were used as measures of team effectiveness. One-way analysis of variance procedures were used to compare the leadership characteristics of male and female coaches. Multiple regression procedures were employed to examine the relationships between various leader characteristics and team effectiveness of teams coached by males and females, respectively. Results indicated that male and female coaches display different leader characteristics. However, teams coached by male and female coaches are equally effective in terms of win-loss records.

The popular image of a coach is that of a gruff, authoritarian, male taskmaster with the single focus of winning ball games. The athletic world has been described as a quasi-military environment in which players are expected to perform as foot soldiers under a field commander. The success of well-known professional and collegiate coaches has inspired coaches and would-be coaches to imitate their presumed autocratic coaching styles. Moreover, the notion that coaches are responsible for the success of their teams is as widely accepted as is the assumption that this accountability for winning ball games permits or requires the exercise of firm control. The number of high school, college, and professional coaches hired and fired each season is testimony to the belief that the coach is primarily responsible for the success of the team. Those who have studied coaches acknowledge that one seldom finds a coach with more than 5 years experience who has a losing record (Tharp & Gallimore, 1976; Vander Velden, 1971). The high visibility of interscholastic sport with the accompanying emphasis on producing winners has eliminated almost all losing coaches.

Despite beliefs that a coach is responsible for the play of the team, there is very little specific information available about coaching styles and behaviors. Small group studies indicate that factors such as cohesiveness, status consensus, and task ability are related to successful team performance.

However, the coaching characteristics and behaviors that contribute to the development of the factors associated with winning teams are not clear. It is ironic that individuals are appointed to such highly accountable positions and released whenever they fail to turn out winning teams when there are few specifics in the job description for coaches. The fact that coaching success is defined so simply in terms of wins and losses suggests that coaches must have extensive control over everything that contributes to winning, from player selection and skill training to team cohesiveness.

Complicating any understanding of coaching, generally a masculine endeavor, is the increasing number of women now involved in organized sport both as coaches and as players. Whereas the prototype coach has been described as highly masculine and one who will make "men out of boys," the presence of female athletes and coaches challenges these assumptions. Now that coaches may sometimes be female, athletics may also have some influence on making women out of girls.

Since Title IX of the Education Amendments Act of 1972 was implemented in 1975, the growth of athletic participation and competition by females has been unprecedented. Administrators and policymakers have recognized the need to provide resources to improve the number and quality of athletic opportunities for females at all levels of participation. Following a more than sixfold increase in female participation at the high school level, the demand for qualified coaches for females now exceeds the supply in most areas. However, little systematic investigation of the coaching styles and behaviors of the female coaches or coaches of female teams has been undertaken.

Historically, women have not been encouraged or prepared for full participation in the world of competitive athletics. In fact, women may have learned not be be athletic (Walum, 1977). Other researchers have found differences between the sexes in attitudes toward sports involvement. While involvement in sport by men is viewed positively by men and women, women have experienced role conflict and ambivalence about their participation in sport, especially those in team sports (Sage & Loudermilk, 1979; Snyder and Kivlin, 1977).

The ambivalence of female athletes may contribute to a distinctive pattern of leadership functions for women in athletics. Previous descriptive research as well as prevailing stereotypes suggest that socialization patterns encourage and develop leadership functions in males to a greater extent than in females (Maccoby & Jacklin, 1974; Walum, 1977). Social-psychological descriptions of leaders in management settings have been highly correlated with similar descriptions of men generally, but not correlated with comparable descriptions of women generally (Bardwick, 1971; Schein, 1973). Most of the theoretical models of leadership have been tested in settings with male leaders and male or mixed-sex groups. In addition, some research has addressed sex differences in leader style and behavior in organizational settings. Chapman (1975) indicated no differences in leader style of men and women, but suggested that differences in behavior that exist might be due to differential socialization and compliance with societal norms. Keane and Cheffers (1978) also found greater differences in leader style within the sexes than between the sexes in a small group of 10 coaches. Bird (1977) studying women and Vander Velden (1971) studying men reported that coaches are generally relations oriented. Keane and Cheffers, however, found that male and female coaches were more task oriented. Additional implications concerning sex differences of leaders may be found in research concerning experimenter effects in motor performance studies. These studies (Rikli, 1974; Rosenthal, 1966; Singer & Llewellyn, 1973; Stevenson, 1964) indicate that male experimenters and opposite-sex experimenters elicit better performances in certain subjects performing certain tasks.

Early attempts to explain leader effectiveness in terms of leader traits were not fruitful but provided the basis for the examination of the actual behaviors exhibited by individuals attempting to influence group behavior in different situations (Stogdill, 1974). The work of Fiedler (1967, 1973) and House (1971) represents situational leadership approaches in which the leader style or behavior interacts with situational factors. Fiedler emphasized leader style as a stable factor representing a motivational structure which limits the range of behaviors a leader uses. The leader operates within this structure to manage contingencies such as task structure, group atmosphere, and leader power, which in turn provide the basis for determining the effectiveness of the group and the leader.

Fiedler classified situations based on (1) interpersonal relations of the group members, (2) task structure, and (3) power of the leader. Combination of these factors provided eight ideal types of situation, ranging from a highly favorable one with positive group relations, high task structure, and high leader power to a highly unfavorable one with poor group relations, low task structure, and low leader power. Extensive research undertaken in military and industrial settings indicated that in highly favorable situations or highly unfavorable situations, groups with leaders whose styles were more task oriented were more effective, while in situations of moderate favorability, groups with leaders who were more interpersonal relations oriented exhibited greater effectiveness. The application of Fiedler's model to a sport setting suggests that, for example, effective basketball coaches should have a task-oriented leader style because, typically, basketball teams represent a favorable situation with high task structure, high leader power, and positive group relations (Fiedler, 1967).

In a sport setting Bird (1977) found that highly skilled players perceived coaches as task oriented if the team was unsuccessful, but regarded them as relations oriented if the team was successful. The perceptions of low-skilled players were the opposite, task-oriented if the team was successful and relations oriented if the team was not successful. Success in the studies involving sport has been determined by win-loss records (Bird, 1977; Vander Velden, 1971). House (1971), in contrast, emphasized the management of "paths" to "goals" through particular leader behaviors which could be elicited without limitation of the personality-related style factor. Both approaches predict specific relationships between situational factors, leader style or behaviors, and group effectiveness. The House approach views the leader as facilitator responding to follower needs.

House designated the role of the leader in promoting performance and follower satisfaction as providing reinforcements otherwise not available in the task environment. He selected 4 of the 12 behavior factors identified by Stogdill (1974) for use in his investigation as particularly relevant to sport settings. They included initiating structure, consideration, toleration of freedom, and production emphasis. The selective use of these behaviors by the leader promotes group success. For example, highly complex or confusing situations seem to require that the leader use initiating structure behaviors to clarify tasks for group members, and thus increase group effectiveness.

Previous researchers explored style and behavior independently. Fiedler concentrated his efforts on relating the underlying motive structure of the leader to situational variables, while the path-goal approach of House suggests that leader behaviors are the important intervening variables in determining and influencing follower motivation. Most previous studies focused on either male coaches and male athletes, or female coaches and female athletes.

Specifically, the purpose of this investigation was to examine the leadership style and behaviors of male and female coaches of male and female teams in order to address the following questions:

1. Do male and female coaches have the same leader style?
2. Do male and female coaches exhibit the same levels of structuring, consideration, toleration of freedom, and production emphasis behaviors?
3. Are female teams more effective when coached by a man or a woman?
4. Does knowledge of leader characteristics improve the prediction of team success?

METHODS

Subjects

The sample for this study included the coaches of 89 varsity basketball teams representing high schools in two large suburban school districts in the mid-Atlantic area of the country. Forty-four of the teams were boys' teams coached by men. The remaining were girls' teams. Twenty-six of the coaches of the girls' teams were women and 19 were men. All coaches were teachers, and all but three taught in the school where he or she was coaching.

Instruments

The Least-Preferred Co-worker (LPC) Scale was used to measure leader style. This instrument was developed by Fiedler (1967) and consists of an 18-item semantic differential checklist. Subjects were asked to evaluate their least-preferred co-worker on a series of bipolar adjectives. Scores for each item ranged from one to eight, providing a possible range of 18–144 as the leader style score. The higher the score, the more relations oriented the subject. Fiedler designated "high LPC" (relations oriented) as greater than 73.8 and "low LPC" (task oriented) as less than 39.6. The LPC scale has been widely used in a variety of leadership studies and group settings. Fiedler reported high reliablility and validity for the scale if used with experienced and mature leaders. The test-retest reliability in the present study was .83, suggesting stability over the season of play of the leader responses.

Leader behaviors were measured with the Leader Behavior Description Questionnaire (LBDQ-XII). This questionnaire was the result of a body of research known as the Ohio State Leadership Studies (Stogdill, 1963) and is based on extensive factor analytic work and field testing. The results of this work were the basis for identifying 12 subcategories of leader behavior. The 4 categories of behavior selected for this study were based on House's selection in formulating the path-goal model. They are initiating structure, consideration, toleration of freedom, and production emphasis. Initiating structure behaviors are those leader activities that define tasks, roles, orga-nize work, and generally provide patterns that assist or direct followers in task accomplishment. Consideration behaviors are those that support fol-lower effort, show appreciation, and encourage or reward the followers. Toleration of freedom behaviors allow follower decision making, latitude in method of task completion, and limited imposition of leader supervision. Production emphasis behaviors are the ways in which the leader makes demands for performance, output or task accomplishment.

Stogdill (1974) reported reliability coefficients for the four subscales—initiation of structure, consideration, toleration of freedom, and production emphasis—ranging from .76 to .81. Each subscale was represented in the questionnaire by 10 items. Subjects assigned each item a score of 1–5, depending on the degree of agreement with the statement felt by the subject. This provided a possible range of 10–50 for each subscale (Halpin, 1957). In the present investigation, the wording of some items was changed slightly to make the terminology sport-specific; for example, performance was used instead of production. The test-retest reliability of the subjects' responses in the present study was .91.

Procedure

Each coach completed the LPC and the modified LBDQ-XII prior to a preseason interview. After the season the coaches completed these scales again. Also, following the season, at least five of the players from each team completed the modified LBDQ-XII. Thus, the behaviors coaches said they used were compared with the players' perceptions of their behaviors.

Interviews with each coach provided information concerning their perceived leader style, preferred behaviors, beliefs and expectations about sex differences in athletics, generally, and their own coaching, specifically. In addition, demographic data including age, playing experience, coaching experiences, and career coaching records were recorded. Season winning percentages were also computed for each team.

RESULTS

Leader Style

The results indicate significant differences in the leader styles of male and female coaches. Table 1 shows the means and standard deviations and the results of the analysis of variance for leader style.

TABLE 1
Leader Style Comparisons

Coach Groups[a]	$\bar{X}$	SD
Boy ($N = 44$)	70.84	18.01
Girl ($N = 26$)	59.00	16.27
Gmal ($N = 19$)	77.79	16.83
	$F = 2.06^{**}$	
Contrasts		
Boy to Gmal	$t = 1.47^*$	
Boy to Girl	$t = 2.77^{**}$	
Girl to Gmal	$t = 3.77^{***}$	

[a]Boy refers to male coaches of boys. Girl refers to female coaches of girls. Gmal refers to male coaches of girls.
$^*p<.05.$
$^{**}p<.01.$
$^{***}p<.001.$

Coaches of boys ($\overline{X} = 70.84$) were significantly less task oriented than female coaches of girls ($\overline{X} = 59.0$). Contrasts of male coaches of girls to male coaches of boys, and male coaches of girls to female coaches of girls were also significant. Interestingly, the least task-oriented coaches were males who coached girls ($\overline{X} = 77.79$) The mean of 59.0 for the female coaches is the only mean in the "low" category (< 64.0) designated by Fiedler, while the male score of 77.79 is in the "high" range ($> 73.$) as described by Fiedler. The coaches' descriptions of their own leader styles indicated that 27 of the 44 men coaching boys considered themselves task oriented, while 17 of the 45 coaches working with girls designated themselves as task oriented; only 10 of the 17 were females. Table 2 displays the self-description of leader style of the coaches.

Leader Behaviors

Leader behaviors for each coach are presented as the mean of the responses of all team members who rated their coaches. Each coach has a mean score for each subscale of the LBDQ-XII. There was positive correlation between the coach scores and the players' scores on each leader behavior subscale. These correlations between coaches' and players' scores on the LBDQ-VII ranged from .68 to .89. Table 3 gives the means and standard deviations for structuring, consideration, toleration of freedom, and production emphasis behaviors. Female coaches scored higher in structuring behaviors ($\overline{X} = 45.15$) than did males ($\overline{X} = 40.23$). Even though male coaches did not use more structuring behaviors than women, they scored higher than female coaches in production emphasis behaviors.

Consideration behavior scores were lower than structuring and production emphasis behavior scores for all groups. Men coaching girls showed the highest consideration scores ($\overline{X} = 41.21$), followed by female coaches ($\overline{X}$

TABLE 2
Coach Self-Descriptions of Leader Styles

Coach Groups[a]	Task-Oriented	Relations-Oriented	Total
Boy	$N = 27$	17	44
Girl	$N = 10$	16	26
Gmal	$N = 7$	12	19
	44	45	89
	$\chi^2 = 7.88^*$		

[a]See Table 1 Note a.
$^*p < .05$.

TABLE 3
Leader Behavior Comparisons

| Leader Behaviors | Coach Groups[a] | | | | | | |
| | Boy (n = 44) | | Girl (n = 26) | | Gmal (n = 19) | | |
	$\bar{X}$	SD	$\bar{X}$	SD	$\bar{X}$	SD	F
Structuring	42.64	3.73	45.15	3.40	44.32	3.51	4.33*
Toleration of freedom	29.71	5.50	31.62	4.73	32.26	4.70	2.10
Consideration	36.80	3.65	37.04	2.86	41.21	5.07	9.72**
Production emphasis	43.96	3.10	40.23	4.43	39.11	4.01	14.62**

[a]See Table 1 Note a.
*p < .05.
**p < .001.

TABLE 4
Leader Behavior Contrasts (t Values)

| Coach Groups[a] | Leader Behaviors | | | |
	Structure	Toleration of Freedom	Consideration	Production Emphasis
Boy to Gmal	−1.70	−1.82	−4.23*	4.70**
Boy to Girl	−2.83	−1.51	−0.26	4.04**
Girl to Gmal	−0.77	0.42	3.64*	−1.00

[a]See Table 1 Note a.
*p = .01.
**p = .001.

= 37.04), with male coaches of boys showing the lowest scores ($\bar{X}$ = 36.80). Toleration of freedom scores were also lower than initiating structure scores for all coaches, but there were no significant differences among the groups (see Table 4).

Coach Effectiveness

No significant differences were found in season winning percentage of male and female coaches for any of the three coach groups (see Table 5). These findings suggest that although male and female coaches differed in certain characteristics, these differences did not influence their effectiveness as measured by win−loss records.

Multiple regression techniques were employed to determine the relationship between leader characteristics and the win−loss records of the teams in each coaching group. Table 6 contains the summary of the multiple regression analysis for each coaching group.

The analysis to identify those coach variables that account for team success indicated that structuring and consideration behaviors were the best predictors of success among female teams. However, these variables were not significant predictors for male teams. This finding suggested that male and female coaches use different coaching behaviors, depending on the sex of the players.

TABLE 5
Means and Standard Deviations for Seasonal Coaching Success by Coach Sex and Team Sex

	Winning Percentage[b]	
Coach Groups[a]	$\overline{X}$	SD
Boy ($N = 44$)	.519	.221
Girl ($N = 26$)	.474	.229
Gmal ($N = 19$)	.537	.242
All coaches	.510	.227

$$F = .493*$$

[a]See Table 1 Note a.
[b]Percentage of games won.
*No significant differences among means.

TABLE 6
Multiple Regression of Leader Behaviors and Leader Styles as Predictors of Variance in Seasonal Winning Percentage

Coach Groups[a]	N	Multiple R	R^2	SE	F
Boy	44	.544	.296	.207	2.85
Girl	26	.756	.572	.214	8.69
Gmal	19	.827	.684	.205	4.34*
All coaches	89	.496	.246	.203	3.58*

[a]See Table 1 Note a.
*$p = .05$.

DISCUSSION

The results of this investigation do not support the conclusions of Keane and Cheffers (1978) who found no differences in leader style between male and female coaches. Further, role definitions for females suggesting that female leaders might reflect the more nurturant, less dominant, less aggressive, and more expressive characteristics traditionally attributed to women were not supported. Rather, the data support previous findings indicating that successful female leaders and skilled athletes exhibit characteristics commonly expected of men. Although these women score higher in masculinity, they are not lower in femininity (Basow, 1981; Kanter 1975). These findings also support the conclusion that social-psychological gender should not be regarded as a bipolar phenomenon (Harris, 1980; Spence, Helmreich, & Stagg, 1975). Because the primary role models for women who coach are men, and because perceptions about coaching are based on what male coaches demonstrate, it is reasonable to expect female coaches to develop attitudes and approaches to coaching that are similar to those of men. Moreover, these female coaches may subconsciously emphasize what they perceive to be significant factors in effective coaching.

Since there are fewer female coaches, they may reflect a specific, unique leader style. They may also feel a need to compensate for lack of experience in highly competitive situations by adopting a high task orientation. This explanation may also be pertinent to the higher relations orientations of men coaching girls. Men have had less experience coaching girls and may be reacting to social stereotypes of girls and women. Stereotypical responses might lead male coaches to expect less of girls, focus on more general goals, and expect lower levels of competition. They may tend to coax rather than demand, and generally provide more social-emotional encouragement.

The leader style measure as developed by Fiedler did not address potential sex differences in responding to the instrument. Therefore, characteristically different response sets may suggest a gender bias in the instrument rather than leader style differentiation. If differential socialization experiences have encouraged more nurturant, expressive, supportive, and social-emotional qualities in women, they might be expected to evaluate people from a more social perspective, that is, tasks may be viewed in an interpersonal context. Such experiences would influence the LPC style measure, because the least-preferred co-worker would be a person who was evaluated as low on these expressive social-emotional characteristics. Concern for the interpersonal context of coaching was further supported by the feeling expressed by several coaches that "girls won't play if they're mad at a teammate." Many coaches maintained that dealing with intrateam relationships was critical and a continual concern with female teams.

The differences between men and women relative to structuring behaviors again may be a reflection of the experiential deficit of female athletes and coaches. Until recently few women had any background in participating, training, or coaching in highly organized, competitive athletics; hence, female coaches may feel the need to emphasize organization (structuring) in their coaching behaviors. Men who coach females may perceive a similar need for development of basic skills and adapt their behaviors for the less experienced, less skillful athletes. Men have greater experience in athletics, and structuring has been built in through prior athletic participation of varsity athletes. The higher production emphasis scores of male coaches in this study may be due to the greater experience of the male players with practice regimens and training procedures, which increases the need to relieve boredom and motivate players to increase output and improve performance.

The greater frequency of consideration behaviors for male coaches of girls suggests again that these coaches perceive a need to modify behaviors because of the sex of the players. During the interviews, the coaches mentioned their concerns for the female players frequently in response to the questions: "What are the differences in coaching boys and girls?" and "How do you find you have to behave differently?" The men coaching girls felt they should be less demanding, more supportive, and less critical with the female players than they would with boys. Coaches considered girls to have less skill and a lower drive to excel, and to be easily distracted by other interests. In short, they thought sport was less important to girls. Bartol (1978), suggested that leader style and behaviors may be constant, but that the experiences and actions of the followers are variable and that more research should be focused on the reciprocal aspects of the follower as the initiator or catalyst of leader behavior. These data suggest that some differences in leader behaviors are influenced by followers. More investigation of the nature of these processes involved is warranted.

Changing their style and behavior in different situations may be necessary for coaches to assure maximum success in specific situations, particularly in opposite-sex combinations of leader and followers. The sex of the followers may be a significant factor in determining effective leader behaviors. Coaches may need to act in particular ways toward girls to elicit the best performance, while these same behaviors may be inappropriate when working with males. Conversely, men may respond to certain leader behaviors that do not work with women.

The similarity in overall team effectiveness is also noteworthy considering that the men coaching girls had the least coaching and playing experience of any of the coaching groups. Thus, the awareness of what behaviors would be effective apparently did not come from their previous experiences as players or coaches. Some of these men were actually seeking opportunities to advance in coaching, hoping to eventually coach what they considered the more challenging and competitive male teams. Many coaches relied on their vicarious impressions of the coaching role and their classroom teaching experiences to design their coaching strategies.

The data also indicated that leader style is not a strong predictor of coaching effectiveness. Coaches seem to make behavior decisions that are not consistent with the characteristic leader style that they exhibit on the test instruments. This suggests that one's leader style does not limit the range of behaviors he or she may use in various situations. Therefore, no predictions concerning behavior can be made based on the leadership style associated with a coach.

In conclusion, this investigation provided limited support for a situational model of leader effectiveness. Leaders in this sport situation seem to vary their behaviors in response to perceived differential expectations of male and female athletes. Moreover, in order to have winning teams they use both consideration and structuring behaviors differently according to the situation. For example, some coaches may find players respond to more rigorous structure with continual considerate behaviors incorporated, while other players perform very well with less structure. The operational definitions of leader characteristics may not have been adequate to fully explore the dimensions of leadership. For example, Fiedler's concept of leader style may be so general that a wide range of behaviors is possible within either orientation, task or relations. Similarly, the concepts of structuring, consideration, and production emphasis were derived from an analysis of the repertoire of all leader behaviors.

Researchers previously have focused on style or behaviors rather than attempting to link them together. However, the critical factor in developing a leadership model is the decision-making process by which the leader (coach) selects the particular behavior to be used in a specific situation. The players respond to their perception of the coach's behavior. Similarly, coaches select behaviors and make decisions about behaviors in response to their perceptions and predictions about players. Players, in turn, attempt to behave as they perceive their coach's behaviors.

Further research should focus on this decision-making process in coaching in relation to selection of the most appropriate (effective) leader behaviors. The development and use of sport-specific instruments for assessing leader decision making combined with the use of direct observation of coach behaviors in a variety of situations is an important focus needed for more complete understanding of leadership processes in sport settings. Finally, leader characteristics of women coaching male players need to be examined to more fully understand the reciprocal influence of gender in coach-player interactions.

REFERENCES

Bardwick, J. (1971). *Psychology of women: A study of bio-cultural conflicts.* New York: Harper & Row.

Barol, K. (1978). The sex structuring of organizations. A search for possible causes. *Academy of Management Review, 3,* 805–815.

Basow, S. (1981). *Sex role stereotypes: Traditions and alternatives.* Monterey, CA: Brooks/Cole.

Bird, A. M. (1977). Development of a model for predicting team performance. *Research Quarterly, 48,* 24–32.

Chapman, J. B. (1975). Comparisons of male and female leadership style. *Academy of Management Journal, 18,* 645–650.

Fiedler, F. E. (1967). *A theory of leadership effectiveness.* New York: McGraw-Hill.

Fiedler, F. E. (1973). Personality and situational determinants of leader behavior. In E.A. Fleischman & J.G. Hunt (Eds.), *Current developments in the study of leadership* (pp. 121–142). Carbondale: Southern Illinois University Press.

Halpin, A. W. (1957). *Manual for the Leader Behavior Description Questionnaire.* Columbus: Ohio State University.

Harris, D.V. (1980). Femininity and athleticism: Conflict or consonance. In D.F. Sabo & R. Runfola (Eds.), *Jock: Sports and male identity* (pp. 222–239). Englewood Cliffs, NJ: Prentice-Hall.

House, R. J. (1971). A path-goal theory of leader effectiveness. *Administrative Science Quarterly, 16,* 321–338.

Kanter, R. M. (1975). Women and the structure of organizations. In Marcia Millman & Rosabeth Kanter (Eds.), *Another voice* (pp. 34–75). Garden City, NY: Doubleday.

Keane, F. & Cheffers, J. (1978). The relationship of sex, leader behavior, leadership style and coach player interaction. Paper presented at the American Alliance of Health, Physical Education, and Recreation National Convention.

Maccoby, E., & Jacklin, C. N. (1974). *The psychology of sex differences.* Stanford, CA: Stanford University Press.

Rikli, R. (1974). Effects of experimenter expectancy set and experimenter sex upon grip strength and hand steadiness scores. *Research Quarterly, 45,* 416–423.

Rosenthal, R. (1966). *Experimenter effects in behavioral research.* New York: Appleton-Century-Crofts.

Sage, G., & Loudermilk, S. (1979). The female athlete and role conflict. *Research Quarterly, 50,* 88–96.

Schein, V. (1973). Relationship between sex role stereotype and requisite management characteristics. *Journal of Applied Psychology, 57,* 95–100.

Singer, R. N., Llewellyn, J. N. (1973). Effects of experimenter's gender on subject's performance. *Research Quarterly, 44,* 185–191.

Snyder, E., & Kivlin, J. (1977). Perceptions of sex role among female athletes and non-athletes. *Adolescence, 12,* 23–29.

Spence, J. R., R.L. Helmreich, & Stagg, J. (1975). Ratings of self and peers on sex role attributes and their relation to self-esteem and conception of masculinity and femininity. *Journal of Personality and Social Psychology, 32,* 29–39.

Stevenson, H.W. (1964). Adult performance as a function of sex of experimenter and sex of subject. *Journal of Abnormal and Social Psychology, 68,* 214–216.

Stogdill, R. M. (1963). *Manual for the Leader Behavior Description Questionnaire—Form XII.* Columbus, OH: Bureau of Business Research.

Stogdill, R. M. (1974). *Handbook of leadership.* New York: Free Press.

Tharp, R.G., & Gallimore, R. (1976). What a coach can teach a teacher. *Psychology Today, 9,* 75–78.

Vander Velden, L. (1971). *Relationships among member, team and situational variables and basketball team success: A social-psychological inquiry.* Unpublished doctoral dissertation, University of Wisconsin.

Walum, L. R. (1977). *The dynamics of sex and gender: A sociological perspective.* Chicago: Rand McNally.

INDEX